# COMPLETE PROPERTY INVESTMENT SUCCESS

## THE PROVEN STRATEGIES FOR FINANCIAL FREEDOM FROM PROPERTY INVESTING

by Nick Fox

ISBN: 978-0-9927817-0-5

First published in England in 2015 by Fox Print Partners

# COMPLETE

# PROPERTY

# INVESTMENT

# SUCCESS

## THE PROVEN STRATEGIES FOR FINANCIAL FREEDOM FROM PROPERTY INVESTING

by Nick Fox

with Sarah Walker

published by Fox Print Partners

# Contents

## HMO PROPERTY SUCCESS

*For my family, friends and business partners.*
*You all inspire me daily.*
*Thank you.*
*Nick*

# About the author

*A prolific and highly successful investor, Nick Fox has been involved with property since his early childhood. Today, his investment portfolio includes more than 200 buy to let properties – both shared accommodation and single household lets – and he has interests in a number of development projects.*

As is the case with so many successful businesspeople, Nick started young. When he was eight, he bought up all the penny sweets from the Scout Camp tuck shop and sold them on to his friends for 2p! His delight at doubling his money on his first business venture signposted an entrepreneurial attitude and launched an enthusiasm for making money on his own terms that has never left him.

His introduction to the property market came not long afterwards, when the caravan that he lived in with his mother burned down. She used the insurance money to buy a wreck of a house, which she did up and sold for a profit, repeating the process until they had a nice home. When he wasn't in school, Nick helped his mother out and began to understand not only what could be achieved by hard work, but also the potential of property as a money-making vehicle. He just needed a bit of capital to get him started.

In 1988, at the age of 19, Nick landed a job with a company that imported computer software from America and sold it into retailers in the UK. It didn't take long for Nick to see the technology boom that was starting and he quickly realised he could do the same thing himself.

Operating out of his bedroom, Nick took out as many credit cards as he could and bought software stock from all over the world. He started off selling into small retailers, then, when the market for personal computers really took off, he moved into proper premises and grew the company until it became the UK's leading budget software company, selling over a million units every month into Dixons, Woolworths and WHSmith.

But by 2002 business had peaked. Technology had gone mainstream and was even available in supermarkets, and things quickly declined for Nick.

2005 was the 'light bulb' moment, when he realised that the income from his various businesses might have paid for his lifestyle, but it was his home that had built equity and given him a lump-sum return. He knew that the quickest and only way he could replace his financial losses was to buy more properties.

By the end of 2005, Nick had five properties, all rented to friends, generating an income and building equity. He started buying larger homes, which he rented as single units to families, and by the end of the following year, Nick had 20 properties and a significant buy to let business.

In 2007, he went into a buying frenzy. Within 12 months, he'd added another 90 properties to his portfolio. Then, as the credit crunch hit and many of his mortgages moved off initial low fixed rates and onto variables, Nick started to look at how he could increase his profits and turned one of his existing family home lets into an HMO. That was light bulb moment number two.

He began to partner with other investors and subsequently doubled the size of his portfolio to more than 200 properties, around 100 of them HMOs. That portfolio is currently managed through the Milton Keynes letting agency he set up in 2010 and achieves 98% occupancy.

*"Everyone thinks I must be constantly working to keep so many plates spinning but, really, I just employ great managers and develop effective systems."*

Nick's HMO investment strategy is now highly regarded within the industry and he is regularly asked to speak at property investment events. His expertise is called on by new clients and fellow professional investors alike and his reputation has enabled him to establish a significant mentoring business.

Over the past few years, Nick has also acquired business interests outside property: a photography company that he's looking to franchise and investment in a local pre-school that serves 80 children and has been rated 'outstanding' by OFSTED.

Nick loves football, tennis, golf and boating and has climbed Mount Snowdon with his partner, Samantha. He is committed to supporting local charitable causes and is also a Patron of Peace One Day. He and Samantha live just outside St Albans with their five children.

# Author's disclaimer

I am not qualified to give financial or legal advice. All related recommendations made in this book should only be considered in consultation with suitably qualified and accredited professionals. Persons giving financial advice MUST be properly qualified and regulated by the Financial Services Authority (FSA) and anyone giving you legal advice should be suitably qualified and regulated by The Law Society and the Solicitors Regulation Authority (SRA) (or the Council of Licensed Conveyancers (CLC)).

# A note from Nick...

This compilation contains my first three books in their entirety. There is, therefore, a little duplication of information but I have left it all in, as it remains very relevant in each case and the precise content does vary slightly. Plus, a little revision never hurts, so stick with it.

And the fourth part: NEXT STEPS contains lots of new information and the opportunity for you to get hold of some free stuff – a good reason to read right to the end!

I hope you enjoy this 'superbook' and do get in touch if you have any questions or would like some advice from me, personally. We're here to help.

EMAIL hello@nickfox.co.uk
TEL 01908 930369
FACEBOOK Nick Fox Property
TWITTER @NickFoxMentor

# PROPERTY

# INVESTMENT

# SUCCESS

## HOW INVESTING IN THE PROPERTY MARKET CAN HELP SECURE YOUR FINANCIAL FUTURE

# Introduction

When I started working, I, like most people, was sold the benefits of investing in a pension plan: "The sooner you start, the better off you'll be in later life"… So I started paying into pensions and ISAs, because 'that's what you do'.

Then I watched as my father's pension provision came crashing down. During his working life, he was Financial Director for a number of major corporations and he'd been very well educated in the wisdom of investing in traditional pensions. But when the time came for him to commit to his annuity, the stock market was very low – not unlike it was in 2008/9 – and he found himself tied in to a very poor level of return. He was genuinely shocked at how bad his annuity purchasing power was. The expectation he'd had for his income in retirement – having paid in a considerable amount of money over the years – was not even close to what he would now realise.

When I started investing in property, my father saw the income returns I was making and used the capital he had not tied up in annuities to buy some properties himself. I manage those properties within my lettings portfolio and my father is now realising many times over the income he gets from the annuity payments he's receiving on a far greater amount of invested capital.

This is not a guide about how to invest for your pension; it's an overview of some of the options available to you, making the case for property as a sensible, reliable, flexible investment vehicle. I'm not trying to tell you where to put your money, just to open the discussion for you by looking at the realities, risks and rewards of investing in property versus going down the more traditional pension provision routes.

I hope you'll find what I have to say interesting and enlightening and that it will encourage you to at the very least think about your current financial provision; at most, to take the first step towards investment property success.

*"More money has been made in real estate than in all industrial investments combined. The wise wage earner of today invests his money in real estate."*

**Andrew Carnegie**

# PART ONE:

# SECURING YOUR FINANCIAL FUTURE

# Chapter 1

# What does financial security mean to you?

The concept of financial security is very personal. Your idea of the amount of money you would need and want in order to consider yourself financially 'secure' and your family properly provided for in the future, will be determined by your lifestyle, the size of your family, current financial commitments and future plans.

A lot of people talk about achieving 'financial freedom', but does that mean the same to you as financial security? Although it would undoubtedly be ideal to know that your investments would continue to deliver an excellent income while growing in capital value, without needing any day-to-day time commitment from you, would something less still give you security?

You might say that's all semantics, but my point is that you need to really think about what income and capital you're going to need for the rest of your life:

a. as a minimum, to ensure your financial commitments are covered and you can continue to have a good lifestyle, and

b. ideally – the amount that would allow you to live the life you dream of.

Once you've got those two figures – and it's going to take some time to work them out properly – then you can start to plot the steps you'll need to take to get there and set some measured, achievable goals that will enable you to build an investment portfolio that delivers on those goals.

## Where are you now?

Far too many people have only a vague awareness of their own financial profile. I meet lots of budding investors who tell me they want to build a property portfolio for passive income so they can become financially free, but when I ask how much they need, why and by when, they have very little idea. All they really know is that they don't have enough right now and want more!

If you're really serious about having a financially secure future, you need to consult with an excellent wealth manager and/or financial advisor, and if they're going to advise you effectively, you've got to be able to give them an accurate picture of both where you are now and where you want to be. As I'll elaborate on in the next two chapters, one reason why pensions are failing to deliver is that many people simply haven't properly calculated what they're going to need in the future. And if you don't have a realistic target to aim for, you can't possibly expect everything to turn out 'fine'.

*Set goals for yourself; if you don't know where you're going, how will you ever get there?*

So, begin with your current lifestyle, financial and family situation, and put together a clear statement of your income and outgoings every month and year. I use Excel to keep a clear track of my assets, other investments, monthly income and expenditure, plus a budget, which I revise every month. However you choose to collate this information, your 'financial statement' should include:

- Monthly income & expenditure, remembering:
  - the spread cost of any one-off or lump-sum annual
  - outgoings, such as Christmas, car servicing and holidays
  - Allowances for eating out and entertaining
  - Income from investments – you may need to put this down as average estimates
- Information on existing property assets - borrowing, interest rate, term of loan, repayment amount, cash flow, etc.
- Details of any other investments
- Your current pension provision (see Chapter 2)
- Credit card and loan rates & outstanding balances
- Any other assets
- All on-going financial commitments, such as school fees.

It's important to be realistic about your expenditure. This exercise is the first step towards establishing how much income you'll need in retirement, so be absolutely honest about how much you spend – and on what.

## What do you need and want?

You can fine-tune your projections when you meet with your advisor, but it's important that you have a clear plan to discuss with them. And remember that your future begins right away - it's not just about retirement - so make plans and calculations relating to the short, medium and long term.

If you've never put pen to paper regarding financial and lifestyle goals, I'd recommend you read 'Goals' by Brian Tracy and 'Goal Mapping' by Brian Mayne. There's a skill to doing it right, much of which comes down to managing your time excellently and committing to doing what you've said you'll do – and neither of those things are as easy as you might think! The vast majority of people need to train themselves to be disciplined and a very big help in succeeding with this is having someone that you make yourself accountable to. It's a bit like sticking to new years' resolutions or diets – telling someone else what you're doing and asking them to keep checking up on you is a great motivator for staying on track.

The other thing that will really help is having a visual representation of what you're trying to achieve. We subconsciously focus on the things we see and hear most often, so when you've got your goals down in black & white, stick some of the key figures, targets and end-game images around your home and office. I've done this for a number of years now and I promise you, it works. Some people talk about having a vision board; I have lots of them, from A5 size on the fridge, to big panels - several feet wide - in my office. That may be a bit extreme for you (!), but do make sure you have some kind of visual reminders of your targets for the short, medium and long-term and something that represents the kind of life you want in retirement.

So, on to your projections. I'd recommend that, using the calculations and information you put together for your financial statement, look at how much income is required to cover all your expenses, and estimate the figures for different timeframes, e.g.

- Over the next couple of years
- In, say, 5 years, when one or more children might be at secondary school
- In 10 years, when you are mortgage-free, but your children are at university and when you perhaps might want to remodel or update your home
- In 15 years, when all your children have left home
- In 20 years.

Include absolutely everything that would allow you to continue to live your current lifestyle, plus a 10% contingency.

Then add in the things that you don't do at the moment, but would like to be able to, for example: additional travel and holidays; investments and provision you might want to make for your children or other family members, perhaps deposits for homes or putting money into trusts; charitable contributions, and new assets and personal items you might want to buy, such as cars, jewellery, art and clothes.

This should highlight the kind of money you'll need and when you'll need it in order to live the life you want – both in terms of on-going income and lump sum capital returns.

## Consult with the best advisors you can find

Now that you have your personal financial statement and your short, medium and long-term needs and plans drafted out, you're in the right position to get professional financial advice. Having all this information to hand means that when you meet with advisors, you can make the best use of the time you're paying for – and they'll be very grateful to have such an organised client! They will be able to help you calculate the kind of savings and investments you'll need to make in order to achieve the income and level of financial security you want.

*Note that all professionals giving you financial advice MUST be properly qualified and regulated by the Financial Services Authority (FSA).*

The first financial professional you should engage is a Wealth Manager. They will look at all your financial affairs – mortgages, savings, investments, earnings, and so on – essentially as a portfolio, within the context of your business, lifestyle, family situation and desires for the future. They'll be able to advise you on the kinds of investment you should consider in order to achieve the right returns, in the most tax-efficient way. If you can find a Wealth Manager who invests in property themselves, that would be ideal.

*Wealth Managers should also have the CISI Masters in Wealth Management (MCSI after their name).*

Assuming that when you've finished reading this book you're still seriously considering investing in property, you should also engage an independent mortgage broker, who has plenty of experience in securing buy to let mortgages, and a property tax specialist. You may already have an accountant, and your wealth manager will certainly be able to give you tax advice, but property tax is quite complex and you need someone who knows what allowances you can take advantage of, when and from where. Make sure they're happy to liaise with your wealth manager, so that you get an accurate picture of how income and gains from various property investments might impact your overall tax position.

*Any person acting as a broker or making recommendations for your mortgage finance must have one or more of these qualifications: Certificate in Mortgage Advice (Cert MA); Certificate in Mortgage*

*Advice and Practice (CeMAP) from the ifa School of Finance; Mortgage Advice and Practice Certificate (MAPC) from the CIB in Scotland.*

*As well as qualifying under the Association of Chartered Certified Accountants (ACCA), your tax advisor should also be a member of the Chartered Institute of Taxation (CTA).*

Clients often ask if I can recommend advisors to them. Mine are excellent and I'm happy to disclose who they are, but I do recommend you find someone reasonably local to you, as face-to-face meetings are always the most beneficial and you don't want to have to travel long distances every time you meet, or when you need to exchange paperwork.

Ask friends, family and colleagues for their experiences and recommendations with regard to wealth advisors in your local area, then make appointments with them in order to see who you feel is going to be the best fit for you and your financial plans. Building your own 'power team' of specialists is very important.

# KEY NOTES

- Put together a complete 'statement' detailing your current financial position: income & expenditure, assets & liabilities, investments

- Research goal-setting techniques

- Project your lifestyle and financial requirements for the short, medium and long-term future

- Get an idea of what financial security would mean for you

- Meet with a Wealth Manager

# Chapter 2

# The problem(s) with pensions

*Savers are being left thousands of pounds worse off in retirement because of a "broken" pensions market. Insurance firms are not encouraging customers to shop around for the best deal, and are making a "significant" extra profit as a result.'*

**The Telegraph, February 2014**

For the last few years, pensions have been at the forefront of the financial headlines: concerns over shortfalls in final salary schemes and investment funds not maturing as originally anticipated; fraud; fees being excessive; annuities being mis-sold – and so it goes on.

As I write, the Association of British Insurers and its members are in the process of carrying out an audit of older pension schemes, overseen by an independent panel. The fact that this audit has been commissioned is an admission by the industry that, for far too long, pension schemes have been flawed and an acknowledgment that something needs to be done to improve the situation of those whose investments are unlikely to mature at an adequate level.

## Your current pension provision

Channel 4's 'Dispatches' programme reported in November 2013, 'Most people can't actually tell you exactly what they've invested in their pension, how funds are performing or how it's likely to mature. They're paying in blindly.' Not only that, but far too many people have no idea how much they're even going to need in retirement. The programme calculated that to have just £15,000 income in retirement today, you need to have saved £150,000 to top up the state pension, and a child born today will need to have saved around £2.4 million in order to have a 'comfortable' retirement.

So how does your current pension provision look?

If you've simply paid into a standard workplace pension and/or have taken an annuity offered by your provider without shopping around, I'd go so far as to say there's no chance it will mature to give you anywhere near the income you'll need – never mind *want* – for a 'comfortable' retirement.

Basic workplace pensions are linked to your salary and we also tend to invest into private pensions based on a percentage of what we bring home. But with wages not rising in line with inflation and life expectancy increasing, have you reassessed how your pension is likely to mature? If you haven't, make sure your Wealth Manager or IFA takes a look and explains to you how much you can expect to receive, based on their projections.

The reason I've chosen to put most of my pension provision eggs in the property basket, rather than into 'traditional' pension schemes is because I believe – as does the Financial Conduct Authority, according to the headlines – that the UK pension system is 'not working' (BBC, February 2014). I think there are fundamental issues with the schemes on offer, particularly annuities, and I don't want to leave my financial future in the hands of strangers managing what I see as very mediocre funds.

But before I go on to annuities and funds in more detail, I just want to stress the importance of understanding your pension – both the options that are available to you and your own needs for retirement.

You may have noticed there's been a lot of talk over the past year about the new legislation regarding workplace pensions. The fact that all employers must enrol their employees in a pension scheme might sound good, but the amount paid in could be so low that the end provision could still be massively inadequate. Two million people were automatically enrolled in a workplace pension scheme in 2013, but I wonder how many of them have bothered to calculate either how the pension will mature or what percentage of their required income in retirement it will actually represent? There is a danger that insisting on workplace pensions could be doing savers a disservice, causing them to think their pension has now been taken care of and that they don't need to worry any more.

So if you haven't already sat down and done the 'financial statement' exercise in Chapter 1, do it now. You simply cannot afford to have the wrong impression about the shape of your finances or your future needs.

## Fundamental problems with annuities

Most people's pension provision is based on their having taken out an annuity - essentially an insurance policy that pays out in retirement. The biggest 'scandal' here, for me, is the fact that single-life annuities – the ones that are sold as 'standard' – die with you. You pay into your pension fund every month so that you will be guaranteed a certain level of income from the fund after you retire, but on your death, regardless of when that occurs, your fund essentially ceases to exist. That's to say, your invested capital is still there, but it reverts to the pocket of your provider; it does **not** form part of your estate and your beneficiaries will therefore get none of it. (A joint life annuity will be passed on, but the overall rate is lower than with single life.)

So, be under no illusion that those who have been selling annuities, working for the provider, have quite possibly been focused not on giving you the most appropriate pension plan, but on securing the best deal for their employer – usually a single-life annuity.

*"It's deeply dysfunctional for the consumer, but seems to be working very well for those who are selling annuities.*

*The mis-selling of annuities could be at least as big as the mis-selling of PPI."*

**Dr. Ros Altman, Pensions Expert, November 2013**

And it's not just the single life annuities that may have been mis-sold. In November 2013, The Telegraph estimated that insurers made around £63m a year by directing unhealthy customers to an annuity designed for 'super-healthy' people. Research data from the Financial Conduct Authority, released in February 2014, showed that while 60 percent of people should qualify for an enhanced annuity because of poor health or an unhealthy lifestyle, just 7 percent of those who held pension savings at one of the ten firms that offer the enhancement had an annuity that took their medical condition into account.

Reporting from the same FCA data, in February 2014 thisismoney.co.uk said: 'around 1,000 retirees a day are being lured into payouts offered by their own insurer and are so confused that they fail to look elsewhere for the best deal.' And by taking the first option offered to them, some people are ending up on annuity deals that are around 20% below what they could get if they shopped around. The article went on to suggest the introduction of a 'pensions passport', where people would have to give information about their current pension provision, plus their health and lifestyle, in order that financial advisors and pension providers could give better, more tailored advice.

*"Not only does [a passport] force the saver to engage with their savings, but it sends the message that this money is yours. It's up to you what you do with it. We've got to break the link between building up your pension savings, then taking them as an income. They are two different things, but are not treated as such — and that is where many problems lie."*

**Tom McPhail, head of pensions at Hargreaves Lansdown**

In short, the industry seems to be admitting that people have not been getting the right pensions advice, acknowledging there is a widespread belief out there among savers that (a) annuities are the only option and (b) brokers are selling them an appropriate product. And that's just not true.

Quite apart from the risk of having been mis-sold your annuity, there is also the fact that the vast majority simply don't give a very good return.

*"The annuity concept was designed for an era when life expectancy was much shorter than today. There is a serious question over whether people should be buying what is a low-risk, low-return product."*

**Otto Thorensen, Director General, The Association of British Insurers, February 2014**

Now that we can expect to live to around 80 and most of us would like to retire as early as possible, you should probably plan for at least 25 years of living on your pension – and by that I mean your savings and various investments. And if you've invested in a traditional pension scheme, your money will be in a fund.

## Fundamental problems with funds

Your (and your employer's / the state's) contributions are invested into funds, usually made up of stocks and shares in a broad range of companies, varying in terms of size, sector and geographical location.

The idea of these funds is that they comprise a balanced portfolio that carries minimal risk, due to its spread of interests, while still offering what is deemed a 'reasonable' return. The assumption is that that's what most people want: the safety of their capital virtually guaranteed, for a slightly better guaranteed return than they could get elsewhere. The problem is, 'reasonable' is likely to be inadequate – after all, it's almost always the case that the lower the risk, the lower the return. If you've only got to get by for ten years or so, the return offered by a standard annuity might suffice, especially if you've built up some other capital. But what about when you're looking at more than 20 years of living a decent lifestyle?

Then, these 'reasonable' returns are taxed and, of course, pension providers and brokers have to make money, so you pay fees for having your money invested and managed. That sounds fair enough, but the reality is you may be paying far more than you should.

In September 2013, the OFT revealed that around £30 billion of savers' money is still invested in 'old, high-charging workplace pension schemes' (those set up before 2001) and in February 2014, The Telegraph reported that fees charged by pension fund managers had risen by 'up to ten percent in two years'. Although the pensions minister has pledged to cap fees from April 2015, I can't help but think that the providers will simply find another way to recoup their subsequent profit shortfall.

And what about the people taking these fees and the companies they're investing your money into?

Periodically, over the past hundred years, institutions regarded as absolutely reliable because they were so big and wealthy have suffered massive drops in value, resulting in black days, crashes and crunches that have had a significant impact on both individuals and entire economies. The point is, companies can fail on an enormous scale, taking your money with them.

The failure of companies and institutions is usually down to human error – either gross incompetence or fraud – and these are people you will never meet. You're far removed from your investments, which are often made by brokers you don't know and possibly managed by other people you've never met, meaning you have very little control. And, because many of us struggle to understand pension products in any detail, we're almost forced to rely on the assumption that the people selling the products are offering us the best and most appropriate deal….and too many simply aren't at the moment.

*"We have the opportunity to develop products and services that really meet people's needs - that are simpler, more flexible, and better value with transparent charges. And the opportunity to change the conversation on pensions so it's simple and more positive."*

**Ruston Smith, chairman, National Association of Pension Funds, December 2013**

That's certainly the right sentiment, but are you prepared to wait until the Government and all the various financial institutions involved finally come up with new options that may only end up being marginally better than the current schemes?

The final kick in the teeth from workplace and other pension schemes is that if you want to cash them in early to invest the money into something else, known as 'pension liberation', the Government taxes the whole value of your pension pot at 55% and the pension company will take a large management or arrangement fee, which could be as much as a third of the total value. For example:

| | |
|---|---|
| Value of pension pot at age 55: | £200,000 |
| Less HMRC tax at 55% | £110,000 |
| Less pension company fee of 30% | £60,000 |
| Amount left for you to reinvest | £30,000 |

In other words, the financial penalties are so high that once you've built up a pension pot, you're essentially trapped in the scheme. Between them, pension providers and the Government have made sure you can't afford to change your mind or access any of **your** money until the originally agreed date – and then it's in small monthly amounts. Some changes to early release legislation have recently been made, but it's still not good enough to temp me to change my mind. This lack of flexibility and locking up of your savings is probably the single biggest reason I don't subscribe to a traditional pension scheme.

## And lastly...

...a quick glance at the State Pension, such as it is. First things first: it's not very much at all. For the financial year 2013/14, the maximum amount a single person can draw is £110.15 a week. I don't know about you, but I certainly wouldn't want to have to try to live on that.

Then you have to think about the fact that there are fewer people paying in than drawing out and the gap between those two figures is getting wider every year. Even if there is still a 'state pension' by the time I retire, it's unlikely to bear much resemblance to what we have now. I'm working on the assumption that it will be such a small amount it's not really worth counting – and that's my recommendation to you: think of it as nothing more than a small added bonus that you may or may not get.

## ADDENDUM:

Just as I was finishing this book, it was announced that savers – under certain conditions - will now be given 'unrestricted access' to their pension funds, with no draw down limits, although tax will apply at certain levels. This is excellent news for those who have an idea of what they would like to do with their capital instead of leaving it in their current scheme and a step in the right direction by the Government. However, I would suggest that pension providers are unlikely to have agreed to take a huge drop in profits, so I suspect they'll still be making money from their investors somewhere along the line…these things are rarely quite what they seem…

# KEY NOTES

- Revisit and question your current pension provision

- If you haven't already, put together a personal financial statement

- Be aware: single-life annuities die with you – there is no capital to pass on to your family

- Your annuity may have been mis-sold, so question your provider

- Are you aware of all the fees, charges and taxes applied to your pension fund?

- Companies can fold and disappear overnight, taking all your money that's been invested in their stocks and shares with them

- You may as well forget the state pension!

# Chapter 3

# Why property?

*"Average [capital] gains of more than £7,000 in the [last] year highlights how property wealth can play a major role in improving the standard of living in retirement. On average, retired homeowners have gained nearly £600 a month, which compares very well with every other source of retirement income."*

**Dean Mirfin, Group Director, Key Retirement Solutions, February 2014**

Property has long been considered a good investment, but why? "Because the value will go up over time" is the most common reasoning, but then people often stumble over being able to say much more, in the same way that they do when you ask why it's sensible to put money into a pension scheme!

What I'm going to explain in this chapter is why *I've* chosen to invest in property and to rely on it for the majority of my future financial security. Property investment success, in my opinion, comes down to understanding these key points, implementing them and incorporating them effectively within your investment strategy.

## Leverage

I'm hesitant to choose a 'top' reason why property is such a good investment vehicle, but if I absolutely had to, then leverage would be it. There is not one other asset class that enables you to profit to the same extent from other people's money, while investing such a relatively low amount yourself, and at such a relatively low level of risk.

Banks and building societies lend against property at such a high Loan to Value rate because it's considered to have a fundamental 'bricks & mortar' value. The higher the LTV, the more confidence it demonstrates they have in the property market, because they will only lend what they can be sure they can recoup if you were to default and they had to sell. As a result of their confidence, you can leverage their money to make a better return on your own capital than you could in almost any other situation, because when the market rises you get to keep *all* the profit (less, tax, of course!), not just the profit on your share of the capital investment.

Let's say there was a rise of 15% across all markets and you had invested £100k in stocks, you would benefit from growth of £15k, i.e. your capital would have increased by 15%. But if you had split that £100k investment capital into 25% deposits on four properties, each worth £100k, that would be a total of £60k growth, representing a 60% increase on your original investment. Even taking into account that realising that profit would involve paying taxes and fees, you would still be many times better off having invested in property than if you had put your money in stocks.

In short, the power of leverage means your money goes further and enables you to invest in assets with a value that's several times that of your actual capital – which brings me on to the next major benefit of property: the ability to refinance.

## Refinancing

The willingness of lenders to loan you such a high proportion of a property's value means that when it increases in value, you should be able to remortgage and extract some of your invested capital. There needs to be sufficient equity for the LTV of the mortgage product and the rental income must 'stack up' (see Chapter 4), but as long as you and the property can satisfy the lender's criteria, this is a great facility.

While there is an administrative cost associated with refinancing – broker fees, lender fees and survey fees – and there are likely to be tax implications down the line, the cost is nothing like the prohibitively heavy penalties you suffer if you want to release lump sums from your pension. I wouldn't recommend doing it on a regular basis, but certainly it's worth looking at the possibility every three to five years.

If you've bought 'well' and treat the property as a medium to long-term investment (and assuming the market continues to rise over time), you should find that at some point you are able to release all the capital you originally put in, leaving you with an appreciating and possibly income-producing asset that has none of your own money tied up in it. You can then take the lump sum you release and either reinvest or spend it.

Leverage and refinancing together certainly make a strong argument for property offering the best potential return on your capital, but add in the income opportunity and that's when property really becomes an exciting investment proposition.

## Income returns

With all other asset classes, you mainly profit from growth on the capital. Although there may be interest payments on other types of investment, I haven't found any that offer the same income potential as property, where your tenants' rent covers the mortgage and other costs associated with the property and there is enough left over, after tax, for you to take a good profit.

The caveat to that is: you get out what you put in. That's to say, in order to get the best income returns, you'll need to invest time and effort and put an effective business management system in place, which I'll go on to describe in Chapter 4. You incur far more costs in running a high income-generating portfolio of buy to let properties – and I'm talking about multi-lets - but the profit is much greater than if you take a hands-off approach.

There's a lot to consider in making the decision about how involved to be in your investments (see Chapter 8), but if you're able and prepared to build a property business, it can give you on-going monthly income at a level that will cover all your own bills, and many of your other outgoings. Put that together with the possibility of refinancing and I'd say that within five to seven years you could be looking at a situation where you have a portfolio of appreciating assets giving you a more or less passive income, with most, if not all of your original capital released. Now that's a good investment.

*'The average £30,000 pot provides an annuity income of around £1,500 a year. In reality, that's a menial top-up to the state pension and it takes 20 years before you get back what you put in.'*

**The Telegraph, 4ᵗʰ February 2014**

In contrast, if you could use that £30,000 to put down a 15% deposit on an investment property, assuming you 'bought well', it's quite possible you would be able to:

- generate at least £125 monthly income, equivalent to the annuity payment
- secure an asset that would appreciate in value, in addition to providing income

- retain the invested £30,000 capital and still be able to access it via sale, equity release or refinancing
- have the option of passing on the whole amount to your family

## Variety and flexibility of opportunities

One of the big downsides of saving in a traditional pension scheme is the inflexibility of it. You're expected to decide, at a relatively early stage in your working life, on a plan that will stay more or less the same until you retire. If you decide – and it may be years down the line - that you want to change to a different plan or gain access to *your* money, the financial penalties can be huge. You are also in the hands of other people and have very little control over where your money is ultimately invested.

Property, on the other hand, is a brilliantly flexible asset class. Not only do you decide on the type of property you buy, but also what you do with it and when. That means **you** have control over how you make your returns and when and how you take them.

While you can't control the market as a whole or mortgage rates, you *can* choose:
- residential or commercial property
- the type of property
- the location of the property
- your mortgage product

- how much you invest in improving/refurbishing
- what type of tenants you accept
- the rent you charge (to a certain extent)

All that means you have a very high degree of control over income and expenditure, and therefore profitability. Your income is not at the beck & call of the stock market, as are annuity payments.

Although there are planning issues to consider, which will limit your options, a property is essentially square footage, which you could look at as nothing more than a potentially profitable box. That means you can, to a certain extent, change your mind about how you make money from it and move with the demand from the market.

For example, there is currently a very high demand from young working adults for rooms in shared houses, with an all-inclusive rent package. As a result, some landlords are turning what were previously let as family homes, into multi-let accommodation, satisfying local demand and increasing their income in the process. There is also the opportunity in many areas to convert commercial premises into residential accommodation, as well as deals to be done to raze an existing property to the ground and either build a new property yourself, or simply gain planning and sell on.

I thought carefully about the way I wanted to structure my own portfolio and my property knowledge has meant I've been able to make better decisions in my other businesses, to give me greater financial security.

In addition to the single and multi-let rental properties I own, I also took the decision to buy premises for my childcare business, rather than renting. As a result, my business pays me rent and I have chosen a property that will also let well as a House in Multiple Occupation, should I move the business in the future.

Having this level of control and such a variety of options is yet another key reason why so many people use property as a wealth creation tool. Your future financial requirements change as your life circumstances change, and property allows you to change your mind accordingly.

## A tangible, appreciating asset

The last point brings me back to where I started – with the fact that property has always gone up in value over the long term. People will always need a roof over their heads and there's a finite amount of land available for development. Of course, not every property in every area will increase in value at the same rate – and some will undoubtedly fall, for a variety of reasons – so calling property an appreciating asset comes with a caveat: it's all in the buying.

Properties appreciate in value because they're in demand and there is a skill in identifying a property that you can be confident will remain in demand into the future. Even if your focus is on buying properties that will primarily give you income, you need to be as sure as possible that they will also increase in value so that your investment at least keeps pace with the market. That requires good local area knowledge and contacts, market research and an understanding of some fundamental economic principles….all of which you should be perfectly capable of acquiring yourself.

And that ties in with my previous points about having control - you can decide exactly where you put your money; you're not relying on anyone else for your investment. Now, you may see that as a good or a bad thing, and you're quite right! Because if you really don't know what you're doing and don't have the time or the inclination to carry out the necessary research, property may not be the best investment vehicle for you. You don't get something for nothing (I'll discuss working with companies that offer 'passive' investments later in the book) and, like any investment, the best property investments are made through expertise. And the more expertise you can gain yourself, the more control you will have.

And, finally, I *like* that property is tangible. You can see it, touch it, appreciate its aesthetic qualities and anything that is tangible retains an intrinsic value, unlike stocks, which can lose all their value frighteningly quickly. The fact that I can drive around the area and look at my investments, rather than simply figures on a spreadsheet, gives me confidence that I'm building a solid financial future.

*"Real estate cannot be lost or stolen, nor can it be carried away. Purchased with common sense and managed with reasonable care, it is about the safest investment in the world."*

**Franklin D. Roosevelt**

## Demand for accommodation from the Private Rented Sector (PRS)

The arguments I'm making here for property are dependent on one major factor: the presence of demand. You can only refinance, benefit from capital appreciation and secure income from property if you have tenants and buyers demanding a supply of the particular kind of accommodation you have. As such, each different kind of property investment strategy will require research into the specific demand from the 'end customer', which I'll talk about as we look at each one. But the overall picture for landlords is very good: the demand for rental accommodation within the private rented sector has never been higher and that looks likely to continue for the foreseeable future.

*'More people now rent privately than from councils or housing associations'*

**The Independent, 26ᵗʰ February 2014**

*'Fuelled by rising house prices, demographic change and a tight mortgage market, demand for renting has doubled the size of the PRS over the last decade.'*

**The Guardian, 26ᵗʰ February 2014**

Figure 1: Trends in tenure, 1980 to 2012-13

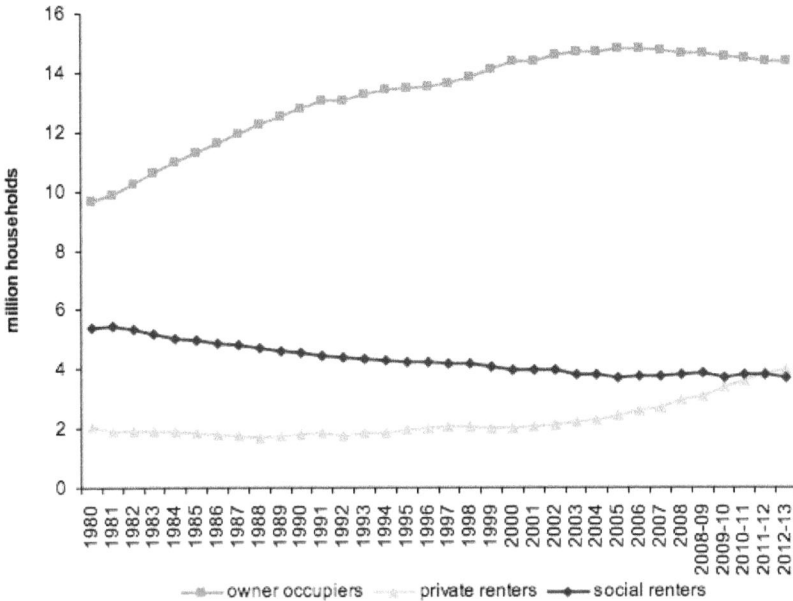

**Source: DCLG English Housing Survey Report 2012-13**

The chart above shows that in 2012 the number of households (and a 'household' can be a family or an individual) renting from private landlords rose above that of those renting social housing for the first time since records began. You can also clearly see that the PRS has been growing steadily over the past thirty years, while levels of available social housing have fallen and the number of owner-occupiers has dropped slightly since the highs of the mid-2000s. But to be able to assess whether this demand will continue into the future – and at least for the lifetime of your proposed investment – we need to understand the key reasons behind the trends.

## Shortage of new housing

The headline fact here is that we have been consistently failing to meet new house-building targets for too long. Taking an average of the figures calculated by various local and national housing and planning organisations, we need to build around 250,000 new homes each year to keep up with the growth in households and ensure prices remain affordable.

DCLG Household Interim Projections 2013 stated that the number of households in England is projected to grow by 221,000 a year from 2011 to 2021. In 2011, total new housing completions stood at 114,000 (only 25% of which was by local authorities and housing associations); from 2011 to 2012 NHBC reported a decrease in new home registrations, and the latest figures show a further drop:

*'Annual housing completions in England totalled 109,370 in the 12 months to December 2013, 5% lower compared to the previous 12 months.'*

**DCLG House Building report, published February 2014**

# Lack of affordability

The fundamental shortage in the supply of new housing has been the key contributing factor to the rise in house prices, which has had the knock-on effect of taking the cost of owning their own home beyond the reach of many people. The average house price in the UK, as I write, is around £170,000* and, while 95% mortgages are available, in order to benefit from what is considered a more 'reasonable' interest rate, you really need to be putting down a deposit of 15%, or more. That means, at the highest rate of borrowing, people need to have an average of £8,500 in deposit funds; 85% borrowing on the average house price requires £25,500. On top of that, there's Stamp Duty Land Tax, removals, legal and mortgage fees and other variable moving costs.

In 1983, the average deposit was around 12% of average national income. Today, that figure stands at 82%**.

And after the introduction of the 'Help to Buy' schemes and various incentives designed to get the property market moving – and particularly aimed at getting first time buyers on the ladder – it has recently been announced in the media that mortgage lenders have tightened their criteria, to ensure borrowers will be able to afford their repayments on-going - the assumption being that interest rates can only increase. Financial commitments, such as gym memberships and childcare are likely to be taken into consideration, as well as other 'lifestyle' outgoings, including what's regularly being spent on travel and entertainment.

In short, it seems that after the last credit crunch crisis, the Financial Conduct Authority (FCA) is keener than ever to ensure banks lend responsibly. And while that's certainly a fundamentally good position, it means there's going to have to be some more creative thinking about how to address the affordability problem.

(* Source: Land Registry, February 2014; ** Source: The Telegraph, February 2014.)

## Shortage of social housing

Some of the increase in demand has come from those who can't afford to buy their own home – and there is a particularly high demand from those in their twenties and thirties, as a result of a big jump in the birth rate in the 1980s - but there is also a significant demand from those who are fundamentally unable or unwilling to buy a home.

The Thatcher government's legislation allowing council tenants the 'Right to Buy' their homes is often cited as a reason behind the current lack of supply of social housing but, while it's a factor, I don't think it's the biggest cause. Around 1.5 million homes have been bought under the scheme, reducing the stock that would have become available as existing tenants died or their circumstances changed and they were able to move on. But from 1980, when Right to Buy was introduced, to 2012, the population of Great Britain increased by around 7 million, and it's this population increase that has had far more of an impact, in my opinion.

While the building of social housing has fallen way short of targets, the number of households needing it has grown faster than anticipated. Between 1991 and 2012, 3.4m people migrated to the UK – that's more than half the total population growth figure for that period – and many of those have needed to be housed by local authorities, on top of the demand from UK nationals. According to Shelter, 'there are more than 1.8m households waiting for a social home – an increase of 81% since 1997'.

And so, because of this lack of supply of social housing, there is a huge demand for affordable accommodation from the private rented sector. While the rent that can be charged to social tenants may not be quite as high as could be asked of private tenants, many local authorities will make payments direct to the landlord and take out long-term agreements, so the issues of rent defaults and void periods are virtually eliminated. As such, many private landlords are accepting social tenants and finding it a solid proposition – and something they can rely on into the future.

## Transient working population

And finally, there is the way our working lives have changed. Many more people than ever before move around the UK for work and/ or are on short-term contracts with no certainty over what the next job or contract will be. And so there is an on-going demand for short to medium-term rental accommodation from working adults who need the flexibility to be able to move on quickly and easily, sometimes at short notice, as their work changes.

These people are often perfectly able to pay rent at the top end of the market and are quite prepared to do so for good-quality accommodation. Those who can't afford to put down large deposits and don't want to have to worry about variable costs and rising bills are often very keen to take an all-inclusive rent package within a shared house. In short, there is demand from the transient working population for a variety of rental property and it's a demand that seems likely to keep growing.

# KEY NOTES

- Property is the only asset class against which you can borrow at such a high level and benefit from **all** the capital growth (less tax, of course!)

- You should be able to refinance at some point and could end up with an income-producing asset that's growing in value, with none of your own money invested in it

- Property is an incredibly flexible, tangible investment vehicle

- You have a high degree of control over your asset and its associated income and expenditure – and, therefore, profit

- There is a very real shortage of housing stock and an increasing demand

- On-going lack of affordability of home ownership means a stable on-going rental demand

# PART TWO:

# YOUR PROPERTY INVESTMENT OPTIONS

# Chapter 4

# Investing for income

A lot of people think about property primarily in terms of capital appreciation and consider their current property assets as something to be held and then 'cashed in' through selling or releasing equity. Lump sum returns of that kind are great and should certainly form part of your investment plan but, in the same way that businesses survive on cash flow, so do we!

The main concern most of us have for our retirement is: when we stop earning a monthly salary, where is our regular income going to come from? Well, depending on what you buy and how you let it, property can deliver anything from a pension top-up to a monthly income that exceeds what you earned as an employee. That's why increasing numbers of people are now using property as their primary investment vehicle.

The income strategy depends on a demand for a certain type of rental accommodation, because the best returns are usually achieved through offering shared housing, where tenants rent individual bedrooms and share the other living facilities. By renting out a property in this way, you can expect to bring in two to three times the rent you would receive from letting it as a single unit. With all buy to let you need to carefully analyse the demand - what it's like now and what it's likely to be in the future – but if you're looking to generate income, your research is especially important. If you make a mistake with this, you could find your standard of living compromised. That being said, there's no reason why you should get it wrong if you do your homework!

Be under no illusion; property investment – particularly when you're talking about an income-generating portfolio - is a business and needs to be treated as such. I invest in several different businesses – some I'm directly involved with; some I have simply financed – but property is where I spend most of my time and effort. I've got a fantastic team that help me run the business, so I don't need to worry about the day-to-day letting and management of my buy to let properties, but managing that team and taking care of all the administrative and financial implications of owning and trading in assets requires fundamental business skills. Of course, there are options for taking a more 'hands off' approach to investing - and I'll cover those in more detail later on – but if you're looking for income from property, that's a business in itself.

## Houses in Multiple Occupation (HMOs)

Most shared houses are HMOs. The Government considers a property an HMO if there are three or more tenants living there, forming more than one household (i.e. they're unrelated) and they're sharing toilet, bathroom or kitchen facilities. If a building has three or more storeys and is occupied by five or more people, forming two or more households, the HMO must be licensed. Those are the umbrella definitions but, practically, it's a bit more complicated, because precise criteria for licensing can vary wildly from council to council, as can the criteria for needing planning permission for change of use class. What you do and don't need to do in terms of health and safety can also be largely dependent on the attitude of the personnel in your own local council and fire safety departments and there is currently no nationwide system for councils to make checks on HMOs.

And all of that regulation and inconsistency is a big reason why many investors steer clear of HMOs, but I think they're making a mistake. Yes, there's a lot to comply with and keep track of, the management is more time consuming and your costs are higher, but the profit levels really do make it worthwhile, in my opinion.

The best returns, as far as HMOs are concerned, tend to come from renting to working adults. You provide them with a room of their own, at a rate that includes all their utility bills and council tax, and then they share the kitchen, bathroom facilities and possibly another communal area, such as a sitting room. And there's an increasing demand for this kind of accommodation, which gives tenants the security of fixed outgoings and the convenience of more flexible terms, with most HMO landlords only asking for a month's notice if a someone wants to leave. It also provides a sociable environment, living with like-minded people.

## Social housing tenants

For a long time, professional landlords shied away from renting to tenants who are dependent on housing benefit, but these days it can be a good way of ensuring a consistent level of 'secure' rental income. Many local authorities will pay rent direct to landlords and in some areas this can be at a good level, compared with what can be achieved by renting to tenants paying privately. Social housing tenants also tend to stay for longer, meaning less re-letting administration.

The main potential downsides are that if the tenants come off benefits, they may not be used to planning their own finances and may struggle to pay their rent in full and on time. They may also be in the property for more of the day than those who are in work, meaning utility bills could be higher and there might be more wear and tear on fixtures, fittings and furnishings.

I meet a lot of landlords who let at least one of the HMOs in their portfolio to tenants on housing benefit, because they see it as helping the local community, and that's a pretty decent attitude to have. While some people are quick to point out the risks, there are always risks in this business – some of the worst 'bad tenants' are those who seem the most respectable at first. So just do your due diligence, make sure that you're very clear about what's expected and trust your gut instinct when deciding whether to accept someone who's applying to live in your property.

What I would say is, don't mix tenant types. Shared houses work best when people have similar lifestyles and it's much easier to manage tenants when everyone's more or less on the same page.

## Student letting

The most common perception of HMOs is that they're student houses and in college and university towns and cities student letting can be very profitable.

People often take the attitude that students treat properties badly, party all the time and can't afford to pay very much rent, but, in reality, the reverse is true. You can usually insist on parents acting as guarantors, which means you have security for payment of rent and are highly unlikely to get defaults. Also, they're usually under one AST, so are jointly and severally liable for the rent, which gives you an added layer of security, as students will generally ensure everyone pays! They also tend to treat the property quite well because they – and their parents! - want their deposits returned.

Another reason landlords often give for not wanting student lets is the risk of voids between academic years, but many students – particularly those in their final year – prefer to hold and/or stay in their accommodation over the summer, for both social and study reasons, particularly if they have part-time jobs. If you do have a month or two between full-time student lets, you may be able to offer short-term lets to foreign students on summer language courses. A short gap also gives you the opportunity to carry out repairs and refresh the property so that you can re-let quickly at the best price and have your pick of prospective tenants! Students almost always want to secure accommodation well in advance of the new academic year, so if you can assure them they'll be moving into an updated home, you should attract a lot of enquiries.

And don't be tempted to think that you can get away with spending far less on refurbishment and maintenance, simply because 'they're only students'. Students these days have an increasingly large choice of where to live and the condition of the property is a big factor for them, so give them a nice home. A good yardstick is, would you be happy for a child of yours to live there?

The main risk in student letting is that areas can end up with a big over-supply of property if colleges and universities decide to build their own halls/accommodation. You may be able to switch your HMO tenant type to working adults but it's likely that the area won't be right if there's a heavy student population. In short, before you buy a student property, check the future plans for the university/college and the area very carefully.

# NUS research into students' experiences of renting

In March 2014, the National Union of Students published the results of the first ever piece of research commissioned into student letting. It looked at their needs and made recommendations for how the experience could be improved for them, at every stage of the rental process. Some headline facts and figures:

- 44% of students rent from the PRS
- Choice between PRS or other accommodation is based on 1) location, 2) cost, 3) ease of rental
- They choose a specific PRS property based on 1) price, 2) location and 3) condition
- Three quarters of students have had to complain about a property's condition – usually about damp and cold
- Around 20% felt pressurised into either signing a contract or paying a holding fee before they'd seen the contract
- Around half didn't know whether they'd had a copy of the EPC
- More than a third went into debt to secure a property
- Around half had to pay fees they didn't know about in advance
- Only just over half were sure their deposit had been protected.

Most of the students surveyed were happy overall with their PRS accommodation, but the vast majority thought there should be a minimum condition standard, a ban on fees and more services to ensure landlords fulfilled their responsibilities.

## Systemisation

I've already said that letting for income is a business and the key to building a profitable portfolio is systemisation. There is a lot of work to do and, while you can probably handle it yourself for the first few properties, it can quickly become a full-time job if you're not careful. The idea of investing in high-income generating properties is that it gives you a greater level of financial freedom, not that you kill yourself achieving it!

You need to build a team who can keep the business ticking over nicely without you having to be there every day. The success and effectiveness of that team will depend on there being a system that they understand and follow, for every stage of the process, from sourcing to marketing to on-going management, and everything in between.

You can either spend some time with people like me, who have been there already, refined systems through trial and error and have an effective system in place that you can replicate, or you can go through that process yourself. It's certainly possible – I did it! – but you'll get there a lot more quickly if you take advantage of someone else's experience.

## Expanding your business

Once you have the right business model and the right people in place, your main role should simply be managing those people and the profits, whether that means choosing where and how to reinvest them or spending them. And having a good system means it's easy for you to scale up your business and add more properties to the portfolio.

In addition to buying more properties of your own, a simple way to generate more income is to take on the full management of other landlords' properties. You're already got the system – you're just adding more accommodation to it. A greater variety of accommodation will attract more tenants, which will raise your profile as a high-quality landlord. And that should contribute very well to helping you maximize profitability.

Yes, a multi-let property portfolio will never be quite as 'hands off' as most other investments, regardless of how good your systems are, but the income and capital appreciation should more than make up for that. I'll move on to more 'passive' investment options in chapters 6 and 7; next, let's take a look at lump-sum returns in the short to medium term.

# KEY NOTES

- You must appreciate that investing for income is a business in itself

- HMOs are a very specific type of rental property and subject to specific governance, which has both national and local regulations

- Research really is key when you're relying on property to generate a certain level of on-going income. Take the time to properly analyse the local market and the demand for shared housing.

- Look to other successful portfolio landlords who have established business systems in place and replicate those systems

- For much more information about HMOs, read my first book, **'HMO Property Success'**

# Chapter 5

# Investing for lump-sum returns in the short to medium term

The perfect investment for most people would be one that gives a healthy income and also grows well in value. Unfortunately, it's *very* rare to find something that can deliver both at a good level, so how those two things are balanced will depend on your personal needs and investment goals.

Generally speaking (and I'm taking London out of the equation), if a property is in an area where multi-let rental prices are high, it's unlikely to be the kind of highly desirable area where capital values rise quickly. Similarly, when the property market is on the rise, it's owner-occupied homes that are in demand and those don't tend to be the kind of properties that deliver brilliant income.

So you need to be clear on your main focus every time you buy a property: is it primarily for income or for a lump sum return? And if it's the latter, **when** do you want your return and **how much** do you need? I'll cover investment planning in more detail in Chapter 10; in this chapter, we're looking at how property can deliver you a lump sum return in the short to medium term – by which, I mean 1-5 years.

As a general rule, you should view property as a medium to long-term investment because it takes time for average property values to rise and most people have chosen to invest in property because they're confident of that increase in equity over time. However, it's useful to work some options for shorter-term returns into your investment portfolio, if for no other reason than to spread your risk. Plans are great, but they can change and you don't want to find yourself 'trapped' and unable to access some capital if you need to.

## Buying to improve and sell

This strategy was incredibly popular in the 1990s and early 2000s. Prices were increasing at such a rate that anyone with some capital to invest could buy a property that needed work - from simple cosmetic improvements to complete renovation projects – and sell as soon as the work was done for a significant profit.

Programmes like 'Changing Rooms', 'Property Ladder' and 'Trading Up' on television fuelled people's imaginations and sold the dream that anyone could make money by improving a property, which a great many did. However, exactly how much of the uplift in value was due to the extent and quality of the work and how much was due to the naturally rising market was never explored, and that's why you need to be very careful with this strategy. You don't want to end up spending more time and money than it's worth, once you've factored in inflation.

## So what should I buy?

You usually make the most money by buying a property that most people don't want and selling it on once you've turned it into something that's in huge demand. What you need to assess is whether you have the capital and the capability to turn one into the other – and what return you're likely to get for your trouble.

Nowadays, you really have to try to find projects that need as close to a complete renovation as possible; you can't just do cosmetic work. DIY stores and suppliers have come a long way in the last 20 years in terms of the range of products, tools and services that they offer, and most people are prepared to tackle re-plastering, new kitchens and bathrooms and redecoration themselves – it's not something they'll pay over the odds for. So look for a property that needs more serious building work, new electrics and plumbing – the kind of work that requires specialist contractors and a good amount of capital spending on it.

Often, people look at auctions for this kind of property, although more and more people are looking for something they can make into their own perfect home, so bear in mind you could find yourself bidding against people with an emotional investment, who are therefore probably prepared to pay over the odds. So make sure you do your research, work out the maximum price at which the property would still stack up as a good investment and don't get lured into a bidding war!

A few other points to bear in mind if you decide to buy at auction:

- When the hammer falls you are liable for a 10% deposit in cash, so you need to have it instantly available
- The sale is immediate and there's no come-back if you find the property is in worse condition than you thought, so make sure you carry out a survey and any other research ahead of the auction
- The 90% balance is usually due within 28 days of the sale, therefore you need to have a mortgage agreement lined up and be confident that your broker or FA can push the transaction thorough in time, otherwise there will be penalties.

A great many complete renovation projects were bought and completed in the last 10-15 years and there simply isn't the amount of stock needing 'serious attention' that there used to be, so there's likely to be competition from other investors for this kind of property. Builders in particular, who can get materials at cost and labour for free, might get the property you want because they can afford to pay slightly more for it and still make more profit than you would! So it might take some time to find the right project that stacks up financially and that's why, if you're looking at a buy/improve/sell strategy, it's a good idea to have something else in the works as well or you can get frustrated at not having an investment underway.

## Don't put all your eggs in one basket...

Before I move on, I just want to stress that it really isn't a good idea, especially in the current economic climate, to rely solely on this property investment strategy. Because of the costs you're incurring over a relatively short period of time, you really should only buy and sell quickly in a rising market, where natural price inflation helps insulate you against anything going wrong with your plans. Having other income-producing properties up and running before you embark on buying to improve and sell is certainly the smart move, as far as I'm concerned.

## Buying below true value, holding, then refinancing or selling

You've probably heard about 'BMV' deals, usually linked to 'dodgy passive investment companies'. Six or seven years ago it was possible to buy a property at one price, secure a valuation at a significantly higher price and refinance on the day you completed with a mortgage based on the higher valuation, essentially buying 'no money down'. Plenty of people took advantage of this loophole and so-called 'professional' individuals and investment companies sourced and facilitated deals for investors and themselves, building portfolios that had none – or very little – of their own capital invested in them.

The days of 'no money down' are over and that financing option, along with a number of other 'creative' alternatives that achieved much the same result, is no longer available.

However, if you're in a strong buying position – with nothing to sell, a good team of legal and financial advisors behind you and money to invest – and a vendor **has** to sell, for personal or financial reasons, you can still negotiate a good deal for yourself. You'll get the best discounts when the market is at its peak, with an excess of supply over demand, but I've found that there are always deals to be done if you have the right approach.

When I say 'true value', I don't mean the asking price, I mean the value a surveyor would put on it. When you've researched properties in an area and after you've bought one or two, you develop a gut instinct for what they're worth, but what's important here is the value a surveyor would pass on to a mortgage company.

*I cover how to assess a property's value, negotiation techniques and putting forward offers in my first book, 'HMO PROPERTY SUCCESS', so visit nickfox.co.uk to find out how to get hold of it, in paperback, digital and audio versions.*

So this strategy is, essentially, buying something that has equity built in from the outset and either refinancing to release that equity or selling to realise the profit. Most lenders will make you wait at least 6 months before you can refinance and, even then, there may be redemption penalties to pay, so make sure you check those implications with your financial advisor or mortgage broker when you're assessing the deal.

Typically, the best discounted deals are achieved on modest properties that are suitable for a single let, rather than larger property that you could let as an HMO. That means you're not likely to achieve much, if any income while you're waiting to release your money. However, you do need to do your research to ensure you'll be able to let it at a rate that at least covers your mortgage repayment and any other on-going costs. That means you should be able to afford to hold the property until any mortgage redemption penalty period has expired and maximise your return.

The kind of properties that you can buy at a discount also tend not to be in the best state of décor and/or repair, so while you're waiting to refinance or sell, you may be able to force some extra appreciation by making a few improvements. It's a good idea to speak to a local estate agent before you start, to find out exactly how much work it's worth doing; as with the 'improve & sell' strategy, you don't want to spend more than makes financial sense.

## Self build and development

A lot of people dream of building their own home, but I'm not talking about the kind of thing you see on 'Grand Designs', where budgets get blown on making something fabulous and individual. The kind of new property that will make you good money is simple housing stock.

This country's Government has failed to even come close to its targets for new housing for several years now and the population is continuing to increase (see **Chapter 3: Shortage of new housing**). So there's no doubt the private sector needs to help out now, more than ever, in the supply of housing.

If you've got a decent amount of capital to invest in buying some land to develop, you'll get the biggest uplift in value by buying a brownfield site for which you then get planning. Planning is the main issue when you're acquiring land for development and, as with most investments, you win biggest when you take the biggest risks. I haven't yet bought any land on that basis, but that's not to say I wouldn't consider it in the future. You would need to know the area well and develop a good relationship with the local town and country planners to make sure it was as certain as possible permission to develop would be granted – and granted for the kind of housing you wanted to build. The last thing you want to end up with is a piece of land on which planning has been refused.

You should also look at the potential that could be unlocked in the land attached to any properties you either already own or are considering buying. If you have a property that's already giving a good return, you have little to lose in applying for planning. That will cost a few thousand pounds but if you get as good an idea as possible from the local planning department before you apply, then it could be money very well spent.

I have two gardens that I split from buy to let properties I own. With planning, a garden that hadn't really held much material value suddenly represented a extra £120k in equity! I haven't moved forward on this project yet; my current thinking is to sell to a builder and simply realise and reinvest the money, but I may partner with another investor or developer, or simply complete the build myself.

That's the beauty of investing in land – it gives you so many options and a variety of ways of making money. You can simply sell to a developer for a relatively quick and easy return; build yourself and sell the property on as soon as it's completed; partner with a developer or other investor to complete a build and then sell, possibly retaining the freehold; you may even decide to build high income-generating property, such as flats or HMOs, refinance the buildings on completion and keep hold of them for income. Then you're a real property tycoon!

*"Buy land, they're not making it any more."*

**Mark Twain**

# Remember the cost implications

Before you get excited about the amount of money you could make on your investment over a relatively short period of time, remember to factor in all the costs. They're likely to include:

- Stamp Duty Land Tax on purchase
- Survey fees on purchase and possibly on renovation
- Planning & architects fees, possibly other building consultancy costs
- Legal fees on purchase and sale
- Estate agent fees
- Capital gains tax on disposal of the asset
- Possible penalty fees on early repayment of mortgage

…not to mention the costs of the actual renovation or construction.

It really is essential that you sit down right at the start with a financial advisor who is used to dealing with property investments or, even better, a wealth manager, so that you can plan the best investment route to take.

*RICS' report says house prices will rise everywhere over the next five years, from 2 per cent a year in the North to 9.3 per cent a year in London.*

*Savills sees house prices rising by 25 per cent over five years across Britain, but adds that some areas will outstrip that.*
**thisismoney.co.uk, April 2014**

# KEY NOTES

- The short-term return strategy is a relatively risky one

- It tends to be capital intensive, so you will need some money behind you

- I would only recommend this strategy when you can be sure the market is rising at a good rate

- There is usually a lot of competition from other investors for the kind of property that will give shorter-term returns, so make sure you're in the best possible position to negotiate a purchase and keep persevering!

- Check out all the tax and mortgage cost implications with your financial advisor

- If you're looking to develop land, spend some time doing specific research and building a relationship with the local town and country planner(s)

- You might consider partnering with a local developer who already has the contacts to proceed efficiently with a build

# Chapter 6

# Investing for returns in the longer term

This really is the easiest property investment 'strategy'. If you're looking for long-term returns, property is a very low risk investment vehicle because virtually all property will give a decent capital growth return over a period of fifteen or more years. You'd have to be extremely unlucky not to make money from property simply by buying and holding it.

As I've said before, that's a key reason why property makes such an excellent investment. You can build a portfolio on the basis of an income strategy and make money month-on-month from buy to let, knowing that you'll also benefit from natural capital appreciation over the long term. The capital increase may not be as great with a multi-let property as it is with a more 'traditional' home, but that's why you should build a varied portfolio; so you can get different returns in different ways at different times.

## Single-let units

This kind of property investment can be anything from a studio apartment to a large family home. The difference between letting a property to one individual, couple or family and letting something as an HMO is the monthly rental income. There are exceptions to the rule - mainly when you're talking about capital cities, where corporate let apartments and exclusive high-earner-style homes attract a premium – but, in the main, people invest in single lets as more of a pension pot. The rent might produce a little income, but it's the capital appreciation over the long term that investors are relying on.

It's virtually impossible to guarantee what kind of property is going to appreciate by the greatest percentage over the long term, but you can give yourself the best possible chance by following some fundamental principles. Properties that are short on supply and highly in demand from people who can afford to buy are the ones that will realise the highest gains, so it's a case of how to predict that future demand.

## Assessing future demand

In the absence of a crystal ball, this means doing some solid research. The good news is that these days there are some very good information portals online. Take a look at your local council's development plans on their website, which will show all new job creation and infrastructure projects that the local authority is working on. Several estate agents and property consultants are also doing excellent research themselves, much of which is freely available to you. Savills, in particular, have a first-class department dedicated to analysing markets and producing reports, so it's well worth going into the nearest branch and speaking to them.

Look at where affordability is reasonable, in the middle range of the market, as these are the areas where most of the working population tends to settle and where they're likely to remain for the foreseeable future. Schools, hospitals and shopping centres don't tend to move, so properties with easy access to all three will probably be a very safe bet. Houses within the catchment of schools that have had a good reputation for a number of years are particularly desirable, tending to increase in value well and sell quickly.

I'd also recommend going for a property with a minimum of two bedrooms. Affordability for first time buyers has been an issue for around a decade now, whereas families and friends are more likely to be able to afford to buy together. And as people live longer and the availability and cost of care becomes more and more of an issue, we're seeing a trend towards elderly relatives moving back in with their children, so homes with three or more bedrooms and/ or the potential for an annexe will be what middle-aged buyers will increasingly look for.

The other thing to bear in mind is that you may want or need to access the equity sooner than you planned to, so buying something that has a unique or at least rare quality will help give you the 'edge' if you need to sell quickly. They're not building Victorian or Edwardian properties any more, so going for a nice character property is a fairly safe bet. If you're going for a more modern home, perhaps something in a block or on a development, try to get one with a corner plot, extra parking or at the end of a cul de sac – just something that makes it a little more desirable than the neighbouring properties.

Those are some generally good principles but the fact is, each area has its own market and the property professionals working in that market are best placed to inform and advise you, so the most sensible thing for you to do is start building relationships with them.

## Making sure you cover yourself in the meantime

Going hand in hand with your research into future demand in the sales market must be research into the likely rental demand from now until you're planning to dispose of the property. While your main focus for this investment is its capital gain, you must make sure the rental returns at least cover the costs of holding and maintaining the property, as well as keeping up with inflation. If you have to start subsidising the investment every month and/or the rent you can charge starts to be worth less and less to you in real terms, that's not a good investment.

Again, speaking to local letting agents should pretty much tell you all you need to know about the market, and do make sure you ask

Complete Property Investment Success

the simple question: 'What do you always need more of?'. In every area there will be a type of property that letting agents always wish they had more of on their books, so see whether that type of stock matches up with the type that looks like a good long-term sales prospect and you should have an ideal investment.


## Beware the 'sourcers'

It may sound like a lot of work for you to research the investment yourself and there are plenty of companies and individuals who would be more than happy to put together deals for you. I'd steer clear. It really doesn't take much more time and effort to find properties yourself than it would take to check out the pedigree of these companies and deals. If this is their business, they're making a good profit from some stage of the deal – profit that you could be keeping for yourself.

I always recommend buying reasonably close to where you live, so that you can really get to know the market and build relationships, and you'll find that if you do that properly for your first investment, it'll be much, much easier when you come to make a second. Sourcers tend to either charge you a flat fee up front or take a percentage of the value of the deal, which means they have their money and it doesn't make any difference to them whether the investment works out or not. There are a few companies that retain an interest in the property and offer to manage the whole purchase process and management for you but, in my opinion, these are

www.nickfox.co.uk

usually incredibly bad value for money. I've yet to see one I'd recommend to anyone.

## Commercial property

A buzz about commercial investing began a few years ago in the investment community, I think mainly because people were looking to diversify their portfolios and fancied something different to residential buy to let.

Investing in commercial property is certainly a good way to diversify your portfolio, as it's a different kind of property market. The value is based on not just the bricks and mortar value of the property itself but also on the quality of the tenant and length of the lease. That means there is the potential to buy something with a short lease remaining and modest rent, make some improvements to the property to attract a better, different kind of tenant and add significant value to your investment.

Commercial lets are often said to be more stable than residential, because leases tend to be anywhere between 5 and 25 years in length. Most commercial leases are 'insuring and repairing', which means the tenant is responsible for everything for the duration of their lease so, unlike with residential buy to let, you have no on-going maintenance or repair bills. With these longer leases, you may also be able to set periodical automatic rent increases at the start, making it easier for you to plan ahead.

In terms of natural increase in capital value, assuming you don't make any improvements, commercial properties don't tend to rise at the same rate as residential homes, mainly because of the difference in demand. As the population increases, more and more homes are needed, but with businesses always looking to consolidate, there's not the same proportional rise in demand. However, yields for commercial properties are usually slightly higher on average than for standard residential single-unit lets, which makes up for that, to a certain extent. And, because the leases are longer, you don't have the same risk of void periods as you do with residential.

## What should I buy?

As with any property investment, you need to be very careful about what you buy and the type of business your tenant is in because the commercial market is much more vulnerable to economic fluctuations - people don't need warehouses and office blocks in the same way that they need a roof over their heads. That being said, there is currently a lot of evidence that UK commercial property is a fairly safe bet.

*'In June 2013, Investec Wealth, the wealth manager, announced it was moving its discretionary clients to an overweight holding in UK commercial property over the next 12 months, with the best opportunities outside London.'*
**FT.com, August 2013**

The FT also reported that construction output levels are still very low and suggested that the supply of new commercial premises is likely to be extremely limited over the next 5 years.

And in July 2014, Savills Research UK Commercial reported:

*'UK commercial activity expands at sharpest pace in four months.'*

Because of the lack of new build office space, it seems that there is certainly money to be made in buying 'tired' existing office premises and bringing them up to a sharp, modern standard. As with any renovation project, you will need to invest a good amount of capital, but the uplift in value, combined with the rent you should be able to charge the right tenant, should more than compensate you.

Probably the most common kind of commercial investment for private individuals in the past has been a shop with residential accommodation above, because the letting of larger office buildings and industrial units is more complex and demands more specialist knowledge. But I have a couple of warehouses that I've let for a few years now, without any trouble, and I'd suggest it's well worth looking at all commercial opportunities in your area that fall within your affordability.

You will need to spend some time understanding the commercial market and find specialists in commercial financing, surveying and letting to advise you. I'd recommend investing locally, as you'll already have an awareness of the shape of the economy. Just as the demand for residential rental varies from area to area, so certain commercial propositions will be better than others, depending on local market forces and future plans.

*Bear in mind...*
- In terms of financing, you'll probably need to invest more capital than you would in a similarly-priced residential property as LTVs are usually a maximum of 65%
- Banks will generally put some restrictive covenants on commercial lending
- It can be very difficult to remove a tenant during their tenancy
- Roughly half of all new businesses fail within the

first three years (you'll find a variety of figures quoted by different sources, but 50% seems to be a fair approximation) so check your tenant out thoroughly before agreeing the lease terms

- If you want to refinance, the banks will take into account the quality of the current tenant when valuing the property and its lease

I've talked here about buying and holding a commercial property but there is also the option of turning your investment around more quickly – although that's less common. You could simply improve the property and the value of the lease and re-sell, but when yields are perceived as generally good and you can factor in rent increases, why not hold on to it. If you buy right, you could be sitting on a very profitable piece of prime real estate!

## Land banking (via companies)

I'm going to be brief here, because land banking is purely speculative – it's like gambling. As with investing overseas, which I'm going to cover in the next chapter, it's only for those with money to spare.

The concept is that you either buy a specific plot that you own yourself or, as is more common, you form part of 'consortium' that funds the purchase of a larger piece of land. The land doesn't have planning permission and has been selected because someone believes that it will be possible to secure planning for a significant development – either residential or commercial – in the future.

There are a lot of land banking companies offering plots for investment, where your capital is usually tied up for an absolute minimum of 5 years. There's no certain medium to long-term outcome and, because all you have is a piece of unused land, you're not getting any income in the meantime. I don't consider that a sensible investment because if capital growth isn't assured, you need to be getting a decent monthly return.

*"Plan and prepare for the future, because that's where you're going to spend the rest of your life."*

**Mark Twain**

# KEY NOTES

- Buy in a location where the infrastructure and local economy are sound, and local services are within easy reach

- Character properties or homes with distinguishing features tend to sell on well

- No matter how good the purchase deal, make sure the investment stacks up on the rental front and gives you an on-going return that's at least as good as you could get from a savings account or other more traditional investment

- Consider commercial property but bear in mind you'll need specialist advice – see Chapter 9

- Steer clear of land-banking companies!

# Chapter 7

# Investing overseas

Investing overseas is an odd proposition. It's probably the most risky type of property investment you can make and the most difficult to get right. Ironically, it's the people who are least prepared and least equipped to make the decision to invest overseas who often end up doing it. They get blinded by impressive marketing and sales patter, jump in and usually find themselves stuck with something that bears no resemblance to the deal they thought they were getting; in the worst cases, losing all their capital.

It's not a reliable income strategy, because the associated management costs - not to mention the cost of you travelling to the property when necessary – tend to be so high, so if you're considering an overseas investment, it should be based on capital appreciation. And that's something of an issue, because projecting how a relatively new market is likely to perform over the coming years is very tricky.

## The dream
Most people who are interested in property and have money to invest have been targeted at some point with overseas 'opportunities', so

you've probably seen the dream yourself. It's the promise that if you put your money into land and/or new developments in up-and-coming 'hotspots', you'll be able to sell in a few years for a huge profit and benefit from great rental returns in the meantime. Often, the projected rental returns come with a 'guarantee' and there may also be a financing option on offer that means you can make all this money in return for very little investment of your own capital.

The brochures, scale models and locations make the properties look glamorous and high quality. Impressive facts and figures about huge demand and a stream of locals or tourists begging for just this kind of accommodation will be forthcoming and the focus will be on the dazzling potential returns.

## The reality

The success stories and instances where investors have really made a lot of money in overseas markets are few and far between. That's because it takes a lot of effort and expertise to be able to identify a market that's right at the start of its growth spurt and, to get the best returns, you need to make your investment at a very early stage. And when a market is at that early a stage in its cycle, you're unlikely to be able to secure financing, so it means you'll be funding your investment 100% yourself. That's a heck of a risk to take.

The people who take these risks spend a lot of time on planes, visiting countries, meeting and building relationships with local developers and officials. It really does take money to make money overseas and I'm confident in saying that all the truly successful overseas investors have also lost a good deal of money. But, because they're well capitalised, they can afford to gamble and when they win big it more than makes up for any losses along the way.

These are the people who are selling deals to you. By the time they've secured planning permission and put financing schemes in place, it's been two or three years since they made their own investment and the initial opportunity for big profit has passed.

So when you're presented with something that looks almost too good to be true, you have to ask yourself: if it's such a great deal and the profits are so certain, why aren't the developers keeping it for themselves? Because they can make a lot more money from selling to naïve investors at inflated purchase prices that no local person or large investment institution would dream of paying – that's the reality much of the time.

Financing schemes usually consist of some kind of personal loan that is secured on an existing asset, probably your own home, and the 'guaranteed' rental returns will be fixed in some way, certainly built into the price you're paying. When the period of that guarantee comes to an end, most return slump. Then, because all the virtually identical units have been sold to investors under the same investment principle, you find everyone wants to sell at the same time. The result is a flood of property to a market where locals can't afford to pay inflated prices and other investors want new builds, not second hand properties in a location that's yesterday's news.

I realise I'm painting a biased and sceptical picture, but I honestly have yet to see an overseas deal that meets my own risk/reward criteria. Investing in so-called 'emerging' markets is not something I've done myself, or would ever do.

But if you think it's worth taking the risk for a potentially excellent return that can't be matched by any UK-based property investment, read on.

## Types of opportunity

There are three main types of investment you can make:

### Land

Buying land in an area where the market cycle is in its absolute infancy and being as sure as you can be that there will be an economic infrastructure in the near future to support it is how you'll make the best return. As I mentioned above, it does carry high risk, because you'll probably be buying before planning permission has been secured and will more than likely need to buy the land for cash.

You can make smaller investments by buying a small piece of land on your own or a larger plot as part of a consortium; if you have a lot of capital, you can enter into larger ventures. For that, you would need to take the time to research and secure local business partners, and that's a major investment that very few people would enter into on their own.

The investment plan is usually for a lump-sum return, either within a couple of years, through selling the land at a significant mark-up, or in three to five years, by building it out and selling the development. Some developers choose to keep an interest, either by retaining the freehold of the whole site and/or ownership of an income-generating asset, such as a restaurant or hotel.

Pro: Because you're getting in at a very early stage, there is the potential for excellent short to medium-term profit.
Con: It's very high risk and capital intensive.

**Off-plan**
This is probably the most common type of opportunity you'll be offered. You're usually investing at the stage where planning permission has been granted and the architects' designs, scale models and artists' impressions have been created. Work may or may not have started on the development.

There are a few things to be very wary of. Firstly, what you're looking at is an idealistic, sanitised version of the end result. And this is just one reason why I don't like buying off-plan – I like to be able to look at and around a property and see exactly what I'm putting my money into. Secondly, planning permission has not always been fully granted, so make sure you find that out, or you may be investing into a pipe dream. Thirdly, there's the timescale. Building projects invariably take longer than planned, so your rental returns are unlikely to start rolling in when you expect them to.

Finally, and most significantly, there are the projected returns themselves. The promised capital gain is likely to be the main focus of the sales pitch, hotly followed by rental returns, but what are these projections based on? You're usually buying into a new market which, as I've already covered, will more than likely have already had its initial growth spurt, so don't be fooled by any of the historical price growth figures – they're fairly meaningless for you.

Pro: None that I can think of!
Con: You're buying an idea, nothing tangible. At least when you're buying land, you can see the ground!

**Existing developments**

This is where you can see exactly what it is you're buying. It may be almost finished, recently completed or a second-hand sale. The 'red flag' with this is the fact that it's available at all. Generally speaking, when an overseas opportunity is genuinely that good, the whole development is sold at the off-plan stage. Developers want to get their money back as soon as possible, so it's highly unlikely any of them would deliberately hold back on the release of units until they're fully built.

And by the time a development is complete, the market cycle has usually already slowed right down or plateaued entirely, which means you've missed the boat as far as decent capital growth is concerned. I'd suggest the only people who should be buying at this stage are those who want a holiday home for themselves that they can rent out the rest of the year to keep things ticking over money-wise. It's unlikely to be a financially rewarding move or a viable investment opportunity for the pure investor.

Pro: You can at least see the property as it really is.
Con: The market has probably already emerged and shaken itself dry, so returns are unlikely to be worth the effort and cost involved in buying overseas.

The long and short of overseas investing, in my opinion, is that it's only for the well-capitalised and well-connected speculative investor - or the holiday home buyer. Yes, the potential returns if you get in early enough may be better than anything you could achieve in the UK, but you also run a far greater risk of losing your investment.

However, you may still think it's worth a go, in the interests of diversifying your portfolio and having somewhere you could holiday yourself. In that case, there are a few key things I'd suggest you look at very carefully before you take the plunge.

# Be very wary of...

## The proposed exit strategy

Generally speaking, units in overseas developments are sold to the same kind of investor: someone who wants a decent lump-sum return in around 3 years. I'm always amazed that it occurs to so few people to question who, exactly, is going to be there to buy what they're trying to sell. As I've already said, locals either can't afford to buy or don't want what's being sold and other investors want the latest new build, not a second-hand unit. For the very few buyers who might be interested, they have such a choice that the price can be driven right down.

A very good example of this is the coastal apartment craze in Spain in the early 2000s, when investors snapped up units on the new developments that were springing up by the sea. And yes, a few lucky people who'd got in right at the start managed to make a decent return. But by the time most people came to sell, the realisation dawned that there was no resale market as investors had moved on to the new 'hotspots' - Cyprus, Romania, Cape Verdi... Spain was old news and they'd be lucky if they simply broke even because the market was flooded with identical properties that nobody wanted to buy. Many have simply been left with an unwanted holiday apartment that costs them money every year.

So the first questions you should ask when you're looking for a lump sum return is: who's going to buy it, why, and how are they going to be able to pay what I want for it?

## Forecasted returns

You'll be tempted by some excellent-sounding returns, but make sure you ask what they're based on. What happened in the previous couple of years is irrelevant, as there's no guarantee that kind of growth will continue. Just as when you're investing in a new area in the UK, you need to be asking questions about the local economy and infrastructure: are there currently or are there plans in place to build schools and shops, are businesses moving into the area and does it have decent transport links?

## Guaranteed returns

Approach guaranteed returns with a healthy scepticism! If a developer is offering to guarantee a certain level of rental income for the property (usually for the first year or possibly 18 months), it suggests to me that they're not confident in the market. If it really was an excellent property for which there was huge demand, why would they need the 'carrot' of a guarantee to tempt you to buy? And they're not doing it out of the goodness of their hearts, so be aware you're paying for it somewhere along the line, either in the purchase price or the maintenance charge.

## Price

Where have they got this from? It's quite tricky to accurately value a new build in the UK, and we have a very established and secure economy and property market. Trying to put a definite value on a new kind of accommodation that's being offered in a very young market is virtually impossible. The developer or agent will have their own team of surveyors and will put forward all kinds of evidence to support the price, but it's highly advisable to get your own, independent second opinion.

## Legal and financial professionals

The opportunity is usually packaged nicely so you don't have to 'worry' about anything. The developer/agent will put you in touch with their finance people and legal team who are well acquainted with the way this deal is structured and have all the right contacts on the ground to ensure everything goes smoothly. You may even be assigned a personal consultant who will keep you up to date every step of the way.

We're back to the old, 'if it looks too good to be true...' Companies selling investments want to make it as easy as possible for you to part with your money because they're in it to make a big profit themselves. So, while you shouldn't have to 'worry', you absolutely must do your due diligence. Have your own independent financial advisor or mortgage broker look at the financing and instruct your own legal representative, ideally one from a firm that has offices and staff trained in both the UK and whichever country you're looking at investing in.

**Get on a plane**
You'll probably be told this is an ideal 'armchair investment', where you can make a lot of money for very little effort yourself, and I simply don't believe that's possible. I'm a firm believer in gut instinct and I would never buy a property unseen in an area I hadn't visited. You get a feeling for a place, so if you truly believe the opportunity you're being offered is a great one, spend a few hundred pounds on seeing the plot or the development for yourself.

## In summary
You'll have gathered I'm not a fan of investing overseas. Yes, it is possible to succeed and make a lot of money, but if you're going to do that effectively it's pretty much a full-time job. And that's not what about making investments to secure your financial future is about.

Really look at all the costs involved and work out whether the returns look good enough to risk buying in a largely untested market, with a legal system, language and culture you may not understand, a long way from home. And when you're calculating profit, make sure you talk to someone who's a financial expert in overseas investing, because there are likely to be tax implications in bringing money back to the UK, not to mention the risk of exchange rate fluctuations. The returns that have been dangled under your nose may not be quite as attractive when you look at what you're actually likely to net.

As far as I'm concerned, the UK offers such a wide range of ways in which you can make money from property, there's no reason to go to the trouble or take on the risk of buying abroad. We have a solid economy that supports one of the most stable and secure property markets in the world and there are a plethora of opportunities very close to your doorstep.

# KEY NOTES

- The only reason the returns are higher in emerging markets is that the risks are higher

- Approach any company selling you an opportunity with a healthy skepticism!

- If you decide to buy off-plan or an existing property, go for something unique, e.g. a one-off design, a penthouse or a corner apartment with a larger balcony

- Tourist and investment trends can come and go, particularly when you're talking about 'emerging markets', so make sure there's a solid local economy and demand to support the exit from your investment

- Use your own, independent team of legal and financial advisors, who have offices both in the UK and in the country in question

- Spend time with an overseas tax expert and understand the implications of bringing money back into the UK

# PART THREE:

# PUTTING IT INTO PRACTICE

# Chapter 8

# What kind of investor are you?

Understanding something about the array of property investment options available to you is one thing; choosing which will suit you is quite another. I've heard it said many times that not everyone is suited to property as an investment vehicle, but I don't agree. While not everyone can necessarily make a success of building and managing a portfolio of HMOs, property is such a varied form of investment that you're bound to find a path that works for you.

All that being said, assuming you're planning to take my advice and source your own properties to build a portfolio – whether big or small - you need to have the right personality and skill set, an appropriate attitude to risk, sufficient time available and a decent amount of money to invest. If you'd rather let someone else handle the acquisition and management of property assets for you, then your own skills, experience and time needn't come into the equation. Mind you, I hope I've already been clear that if you'd rather take the hands-off approach, you do run the risk of ending up with properties that aren't necessarily going to deliver what you want and need and your profits certainly won't be as great.

*"An investment in knowledge pays the best interest."*

**Benjamin Franklin**

## Your financial position

I'm starting with this because the amount of capital you have and your ability to borrow will obviously govern what kind of investments you can make.

Property investing nowadays is a fairly capital-intensive business. With pretty much every other form of investment, you put your money in at the start and that's that. The capital value might go up and you may get regular interest payments or dividends, or the capital value might drop, but it's highly unlikely you'll be expected to top up your initial investment.

Property, on the other hand needs maintaining. Even if it's freshly renovated or a new build, there will still be things that need doing down the line. If you have void periods, where the property is un-let, you still have to pay the mortgage and possibly other bills, such as council tax and utility bills. If you have HMOs, you'll probably be responsible for on-going general maintenance and if it's a leasehold property there will be a service charge and ground rent to consider. Yes, you work all these costs into your budget and ensure the rental income is such that you're not left out of pocket every month, but you need to prepare yourself and put money aside for the larger jobs that come along every 5, 10 or 15 years, such as new boilers, kitchens, bathrooms, carpets and redecoration. So you need to plan and budget ahead.

**Buy to let mortgages**: On average, a lender will want to see a surveyor's rental valuation equal to or greater than 125% of the mortgage repayment amount. For example:

| | |
|---|---|
| Purchase price | £200,000 |
| Mortgage at 75% LTV | £150,000 |
| Monthly interest-only mortgage at 5% | £625 |
| Surveyor's valuation must be at least | £781 |

Note that, while the mortgage is based primarily on the rental income, the lender will also want to see your personal income at a certain level, usually £25,000 or more.

And at the start, there's the initial deposit and purchase costs for each property. Buy to let mortgages at reasonable rates will probably be at no more than 75-80% loan to value (LTV), so you'll need enough capital available to cover 20-25% of the purchase price for the deposit, plus:

- Stamp Duty Land Tax (likely to be 1% for the average buy to let; 3% over £250,000)
- around 1% of the purchase price for all your other fees and services

- potentially tens of thousands for renovation and refurbishment.

If you've researched your purchase and the market properly, all that money should represent simply an initial and then further investment – it's not as though you're losing it; you're just 'moving' it from the bank into bricks and mortar....which brings me nicely on to my next point...


## What's your attitude to risk and debt?

If you're buying property at the current UK average of approaching around £200,000, you can easily find yourself with mortgage debt of £160k and £50k of your own capital tied up in each property (80% LTV, plus assuming some refurbishment). If you're building a portfolio, you will quickly pass the million pound mark in terms of borrowing and you are responsible for making the mortgage repayments on that debt every month.

The common perception is that property is low risk, 'safe as houses', but in the investment market it's regarded as medium risk. Prices can go down and if you don't keep up the repayments on the mortgage, you could be in danger of losing your investment entirely. That being said, the likelihood of it actually happening to you is incredibly small, unless you made a truly terribly error in judgment on purchase.

The key to successful investment is taking a **calculated** risk and a great benefit of investing in property, versus something like the stock market, is that it's within your power to minimise that risk. Letting a property for a level of rent that covers the associated costs each month and gives you some profit on top means you shouldn't ever have to subsidise the mortgage repayments – your borrowing is 'good debt' rather than 'bad debt'. And as long as you did your research properly before you bought it and maintain it well, you shouldn't have any nasty surprises down the line.

The caveat is that you do need to cover yourself, just in case. Never spend all your profit; keep a proportion aside so that if the worst should happen and you end up with an extended period without a tenant or an unexpectedly large bill for work on the property, the money's there.

Planning for the best but preparing for the worst is simply a sensible way to approach business and although property investment carries risk, I would certainly say that well-planned property investment is less risky than many other options for your money. Yes, prices can fluctuate and demand can change, but buildings are flexible things. You can change the type of tenant, type of let and the way the accommodation is laid out (subject to local council regulations and planning permission, of course), letting for as long as you want or need, then refinancing or selling when the time is right.

So how's it all sounding to you so far? Hopefully good, but if you have any doubts, please take some time to think about what you're looking at getting yourself into. I'm sure I've said it before, but I'm going to say it again: I love property – and I've got loads of mortgage debt! I'm really happy with my investment plans and I have good systems in place for my property business so I'm confident that on the risk:reward ratio, reward is winning by a mile.

But that's me; you might feel differently. And there's no point in leveraging yourself to the hilt with an income-generating portfolio that makes you good money month on month if it also gives you anxiety and sleepless nights because you're so worried about how much you owe the bank and how you'll manage if all the tenants leave and five properties turn out to need new roofs. So have a good think.

## More about you...

Much of life and business is about selling, negotiation and problem solving, and successful property investment demands that you're good at all three. In short, you have to be good with people: intuitive, diplomatic and personable.

To a greater or lesser extent, depending on your investment strategy, you have to be able to build relationships with estate agents (after you've worked out which are going to be the most useful to you); present yourself to vendors in the best light and negotiate purchases; work effectively with legal and financial advisors; attract, screen and manage tenants and their problems; deal with contractors....

all of which you'll be far more successful at if you're a 'people person' with great communication skills.

There are certainly people operating in the property investment industry who are anything but diplomatic and personable – they're simply skilled at persuasion and manipulation – and who are nonetheless perceived as successful. Those kinds of people tend to either do a series of one-off deals so that they're working with new people each time or act as the 'charming' face of a company but get other people to actually handle the business. They enjoy bouts of short-term success but usually also suffer big losses periodically and many have been declared bankrupt more than once or had their companies put into administration.

But when you're making an investment for your long-term financial security, you can't afford to be like that, especially if you're going to trust other people to handle the various different aspects of your portfolio and financial affairs – something I'll come on to in detail in the next chapter.

## How are your business and admin skills?

I've said already that if you have a buy to let property portfolio, you have a property business. If you're investing in a series of single-let properties that an agent is letting and managing for you, you won't have too much administration to handle yourself, but if you're carrying out renovation, self-build or building a portfolio of HMOs, there is a huge amount of paperwork and other jobs that need to be carried out.

To give you an idea, here are some of the main administrative and business elements of investing in property:

(a) Regardless of how you let, refurbish and sell or build, you will need to be concerned with:
- Initial wealth / investment planning with a suitable financial advisor
- Investment research / documentation
- Legal and financial purchase paperwork
- Survey report
- On-going bookkeeping, tax returns and capital gains matters

(b) If you refurbish:
- All of (a)
- Quotes and bills for refurbishment
- Dealing with the local council for building regulations compliance and planning permission, as necessary, particularly so if the property is to be an HMO
- Engagement and management of contractors
- Receipts, warranties, etc for work

(c) If you're having an agent manage your buy to lets for you:
- All of (a)
- Possibly all of (b)

- Ensuring the property is health & safety compliant (installing smoke detectors, correct ventilation, etc.)
- Gaining gas safe, electrical and energy performance certificates
- Possibly furnishing the property
- Sourcing a suitable agent
- Agreeing tenancy terms
- Signing off larger maintenance and repair jobs
- Checking monthly rent has been received

(d) If you're self-managing a single let:
- All of (a)
- Possibly all of (b)
- Ensuring the property is health & safety compliant (installing smoke detectors, correct ventilation, etc.)
- Gaining gas safe, electrical and energy performance certificates
- Possibly furnishing the property
- Advertising for, interviewing and referencing tenants
- The tenancy agreement
- Checking tenants in and out and taking or organising an inventory
- Protecting the tenant's deposit
- Collecting and chasing rent, as necessary
- Dealing with tenant and property issues
- Rent reviews, renewals and re-lets
- Maintaining the property and liaising with contractors – as

well as building a good relationship with them
- Organising annual gas safety checks and periodical electrical and fire safety checks

If you're self-managing an HMO:
- All of (a), (b) and (d)
- Possibly getting the property licensed, depending on local authority requirements (definitely, if the property has 5 or more people living over 3 or more storeys)
- Several time over the amount of paperwork and probably maintenance as for a single let
- Paying council tax and probably utility bills and a TV license
- Organising cleaning services
- Managing a team. As your portfolio grows, you will certainly need to take on some staff – assuming you don't want to run yourself into the ground! – so will encounter all the administration that comes with having employees.

If you decide to go into self-build and/or development, that's a small business turn-around in itself.

In consultation with your financial advisor or wealth manager, you may also be dealing with:
- Setting up and assuming directorship of a limited company
- Trusts
- Other tax-efficiency and inheritance planning

…the list goes on and the above is by no means exhaustive. There is a lot to do so, while you can learn as you go along, it's a great help if you've already had experience of running a business, no matter how small, and are very organised with a keen eye for detail.

You're also going to need to be self-motivated. Once you've been investing for a few years and have built a good local reputation, some deals will come to you but, for the most part, you need to go out there and find them for yourself. You've got to be keen enough to really make a success of your property investments to keep looking for ways to refine your portfolio and make it as profitable as possible, without compromising on quality, care or your legal obligations. And nobody's going to be there making you do it!

## How much time do you have?

This is a big factor in deciding what kind of investments will suit you.

I've chosen to dedicate most of my time to property investment because I'm sure it will pay dividends in the future. However, I'm in my early 40s and have been investing seriously for the past nine years; you may be in a different position and if you're coming to this later in life, or you already have a busy job that you love, you may not want to dedicate as much time as I have.

To build a portfolio, particularly an income-generating one, the first few years are very hard work. If you're taking on any building work - from even minor refurbishment to a new build – you can't underestimate the amount of time you'll need to dedicate to the project. If you choose to self-manage your buy to let properties, you not only need to set time aside for carrying out admin and viewings, but also accept that you'll need to be 'on call' for any problems or things that need your attention at short notice.

Again, I'll say that I think the hard work in the early days is well worth the time investment, because of the financial benefits, but you might feel differently.

## What's your time worth?
A big part of deciding what kind of investor you want to be comes down to the value you place on your own time, both financially and emotionally. Broadly speaking, you'll make more gross profit the more hands on you are, but your time has a value and, while that might sound like an obvious thing to say, it always amazes me how many people forget about it.

You'll have seen people on 'Grand Designs' and 'Property Ladder' talking about the equity they've got or the profits they've made at the end of six months, a year, two years….but what about all the time they've spent on the project themselves, often working very late into the night, not going on holiday, sacrificing time with friends and family, taking time off from their 'day jobs'…? I often look at them when all the work's finished, they're exhausted and I think,

"Was it worth it?". Yes, it costs money to pay project managers and get contractors in to carry out every job, and I understand that sometimes people simply don't have the money in the bank to pay someone else, but a lot of the time it really is a false economy.

So think what else you could be doing with your time and what that's worth to you. It might be working on souring a new, profitable property deal; focusing more on your existing career; spending more time with friends and family; taking more holidays; pursuing sporting interests or other hobbies…all those things will have a value, whether monetary or emotional and you need to work out which tasks benefit you more.

There will be certain things, such as paperwork, bookkeeping and dealing with tenant problems, that you're not all that good at or that you don't feel confident about handling yourself. Now, you could train yourself to be better at those things – or you could simply employ someone else to do them for you. I'm a firm believer in playing to your strengths and find that investing my time in becoming more skilled at things for which I already have an aptitude is a far better choice than struggling through, trying to get to grips with something that doesn't come naturally.

*"To avoid your strengths and to focus on your weaknesses isn't a sign of diligent humility. It is almost irresponsible. By contrast the most responsible, the most challenging, and the most honorable thing to do is face*

*up to the strength potential inherent in your talents and then find ways to realize it."*

**Donald O. Clifton, Psychologist**

For me, the decision about how to manage my property investments comes down to three things:

1. Much of the admin and management is repetitive and can be irritating and quite disruptive to any daily routine. Some people like letting properties and managing tenants – a number of my clients find they get a great deal of satisfaction from having a system that works and making sure their tenants are happy – but that doesn't suit my temperament or personality.

2. I want to make sure my choice of investment improves the quality of my life and helps me realise my goals, one of which is to spend as much time as I can with my family, either at home or abroad. In order for that to happen, I need a system that can keep things running smoothly, whether I'm there every day or not; a business that continues to be profitable even when I'm in Spain for a fortnight!

3. I'm at my most effective when I'm helping others and finding new deals – those are the things that excite me and bring me the greatest financial rewards over the long-term. My time is best spent negotiating and mentoring; I can't afford to be spending the majority of the day in the office or

attending personally to the management of my properties...

...which is why I employ other people to run my portfolio.

## Your own business or someone else's?

So, in building a portfolio of investment properties, you have four choices:

1. Source, refurbish, let and manage properties yourself
2. Source properties yourself and employ people to let and manage them for you, building up a small property business
3. Source properties yourself and hand them over to a 3<sup>rd</sup> party letting agent
4. Pay an investment company or property 'sourcer' to find deals for you and then either manage them yourself or through a letting agent

I would never recommend option 4, because you're quite honestly paying through the nose for an investment that's out of your hands. As I said in the last chapter, I'm not a fan of using other people to find deals for you. Property sourcers simply take an up-front fee and have no financial interest in how your investment performs and investment companies usually play with the figures to make you think you're getting property at better value than you really are, then take a disproportionately large fee for their services.

Option 3 is worthwhile if you're going to be away from your investment area for much of the time or if you only have a couple of investments and don't want or feel able to manage them yourself. If you have a larger portfolio, you will end up paying more in fees than it would cost you to employ your own small team.

Option 1 is where you're likely to start out with your first couple of properties, and I'd always recommend getting your hands dirty at the beginning so that you really understand what's needed and what kind of person and skills it takes to be a good property manager. But, as I said earlier in the book, when you get to 5+ properties it can easily become a full-time job and that usually defeats the purpose of making the investments in the first place!

By far the best route to take, in my opinion, is Option 2, but that does demand good business, managerial and interpersonal skills. By building your own small business you keep much better control over income and expenditure; you have a dedicated team working only for you; you can tailor the staffing and business structure perfectly to your choice of type of investment properties and it's very easy to scale up, as discussed in Chapter 5.

But having an in-house team is only part of the picture. If you're going to be successful in property investing you need the right advice and services on many different fronts…

# KEY NOTES

- Make sure you properly 'cost out' the investments you intend to make and understand how much capital you'll need to invest in each property and when

- How do you feel about risk and debt? Are you happy to take on a high level of mortgage borrowing?

- Do your own risk:reward analysis – are you confident you'll be able to choose the right investments for yourself?

- Are you a 'people person'?

- Think about what your time is worth and where it's best spent

- Assess your own business strengths and weaknesses

- Are you able & prepared to build up and run a small property business yourself, or would you rather let someone else who is already established in lettings and management take care of your properties for you?

# Chapter 9

# Get the best advice

While it's a fabulous investment vehicle, property really should come with a warning, because it is a potential minefield. You need to make sure you buy the right things; mortgage rules, criteria and rates change regularly; your properties need to be bought and let out in a way that is legally right for you and your circumstances; there's a huge amount of legislation around buy to let that seems to be constantly updated or amended; you need to make sure management and maintenance problems are resolved quickly and effectively; any refurbishment or building work must be appropriate and approved; you need to be compliant with bookkeeping and tax regulations – in short, there's a lot you need to get right.

And you can't possibly be an expert in all those areas, so the very best thing you can do for your investment business is tap into the knowledge, skills and resources of the people who *are* experts in their own specific fields and surround yourself with some really good advisors, suppliers and associates.

I use the services of more than 25 different people on a regular basis. They're all very good at what they do, which enables me to acquire properties efficiently and for the business to run with minimal daily input from me. I think of these people as my 'team':

- Wealth Manager
- Specialist Property Lawyers
- Independent Mortgage Broker
- Accountant
- Bookkeeper
- Estate Agents
- Property Manager
- Lettings Negotiators
- Project Manager for refurbishments
- Maintenance team and specialist contractors
- Personal Assistant
- Business Manager

No matter how intuitive you are, you won't always pick the right people the first time and I've made a number of changes since I began investing. As you get to know your investments better, you'll realise exactly what skills and expertise you need and be able to refine your team accordingly. I've worked with most of my advisors, suppliers and employees for a number of years now and am happy that it's a very strong line-up.

A really important thing to bear in mind when you're interviewing or assessing the suitability of people you're considering working with is how much you actually like them. A lot of people say that they're not bothered about that – it's much more important that the person is good at their job – but I disagree. We're not talking about a one-off deal where you're never going to have to deal with that person again, we're talking about finding a number of people you can trust to help you invest in the best way for you and help make your future as financially secure as possible. These are people you'll be working with on a regular basis and I have no desire to work with people I don't like.

If you don't like someone, you're unlikely to trust them and there's a high level of trust in what you're asking of your team. Surround yourself with people with whom you feel a natural rapport and don't be tempted to engage someone just because they've been highly recommended to you or have exceptional qualifications and experience. People tend to do more for you, make themselves more available and go the extra mile if they actually like you, so build solid relationships, based on genuine trust and respect, with people whose company you enjoy and it will pay dividends in your investment business.

*"In the end, all business operations can be reduced to three words: people, product, and profits. Unless you've got a good team, you can't do much with the other two."*

**Lee Iacocca, Businessman & Former CEO of Chrysler**

*\*\*All professionals giving you financial advice MUST be properly qualified and regulated by the Financial Services Authority (FSA) and anyone giving you legal advice should be suitably qualified and regulated by The Law Society and the Solicitors Regulation Authority (SRA) (or the Council of Licensed Conveyancers (CLC)).*

## Wealth Manager

One of the most important things to consider is how property fits alongside your other financial interests. A Wealth Manager will look at all your financial affairs – earnings, investments, trusts, etc. – and work to ensure they're all complementing each other to achieve your investment goals and are tax efficient.

You can engage a wealth management firm or take advantage of your bank's wealth management service but try to make sure you're working with someone who either invests in property themselves or already has a number of property investor clients. It'll short-cut your discussions and they're likely to have researched the subject very well indeed.

Take your investment objectives and personal financial statement (see Chapter 1) along to your meeting, so that the Wealth Manager can get a clear picture of your current situation and what you want your financial future to look like. They can then help you decide the best way to structure your investments and, importantly, discuss whether property is even the best place for you to be putting your money. Although it's not terribly common, sometimes a person's existing financial situation and plans and needs for the future are better satisfied by another form of investment.

Importantly, a Wealth Manager can also help you with inheritance planning. Too many people invest in property so they have something to leave to their children, without realising that it can be one of the least tax-efficient ways to pass on money. You'll need to amend your Will and may need to set up Trusts – it's a complex area, and requires specialist advice.

The best advice certainly doesn't come cheap, but in the long run it will save you many, many times over what it costs you.

*As well as being FSA regulated, ideally they will also have the CISI Masters in Wealth Management (MCSI after their name).*

## Property tax specialist / accountant

Wealth management firms are usually able to give you tax advice and handle your accounts, but you must make sure that you've had a proper discussion with someone who is a property tax expert. Your property investment plans will impact your current tax situation - and vice versa - and a specialist will be able to advise you how to invest and set up and run your property business in the most tax-efficient way.

*As well as qualifying under the Association of Chartered Certified Accountants (ACCA), your tax advisor should also be a member of the Chartered Institute of Taxation (CTA).*

## Bookkeeper

You may want to try keeping your own books to start with, but I would suggest that unless you've already got bookkeeping experience and have thoroughly discussed with your tax advisor how to organize your affairs, it's far better to hand over this job to someone who's used to working with property investors. Quite apart form the technicalities of what to put where, the admin can mount up and it's unlikely to be the best use of your time. Bookkeepers needn't be expensive and, as with so many of the tasks you'll end up delegating, it's well worth the investment.

## Mortgage broker / IFA

Your mortgage broker can make or break a deal. You're looking for someone who understands exactly what you're aiming for and appreciates that things often need to happen quickly. Make sure they're independent (i.e. can access all mortgage products in the market) and have worked in the investment market, specifically buy to let, for a number of years, as they're likely to have established relationships with buy to let and HMO specialist lenders.

I'd never attempt to find a mortgage myself by going direct to different lenders, for three key reasons:

1. It can be incredibly time-consuming and I'm not a mortgage expert.
2. Good brokers usually have access to mortgage products that aren't publicised – you only know they're there if you ask about them, and if you don't know they're there…!
3. As an individual, trying to contact lenders to progress an application can be an incredibly frustrating experience and you're unlikely to have any luck moving it along quickly. An effective broker will be able to access the right people and push your application through.

Having a good broker will really add value to your investment portfolio. Being well financed will mean you'll not only be able to act quickly on deals, but also get better deals and therefore be more profitable, and a good broker will always make sure you're one step ahead by periodically reviewing your mortgages and advising you of new, upcoming products that might be more suitable.

If you're looking at self-build or commercial investments, you may need to find a specialist broker for those. Financing for development projects is harder to come by so it's especially important you're working with someone who knows what they're doing and has a good track record.

*Any person acting as a broker or making recommendations for your mortgage finance must have one or more of these qualifications: Certificate in Mortgage Advice (Cert MA); Certificate in Mortgage Advice and Practice (CeMAP) from the ifa School of Finance; Mortgage Advice and Practice Certificate (MAPC) from the CIB in Scotland.*

## Specialist property lawyer

Ideally, they should be buy to let specialists and have experience of dealing with whatever type of property investments you're planning to make. As with your broker, your legal representative can make the difference between a smooth and speedy transaction and a complete nightmare! You can instruct either a solicitor or a licensed conveyancer – both are qualified to handle property transactions – but one of the benefits of engaging a solicitor is that you can choose a firm that also has solicitors specialising in other areas of law. That means your legal representative can tap into the knowledge of colleagues for advice on things like tax planning, Wills, litigation, etc. and you may be able to keep all your legal affairs under one roof.

Some firms have specific case-progression departments; some solicitors/conveyancers will progress things themselves. Both have pros and cons - the important thing for you to establish is:

1. Are they happy to work to a timescale established at the start (unforeseen circumstances aside)?

2. Will they update you regularly?
3. Will you be able to easily speak to the person directly dealing with your transaction?

You should also make sure that whoever you choose is happy to liaise with your broker/IFA and Wealth Manager to make sure the legal purchase structure of your investments is on track with your objectives. I know all this might sound like a lot to ask but this kind of legal professional does exist!

If the only property purchases you've made have been for your own home, there's every likelihood you've engaged a solicitor over the phone or online and have never actually met them. However, now that you're going to be making a number of investments over a number of years, take the time to go and meet a few different people face to face. Your lawyer's performance will be crucial to your success so make sure there's a good personal relationship and understanding from the start.

**...and a legal lettings expert**

Lettings legislation is constantly under review and it's virtually impossible for you to keep up to date with the latest changes and new laws and requirements yourself. If you're employing an in-house property manager, make sure they're experienced and qualified through the Association of Residential Letting Agents (ARLA). That means they have to abide by a code of conduct and you can be confident they're fully briefed and up to date with regulations.

The alternative, if you're self-managing, is to retain the services of a legal lettings expert who can check that your tenancy agreements and management procedures are legally correct, advise and assist in serving notices to tenants and handle any eviction processes for you.

If you're intending to invest in HMOs or undertake any building work, the other person who can really help you stay on the right side of the law is a local planning expert. Planning regulations have a tendency to change rather quietly, so if you can build a relationship with a Chartered Town Planner, they can guide you and help you minimise the risk of falling foul of regulations.

## Your own in-house team

I talked about building your own business and team of employees in the last chapter and the first person you should probably look to take on is a Property Manager. If you choose someone who is able and willing to take on other tasks while your portfolio is small, you can employ them full time from the outset. As I've already said, make sure they're ARLA qualified, or at least in training, and have some experience of handling tenants and property maintenance issues.

If you pick the right person, they should be able to manage other staff you might take on, such as a bookkeeper. Many of you reading this probably aren't planning on building a business as large as a lot of professional investors', so you'll probably be able to manage with just one or two people working for you. If, however, you do plan on building your own investment property empire, you're likely to have four or five employees. Either way, you will need to take some legal advice on employment law; your accountant will be able to help you set things up legally with HMRC.

## Other service providers

Estate agents and contractors are the two main other types of service provider you'll need to build good relationships with. As I said in the last chapter, if you're going to be hands-on in building a portfolio of investment properties, you do need to be a 'people person' and making a good name for yourself as a reliable investor who does what they say you're going to do when you say you'll do it is particularly important here. These people work and live in the local area and you want the only words that get around to be good ones!

### Estate agents

In most estate agencies these days there's at least one member of staff who understands about buying property purely as an investment and you need to make sure you're dealing with that person and that they understand exactly what you're looking for and why. Avoid agents who want to take your contact details before they've even asked what you're looking for – focus on the ones who actually want to have a conversation. You also want someone who knows the area and market well, so try to deal with senior negotiators or the branch manager, as they're more likely to be able to have a productive discussion.

Independent agents are usually owned and/or managed by people who have lived and worked in the area for quite some time. They're often on local boards and well connected, so can be a very useful source of information about upcoming properties and developments, planning and other investors who may be interested in partnering on projects.

Talk to the agents about your plans, show them you have your finances and legal representation in place, then view a few properties and explain exactly what's right and wrong, so they build up a picture of your ideal purchase. This is especially important if you're looking for properties suitable to reconfigure and let as HMOs. Contact and feedback are key; always view properties they recommend right away and keep them posted on what stage you're at in any transactions so they don't need to 'chase' you.

Ideally, you want to get to a position where you have two or three agents that understand exactly what you're looking for and know you'll act quickly and make sensible offers, so will call you as soon as they see a property that might be suitable. The quicker a sale can be agreed and completed, the sooner the agents get their money – you're an agent's dream! – so don't give them any reason not to want to have you at the top of their buyer list.

*Agents MUST be members of The Property Ombudsman. Ideally, deal with agents who are Fellows of the National Association of Estate Agents (FNAEA) and/or the Royal Institution of Chartered Surveyors (FRICS).*

## Reliable contractors

Reliable contractors are worth their weight in gold – and then some. You need a team you can rely on for any refurbishment projects and then a team that can handle on-going maintenance. While you'll probably be able to use many of the same people, some contractors prefer to only handle larger projects and some only smaller ones, which is often the case with electricians and plumbers. The most important thing is that you hire the right people for each job - and make sure they're accredited by or a member of the relevant trade body or organisation and have their own insurance.

You might be lucky enough to find a general builder who already has a team of people he works with regularly; if not, do ask contractors whether they can make recommendations – i.e. does the plumber know a good electrician? The people you use for any refurbishments need to be able to work together – if they all have their own agendas, you can find projects stall or take longer than necessary because they're all blaming each other for not being able to get on to the next stage. Ideally, find a builder who is also prepared to project manage the work for you, then you can go through a clear plan at the start and pay him or her to make sure everything stays on track. That means you only have one person to liaise with, which can save you huge amounts of time and effort.

Your maintenance team – which will include a general handyman (worth their weight in gold!), plumber, electrician and cleaner – are people you're going to need to call on regularly, often at short notice, so do everything you can to make sure they respond to you quickly. A very good way of doing that is to pay them quickly when they invoice. Most – if not all – of these people will be self-employed and/or running small businesses and really can't afford to wait several weeks for payment, so will greatly appreciate you settling their bills right away.

You should be able to find good people by networking locally with other landlords and asking friends to recommend contractors they've used. You can also look on websites such as RatedPeople.com and mybuilder.com, where tradespeople have been rated on their work.

# Building relationships with other investors and businesspeople

If you're seriously considering investing in property, you've probably come across some local 'meets' and been to one or two seminars, or at least heard about them. When I started out, I went to every one I could find, but I honestly didn't find them very helpful, mainly because they weren't focused enough on what I wanted to do and there were too many people simply trying to sell to me. That's not to say you might not get something from going along, but I'd suggest you're selective. Listen to a few speakers and then approach the ones that make the most sense to you. Talk about your thoughts and plans and you may find they're able to offer some valuable advice, but steer clear of the property sourcers and anyone offering 'discounted deals'.

I get lots of good ideas and advice from other investors and businesspeople, quite a few of whom I've found through my local landlords association and independent estate agents. Again, this comes down to being personable and business-minded and having good intuition. There are a heck of a lot of people out there in the industry that are trying to get something for nothing, but there are also a lot who agree that the more you give, the more you get, so share good ideas and good contacts and you'll find people will do the same in return.

And sometimes what you get from other people isn't necessarily what you expect. Countless times I've been at property events and ended up with a good tip, a new contact or an opportunity that's entirely unrelated to property. Holiday offers, car upgrades, a brilliant music teacher for one of my children, another kind of financial investment…all of these have saved me time and money, and I've made a lot of good friends as well.

Property can feel like quite an isolated business if you don't make the effort to build relationships and if you don't gel with your professional advisors, it can all feel like very hard work, no matter how good they are at their job. So I'll say it again: seek out the best advisors but make sure you also like and trust them. And if you have the personality and approach that they like in return, you'll find it much easier to gain and retain the best advice, service and support.

*"The richest people in the world look for and build networks. Everyone else looks for work."*

**Robert Kiyosaki**

# KEY NOTES

- Only work with people you like and trust

- Make your first port of call a Wealth Manager, who can help you put together a solid investment plan

- Choose professional advisors who either invest in property themselves or have existing clients that do

- Seek out estate agents that understand about buying and letting property as an investment

- Always do what you say you're going to do, when you say you'll do it, and pay your contractors and other suppliers on time

- Network with other investors and businesspeople

# Chapter 10

# Summary:  Where & how to start investing

Your question now is probably: "Right, where do I start?"

So, going back to the beginning, the first thing you need to do is look at your current pension provision and see how your financial future looks today. Are you happy with your projections and, more importantly, are you confident that what you've been told about how various funds and investments will mature is reliable information and advice? Map out a best and a worst-case scenario.

If you haven't done so already, review Chapter 1 and put together a financial statement, then write down what you want your financial future to look like, stating how much you need, why and by when – and what you want your life to be like as well. That will give both you and your Wealth Manager or financial advisor a solid place to start planning your investments. Don't forget, with the announcement about pension reforms in July 2014, came an assurance that free, impartial advice would also be available to everyone affected, so perhaps that might be an interesting place to begin, but I would certainly consult your own wealth advisor before taking any action, as the free advice on offer is likely to be quite limited.

Your 'wealth profile', as I'll call it, needs to be considered alongside the kind of investor you are:

- What's your attitude to risk and debt?
- What are your personal and business strengths and skills and how do they suit the requirements of hands-on property investing?
- How much time do you have available? It's really important you think about this in the context of your family life and discuss it with your family because, as I've said, if you want to be completely hands-on, it can be pretty much a full-time job.

Putting your finances, investment goals and personal capabilities together will enable you and your Wealth Manager or financial advisor to come up with a suitable investment plan.

## If you choose to go down the 'active' investor route...

...then this is where the real work starts and you need to find some good people to work with, as outlined in the last chapter. Start networking locally with property groups and estate agents and get to know the market.

Investing successfully in buy to lets demands that you know the local sales and rental markets very well, as covered in Chapter 4 – and there's some more detailed information on market analysis in **'HMO PROPERTY SUCCESS'**, which I'd highly recommend you read if you've decided to invest in income-generating properties. You'll need to be able to estimate as accurately as possible all your initial costs, on-going income and expenditure and assess the financial viability of properties. Then you need to plan how to transform them from what you've purchased into the type of let that will be most profitable in the rental market. If you're investing in single lets, that process will be reasonably straightforward, but if you're going for multi-lets it's a lot more refurbishment work and you'll certainly need to be concerned with planning and other local council regulations.

It sounds like a lot of work – and it is – but once you've gone through the process a couple of times, it becomes a lot easier. You know what to look for and your contacts and advisors will get to know exactly what you need from them, so you'll get better leads from agents and a smoother service from your legal and financial people. And if/when you choose to take on an assistant or property manger, you can hand over pretty much all the day-to-day tasks to them and spend your time finding new opportunities – that's the fun part!

# The 'passive' investor route

I'm always nervous when I hear people talk about 'passive' investments because it usually means they've invested in a property that's out of their own area on someone else's say-so, often without ever having seen the property or location. It's then tenanted and managed by a third party they've never met and the company offering this supposedly great deal takes a significant fee for their trouble.

I've already talked about investment companies at various points throughout this book and you'll have gathered I'm not keen on them. Some offer a comprehensive portfolio-building service and will not only take an up-front fee and charge you for on-going management, but they may also retain an interest in each property. This supposedly incentivises them to ensure profitability and capital growth but, in reality, between the initial fee and the full management service charge, they're already in profit.

Then you have land banking and overseas opportunities, both of which are even more high risk and less likely to be profitable – indeed, there's a good chance you could come out of the deal worse off than when you went in.

Property sourcers / finders will offer to take the 'hassle' out of securing a good buy to let property and tend to dangle the carrot that they've managed to get it well below what it's worth, which is why you can afford to pay their fee and still be 'in profit'. In reality, these properties are often in less well-off areas and there's a reason they're going cheap! Be very, very wary of anyone offering 'discounted' or 'below market value' deals; there are some out there to be had, but you really need to make sure you do your research on them.

All that being said, there are *some* companies and individuals out there that offer a reasonable service, although I'd still advise you that you'll be better off sourcing your own deals and being in control of the management of your own properties. The time you should spend looking into any third party and checking out their business and track record could be spent analysing your own local market – and that's an investment of time and effort that will continue to reap rewards for you.

If you still think you might like to explore 'hands-off' investing, I'd recommend you take these steps before handing over any money:

1. Choose a company that's recommended by people who have been successful. If you can't get any recommendations, then simply trust your gut on your first impression. Usually it's the companies with the glossiest brochures and the slickest salespeople that are the least likely to make you any real money.
2. Check the company's records with Companies House ( companieshouse.gov.uk ), where it's free to do a basic search and you can see how long they've been in business,

whether accounts are up to date and whether any forms of the company have gone into liquidation.

3. Visit the head office premises and see if they're really who and what they say they are.

4. Ask to meet the key people behind the business and ask them some questions about what they're offering, the first of which should be, "Are you investing yourself?" If you get the feeling they're not being open and honest, walk away.

5. Grill them about how they arrived at their valuations and projected figures. Importantly, ask whether they're happy for you to send in your own independent surveyor and use your own legal and financial professionals.

Fundamentally, 'armchair' investing can work, but I don't think you should put that little effort into what are probably the biggest investments you'll ever make and have so little control over your financial future. That's why, as I said at the start, property appeals so much to me – because it IS an investment vehicle over which you can have almost complete control.

## Consider a mentor

There are numerous pitfalls in this industry. You need to get so many things right and, while you can learn as you go along, it will greatly accelerate your success and you'll be more profitable more quickly if you learn directly form someone who's already done what you're looking to do, made mistakes and worked out how to avoid them, and has investment systems and strategies that are proven to be effective. If you're looking at investing in HMOs, I'd say it's even more important.

A mentor will have an 'open doors' policy on their own property portfolio, showing you what they've achieved and how. They'll come and work with you in your own investment area, helping you get to know the market, and should be there to help you find and negotiate your first deal. They'll guide and advise you on how to build and manage a portfolio and how to achieve the returns you need.

To address the obvious, of course I'm in favour of working with a mentor – that's part of my business. But I wouldn't be doing it if I didn't really think it was worthwhile for my clients and they certainly tell me that mentoring has been hugely beneficial to them. There are testimonials to this effect at the back of this book.

I've also gained a great deal myself from mentoring clients and have even gone into ventures with some of them. This is the one kind of hands-off investment I would recommend you make in property: partnering with someone you have got to know, like and trust, and whose business you've seen inside.

Professional portfolio investors run out of money and mortgage facilities at some point and rely on private investors for capital, so it's well worth asking whether your mentor – or other property professional you might have built a relationship with – whether they'd be interested in investing your money for you. These types of deal are usually uniquely structured, on a case-by-case basis, to ensure that both parties get a return on their investment – you on your financial investment and them on their investment of time and expertise – and can work very well on shorter-term projects, such as new builds, or longer-term investments, such as HMOs.

As I said at the start, there are just so many ways to make money from property, you're bound to find one, or several, that suit you. Take the best advice you can, from people who are experienced in the kind of investing you're considering, and there's no doubt in my mind that property will be able to deliver the future financial security you want.

*"Every person who invests in well-selected real estate… adopts the surest and safest method of becoming independent, for real estate is the basis of wealth."*

**Theodore Roosevelt**

# KEY STEPS

1. Go through your current pension provision

2. Put together a personal financial statement

3. Meet with a Wealth Manager

4. Identify your business and personal skills

5. Be sure you're happy with the level of risk in property investment and the level of debt you'll incur

6. Consider how much time you're willing and able to put in

7. Discuss with your professional advisor(s) and family the type of investments and level of personal involvement that will best suit you and your goals

8. Research your local market and start building relationships with people in the property industry

9. By all means consider 'passive' investment, but be very wary and carry out thorough due diligence

10. Consider working with a mentor who can accelerate your success and may be able to offer joint-venture opportunities

# THE SECRETS OF BUY TO LET SUCCESS

## EXPERT TIPS ON HOW TO MAKE MONEY FROM PROPERTY

# Foreword

How many buy to let property investors do you know?

Buy to let was once the preserve of the wealthy few, but in the last 20 years people from all walks of life have become property investors, from your neighbours to your friends – maybe even your parents! Everyone knows a property investor somewhere.

If buy to let is a national pastime, then house prices have become the national obsession. Whether you've been having a quiet afternoon drink at the pub or just bumping into some parents on the school run, the chances are you'll have ended up talking about house prices at some point.

When house prices are going up everyone gets excited; when they're spiralling downwards the national mood sinks with them. There has rarely been a worse period for national sentiment than the great house price collapse of 2008. This was the year when the dream of property prices rising forever died across the UK.

Like all of the lessons you learn in life, 2008 taught us a very valuable one. Property is an investment like any other: prices will rise but they will fall as well. If you own a house, you can't simply use it as a cash machine.

Anyone who becomes a property investor realises this fundamental truth at some point – hopefully sooner, rather than later! - and this lies at the heart of the advantages you will eventually gain on your journey to financial freedom and a retirement free from money worries.

This book is about teaching you the basics of property investment, so that you can take each step one at a time. It doesn't come with a guarantee that you'll become a property millionaire, but what it will show you is the process and the things you need to consider.

My aims with this book are to:

- Help you understand the property investment market
- Make you aware of financing options and how much money you need
- Help you identify the right kind of investment properties
- Show you how to manage your buy to let business

And, of course, explain how to make a profit on your investment!

*"My interest is in the future because I am going to spend the rest of my life there."*

**Charles Kettering, Social Philosopher**

# PART ONE:

# WHERE DO YOU START AS A PROPERTY INVESTOR?

# Chapter 1

# Before Investing

## Why invest in property?

The answer to this should be, why not? You can choose to put your money in a lot of places, depending on your appetite for risk. One place might be in a tin under the bed or you could, like most people, put it in a savings account. You could invest it in stocks and shares or even a start up a business.

So let's take a closer look at these alternatives before we move on to property.

If you opt to keep all your money in a tin under the bed to protect it, you'll find that something very strange begins to happen to that money. It starts to disappear.

I'm not suggesting that someone is opening up your tin of cash and dipping into it now and again. The money disappears without you even opening this tin. This is because of inflation, which raises the cost of living over time. Something that cost you £100 in 1984 would cost you around £300 today. The longer you keep your cash without doing anything with it, the more it will lose its value.

This leaves us with our second option: a high street bank savings account.

This is the option most people take with their money. Haven't we all been brought up to see the bank as the safest place to store our cash? This faith has only been seriously tested once in most people's lifetimes, and that was in 2008, when we all got a reality check:

*Money in the bank is not necessarily ours when it comes to the crunch!*

I'm not going to tell you <u>not</u> to keep your money in the bank or in a tin under the bed because sometimes these may be the best options you have. It is always wise to keep some money by for a rainy day and the bank is probably the best place for it in those cases. Yet even there your money will lose its value over time and, again, that's down to inflation.

Inflation loves to eat your money. The long-term average inflation rate in the UK, based on the everyday things you buy is 5.58%. The best interest rate the bank will give you (even on an ISA) when I last checked in 2014 was about 1.5%.

The stark choice, then, is between losing the full 5.58% of your money over a lifetime or losing an average 4.08% every year (assuming the banks don't suddenly decide to become more generous). So how do you stop your money disappearing?

The answer is to invest money. This can be in a business, stocks and shares or an asset of some kind – such as property.

If you invest money in a business there is always risk. There is a risk that the business will fail and the reality is that most start-ups do fail in the first 5 years. That risk is there, even if you invest in an established business. Look at what happened to Comet, Woolworths, HMV and other high street names we always took for granted, as established 'big' businesses. They have all disappeared, only to be replaced by derelict units with apologetic signs thanking everyone for their custom.

You can't live in a business and it won't put a roof over your head if the cash flow runs dry.

## Why property is less risky

The great thing about property is that no matter how much money you put into it, over time you will almost certainly get a return on that investment. It might take years or it could take as little as a month, depending on what property you buy, where you buy it and, just as importantly, when.

People can manage without money, they can choose where to shop and do business but they can't manage without shelter. Everyone needs somewhere to live and the population in most countries is rising. In cities such as London, the supply of property is under severe strain. Foreign investors and city dwellers are prepared to battle it out for available properties, which inevitably pushes up prices.

Simple supply and demand will continue to raise property prices in the long term, regardless of recessions or economic crises. Investing in property for the long term will protect you from the effects of the economic 'troughs' that inevitably come with the 'peaks', and can give you the level of financial freedom you desire.

What remains something of an unknown is exactly when and by how much prices will fluctuate. Most property agents and sales people will tell you that property doubles in value every ten years. I can confidently put that myth to bed now: it doesn't, at least not always and not in every area. Like any investment, the value can go down as well as up, even if the long-term trend is one of increasing value.

Fortunately, the capital value of property rising is by no means the only reason that buy to let can be such a safe and lucrative long term investment. And that's what I'm going to show you in this book.

# What kind of property investor are you?

All property investors are the same, aren't they? No. Property investors can come from all walks of life. Some will be part-time investors who hold down a day job while pursuing their investment dreams in the few hours they get outside of work. Some will be professional investors who devote their lives to property investment and make a fortune. Others will fall somewhere in between.

Success in property can mean different things to different people, however if you define success as having a million-pound property portfolio, then the distinctions between investor types become more important.

What type of investor are you?

Do you have the right approach that will allow you to reach your goal?

I've met many different kinds of investor over the years - some sophisticated, some downright reckless and others at the point of 'guru' status. Here are some of those people:

### Richard – The Adventurous Investor

Richard is the suave, casual kind of property investor who has money and a licence to spend it. He wears his suit loose with no tie and has no care for conventions. It's his way or the highway and to hell with the details.

Money is no real object to Richard - he has plenty. Richard likes to take risks because it's all about the adrenaline and the thrill of the chase for him. Property investment is a gamble and it doesn't matter if that property is in Albania or Blackburn; if there is a deal to be done you'll find Richard entering the market first, before anyone else.

Richard relies on luck more than judgement and it sometimes pays off. But then that luck runs out or he misses some of the detail in a rental return that sounded too good to be true…and was.

Being an adventurous investor can be seen as reckless and relies on you having enough money not to worry about your losses when a property market goes bad. It also requires a lot of self belief and resilience, to be able to put mistakes in the past and move on to the next big market and that next potential windfall.

Richard's approach is all about short-term gain, which is definitely not a strategy for the faint hearted.

### Suzanne – The Experienced Investor

Suzanne has been in the property business for more than a decade now. In that time she has built up a substantial portfolio of properties that have allowed her to spread her risk. She focuses more on on-going rental returns than on any short-term gains to be made.

Suzanne will study an area and go through every detail about a property before making the decision to invest. She will look to buy at a knockdown price, or unearth a hidden gem in a sought-after area of town that just needs some refurbishment work to realise its potential. She will have a good relationship with a number of estate agents who find her the right properties that will expand her portfolio.

Before choosing her property, Suzanne will look closely at all the details, from location to the likely rental return. She rarely acts on impulse and won't take risks unless they are calculated carefully beforehand.

**Julian – The Analytical Investor**
Julian is like Suzanne in some ways – until he has to make a decision. He is known for overanalysing every situation, often held back by the sheer amount of knowledge he has about property investment.

Julian has read every book, visited every Internet blog and attended his fair share of property shows over the years. The one thing he hasn't done is move beyond his one investment property.

This is because he knows that property markets move in cycles and by the time he feels comfortable that the next up-cycle has arrived, he is already listening to the news and worrying about when the end of it will come.

Julian is afflicted by what some people in the property game call 'analysis paralysis'. He simply doesn't move quickly enough and won't take any risks because his knowledge about the subject gets in the way. And so he misses out time and again on good, solid investment opportunities simply because he's waiting for 'the perfect deal'.

**Graham – The Novice Investor**
Graham works full time as an engineer and has his pet project. The converted old church he has been working on for three years is beginning to look the part but there is still a lot of work to do. His ambition is to finish the project in a year or two and move on to another house.

The property is large and in an up and coming location, so he expects it to generate a good income in time and provide him with a nest egg for retirement. The only problem is Graham hasn't set a goal for when the project will actually be finished.

The house means a lot to him so he has become emotionally attached and there is no real plan in place to address what happens when the property is finished. Will it be sold or rented out? Has all the investment been worth it?

## Why buy to let investors need to be good all-rounders
Each of these investor types has a different motivation for becoming involved in buy to let property. What you can learn from their profiles is that becoming a successful property investor will require a number of skills.

You'll need to be able to separate your emotions from each project and have the ability to take a calculated risk. You will be more successful if you're prepared to work at it, rather than expecting the right investments to simply fall into your lap. Trust me they won't; investing and being a success in property takes work and organisation. And you need to be clear on why you're investing, so that you can put together an investment profile that will help you achieve your financial goals.

Property is a risk like any other investment. It's only by taking a long-term view and having a well-considered plan, that those risks can be reduced.

# Chapter 2

# Timing

## When is it a good time to invest in property?

One of the most common questions I get asked is, when is the right time to invest in property? Well, if you've explored all the other investment options available, compared the likely returns on offer and are convinced that property is the right investment for you, then you don't actually need to ask this question.

It's bit like asking when should I start my weight loss programme or when should I start running to get myself fit? Investing in property shouldn't be something you put in a calendar and say, "I'll start doing it next month / next year". Once you've decided on property and have the means and time available to do it, the time to start investing is now. If you don't make your move now then you're only reducing the potential gains you can make.

If your aim is to make enough money to generate a decent retirement income, then you will need to have invested in property for at least 10 years.

Obviously, your age will be a factor guiding your investment decisions because running a portfolio of investments at 80 years old plus won't be much fun. If your goal is to retire early you're likely to need more than one buy to let property and you will want to be in a position to relax a bit by then.

The great thing about property investment is that no matter when you decide to do it, there is never a wrong time to invest. As you become more experienced, you'll be able to identify better times to invest to maximise your returns, but there are always good deals to be done.

Your ability to look at the economic climate you're in and see how this is affecting the attitudes of both buyers and sellers will have a major impact on how successful you can be in the long term. In theory – the sky is the limit!

At the moment, we're in a climate of growing optimism.

Unemployment is falling, house prices are rising again and there are Government measures in place to help people climb onto the property ladder. Even the banks are more sympathetic if you ask them for a mortgage.

Although the recent introduction of new measures to ensure responsible lending means a more rigorous application process, 95 % loan to value mortgages, unthinkable a few years ago, are now being routinely handed out (with Government help) to homebuyers with decent credit ratings.

As for landlords, most have enjoyed a long period of strong rental growth and low voids while people were hard pressed to buy their homes. Even if they bought prior to the housing market crash, then the money they have made from rent and the increased capital growth they are likely to be seeing now will have more than compensated for any temporary drop in value. And there needn't be much worry about the demand for rental properties dropping because although more people are coming into the buying market, there is still a huge lack of supply for those still looking to rent.

The one thing you may notice is that the window of opportunity is starting to close on the bargains you may have found in the down cycle, but there is still time to find them. Remember, property investment should always be viewed as a long-term investment rather than a get rich quick scheme – I've yet to find one of those that actually works!

## The property market cycle

One of the first things you should be familiar with if you want to get the best out of buy to let is the investment cycle.

Property, as we have established, is an investment. If you happen to already deal with stocks and shares you'll be familiar with an investment cycle, but if you're new to investing you need to make sure you understand this.

## What is an investment cycle?

An investment cycle helps investors identify where a market is at. Imagine a clock face for a moment, with the market peak at 12 o'clock and the market hitting bottom at 6 o'clock. In between these two extremes you will have lots of other things happening that will cause property prices to either rise or fall. Notice I said rise *or fall*? Property prices are always moving in one direction or another!

If you look hard enough, there will always be certain indicators that will help you decide on the best times to buy for high capital growth or strong rental yields. The evidence will be obvious as long as you have the ability to read the signals.

These signals can be extremely valuable and you'll come across them from time to time whether you're watching the TV or out having a drink with friends. I remember one occasion when a friend living in Manchester said to me, "I've noticed some big changes lately. It's easy to get hold of builders and even the plumber turns up on time. Normally when I call them I get an answer machine and they don't return my call."

## Is the builder returning your calls?

So why is it that builders are sometimes more eager to return your calls? The answer is a quiet property market or one that has reached the bottom of its cycle. Builders are only busy when there is a profit to be made from building or renovating houses.

So, naturally, when demand is falling, there is less major building work going on. Builders are now having to go out and find work and this makes them more eager to take your calls and book in your jobs, no matter how small.

That's an example of a fairly subtle sign. Perhaps the most telling signal you'll get is from the people who work at the sharp end of the property market – the estate agents. The life of an estate agent is rarely straightforward. There's always uncertainty around every corner, whether or not the investment cycle is moving up or down.

If you have ever tried to sell your house at the bottom of the investment cycle, you'll notice that the agent will take their time returning your calls. This is because they will have more properties than interested buyers. From an investment perspective, if the agents already have lots of properties on their books, it's a buyer's market and a good time to make your move. There should be a lot of sellers prepared to make a good deal and you should be able to buy something with 'built in equity' ready for the start of the next market cycle.

**The giveaway clues that a property market is reaching a peak**
One telling clue that the property market cycle is about to pass its peak is when the media starts to report the kind of news that sends shockwaves around the world, such as a break-up of the Eurozone or wars.

This kind of news can spread negative sentiment even in previously fast-growing property markets. As I've already mentioned, you must remember that a property market, like any other investment market, is dynamic. It can go in all sorts of directions but it never stands still.

Anything that creates financial uncertainty usually impacts the property market, as people don't want to make big financial decisions when they're not sure how things are likely to look in the near future.

It can be an emotional reason or perception that affects how people behave over property, or it can be a real financial and economic reason. They call can and will keep happening periodically - the important thing is not to worry about fluctuations. When the market has passed the peak of its cycle, this is just part of the rebalancing that will always take place. And when everyone is running for cover because they fear the end of the world, this is usually the best time to invest!

## What happens at the bottom of a cycle?

When a property market reaches the bottom of its cycle, you have a 'buyers' market'. The bottom of the market is a thoroughly depressing time for most of the population but not if you're an investor. When things get really bad and everyone is fed up, this is usually the best time to invest.

The bottom of the property cycle tends to coincide with a national economy that is in recession, negative wage growth, job losses and pessimism about the future. This is the time when people are more likely to be forced into selling property.

You also get a period of low or unstable interest rates. As we have recently witnessed, governments will step in to soften the blow by cutting interest rates, which brings mortgage payments down. Unfortunately, as those mortgage payments are coming down, so is the price of property for many homeowners and this is when negative equity will rear its ugly head.

There is one section of the population who will be having a much better time at this point - buy to let investors! You can now make the kinds of offers on property that would have been laughed off months earlier. I would say that this is actually the best time to invest in property.

Sellers will soon be panicking and dropping their asking prices further and if you time it right, you can reap the rewards of rising prices in the long term. You certainly won't have much competition either. At these times, even some investors will be opting to wait and see.

This is also the stage when rental returns will rise as people put off buying houses until the market recovers and demand for lettings will be high.

**What happens when a property market is in recovery?**
The recovery is when everyone starts feeling good about property again. When the property cycle moves into a recovery phase, selling houses starts to get easier. As prices begin to rise along with demand, the number of people you see looking for homes increases. More buyers will enter the market supported by better mortgage lending conditions and buyer incentives.

The oversupply of properties we saw at the bottom of the market will soon be absorbed as the recovery gathers pace. Many smaller developers and construction companies will have been forced out of business and projects mothballed, adding to the pressure on the supply.

Landlords can still benefit from rising rents during the recovery as supply struggles to keep up with demand. Statistics will alert the banks that asking prices are increasing in some areas and they will have little choice other than to increase their valuations as a result.

Soon you get a property boom where prices start rising by double digits on an annual basis and this can last for several years. It usually slows again when construction levels are at a point where supply becomes more balanced with demand.

At this point, media hype will add more fuel to the boom, convincing people to buy before property prices rise again. Property prices can literally rise in a week. It's not unusual for offers to be made and accepted on the spot, making it almost impossible to negotiate a good deal. Why should an owner take your offer when there are plenty more people willing to pay the full asking price?

**What happens at the peak of the investment cycle?**
When the property market is at its peak, sellers are now firmly in the driving seat. If you have a portfolio and are considering an exit from your investment, the peak of the cycle may be your best window of opportunity to sell. The owner of a property can dictate all the terms. They will be unwilling to negotiate on anything, including price – unless they are in a desperate hurry to sell.

The peak of the market means that affordability will be hitting a peak as well. At this point, the property cycle is about to move into freefall as people start to see property as too expensive and/or find it unaffordable. Those already in property decide to sit tight for the moment and first time buyers or perhaps those between homes decide to become tenants instead, as they can rent a better home than they can buy, while continuing to save a bigger deposit.

At the peak of the cycle, housing developers will still be bringing more properties onto the market. We've seen this happening in recent years with flats, where a flood of new builds at the peak of the market has saturated it, and towns and cities start to have properties standing unsold for months or even years. This glut of stock starts to result in an increase in repossessions as the value of property quickly falls and the banks start getting nervous about mortgages.

The big housing developers who have relied so much on demand being maintained suddenly find that their sales forecasts are way off the mark. The banks, sensing that all is not well, begin to question those forecasts. New properties are soon discounted, which has a knock-on effect on the rest of the market.

As the investment cycle comes full circle and arrives again at the bottom, this will be the time to look for those bargain properties once again.

**TIP:** *The best time to pick up bargains is at the bottom of the investment cycle, when demand is low and you can negotiate hard.*

## What did we learn from the market crash?
2008 is often cited as the year when the credit crunch began, but things were going wrong much earlier than that. The credit crunch

was something very few people believed would really happen and most felt like they had sleepwalked right into it.

That's the thing with ground-shaking events in history; you often don't feel them until they have already been and gone.

The housing market crash that hit the UK in the winter of 2007 could be seen as part of the fall out of the sub-prime mortgage crisis that had gripped the US the previous summer. Sure enough, the ripples of that disaster were hitting the shores of the UK, even before the full effect was felt on house prices.

But it was actually a year earlier that a nervous UK Government started to wonder just how long the housing boom would continue. Was this the first time in history that house prices would just keep rising?

And house prices were rising fast in 2006 – by more than 10% every 12 months. At this time you could have bought and sold a modest 2-bedroom terrace almost anywhere and doubled your money inside five years.

This consistently fast price growth was a matter of growing concern with the Bank of England. So they duly began raising interest rates and did it not once, but five times between August 2006 and August 2007.

Little did they know that the catastrophic financial crisis that was gripping the US at the time would soon become global and the biggest single collapse since the Great Depression of 1929.

So, with house prices starting to tumble throughout the UK in 2008 (apart from a few outposts in Scotland) the situation and outlook was a grim one for both investors and homeowners, who had both grown used to easy credit and easy profit.

Suddenly, investors who had over-leveraged themselves with 'no money down' investments found that the whole stack of cards was about to collapse on top of them. Many went bankrupt and many companies that had made millions on the back of property investors hungry for 'easy money' began to fold in dramatic fashion.

Harsh lessons were learned, we all realised that there really is no 'sure thing' in investment. The property boom had wiped out memories of negative equity and the times when more than 30% was wiped off the value of homes in the early 1990s. This boom was different – or so everyone thought.

If anything good came out of the crash of 2007-08, it was the realisation that houses cannot be used as cash machines. Just as money doesn't grow on trees, property values can come crashing to earth with a bang.

If you want to make money within this cyclic market and succeed in buy to let, one of the most important rules to follow is to invest in property that not only cover its own costs, but also operate at a profit.

If your rental income isn't covering your mortgage payments and running costs and you end up in a down cycle, it can take a very long time to recover. You can't rely on the value of property to rise in the short term, so you must plan to achieve consistent returns from rental profit, while you wait for the capital value to rise over the long term.

## Property investment myths

I still have several books, written by property investment 'gurus', who poured cold water on the idea that a housing market crash was on the horizon. Instead, they preferred to keep selling the 'secrets' of property investment based on capital increases to others who thought house prices would never fall.

With hindsight, it's easy to look back and laugh at the misguided predictions of those who should have seen what was coming. Some did - there were also property experts who predicted the 2008 crash as early as 2005.

Not surprisingly, you don't hear much from the 'no money down, build a million-pound portfolio' gurus any more. Rather, those investors who understood how investment cycles work are the ones who continued to profit throughout the crash and are still around. They will have bought in the early part of the last decade, from 2001 onwards, and reaped the benefits of a buy and hold strategy. They were the tortoises rather than the hares. And in property it's always better to be the tortoise because what goes around comes around, eventually.

Myths are a powerful thing. We all like to hear them, whether they're good or bad. It's human nature to collectively fall in line with myths that are put out there to scare us or persuade us into making certain decisions. But blindly believing myths often leads us to make the wrong decisions and miss opportunities. Here are three big myths that you often hear about the property market:

### Myth 1: Property is overvalued

I picked up the Daily Mail newspaper one morning as I was writing this book and saw a headline that pretty much sums up why people continue to be cautious about investing in property – even in a growing market.

It read:

## 'House Prices To Soar Until 2020!'

## 'Middle Income Earners Will Be Priced Out!'

The myth you will see crop up again and again is the price to earnings ratio. This is the price of property compared to the income of the average working person. The logic goes that the higher property prices rise, the more out of reach houses become for the average person and people then see property as becoming overvalued.

So why then were property price to income ratios more than 4 ½ times the average salary in 2004? People were still buying property and continued to do so in enough numbers to sustain a house price boom that lasted until outside events ended it in 2007.

The answer to this is mortgages. Whether you're a buy to let investor or a homebuyer, unless you're lucky, you will be relying on the bank to give you a mortgage. The amount of interest you pay on that mortgage and on what terms is the most important driver of a property market.

If people have the means to buy property and the bank is confident enough to lend that money, then they will buy.

For example:

Mr Stevens invests in a property.
He borrows £100,000 and his annual mortgage interest payment is 10%.
The interest costs him £100,000 x 10% = £10,000 a year.

Then the banks and lenders lower interest rates.

Mr Stevens invests in a larger property, borrowing £200,000 and his mortgage interest is 5%
The interest costs him £200,000 x 5% = £10,000 a year.

The mortgage borrowing has doubled, even though his costs are the same.

In recent years we have seen a historically low interest rate environment. Those investors who are able to lock in low interest rates on their mortgages will benefit from lower monthly payments. So the price to income ratio argument fails to stack up.

**Myth 2: Property prices will take decades to recover**
This is one of my favourite examples. It's the kind of myth you might hear people talking about down at the pub. Anyone who is struggling to sell their property will latch on to this myth, even though historically there has and always will be cause for optimism.

A case in point was Florida in the USA. House prices were predicted never to recover as recently as 2010, such was the impact of the sub-prime crisis. But as soon as the banks started lending again, people started buying again. Some of the worst-affected cities in Florida between 2007 and 2009 are now seeing property prices rising by more than 20% a year!

It would take a catastrophe of global proportions to alter a long-term trend of rising prices, and that's been the case for as long as anyone can remember. This is a key factor in making property such a great investment.

## Myth 3: Property prices and rents are rising

When I hear anyone say that property prices and rents are rising – at the same time and at the same rate - I immediately smell a rat.

The reason? As we've established, property markets move in cycles. When prices are falling, it generally means people have stopped buying because they are unable to get a mortgage. This is when we see a surge in rents.

Post-2008 in the UK saw 7% per annum rises in rents, as people who should have been first-time property buyers found it almost impossible to get a mortgage.

In areas where property is in demand, rents naturally rise when the average person is not in a position to buy. This is why buy to let investors were able to capitalise on a rental bonanza as most of the country was struggling through a recession.

During a recovery, which, let's face it, is usually supported by a boom in house prices, people are out there buying again. When people can buy, armed with Government incentives such as Help

To Buy, they are less likely to want to rent. In this case, rental growth begins to slow.

This explains why you're unlikely to see rising prices and rising rents at the same time.

The good thing from an investment point of view is:

Whatever the economy is doing, you can still make money.

*"The best time to plant a tree was 20 years ago. The second best time is now."*

**Chinese Proverb**

# Chapter 3

# Raising Finance

You don't need to be wealthy to be a property investor, but it helps!

That doesn't mean that it's impossible to make money in property if you're not wealthy; the trick is to find a way to get your hands on some financing. In terms of your own cash contribution, this may be earnings from your job, profits from a business venture or the savings you have built up and put by over the years. You could even re-mortgage your home if you have enough equity in it.

Another possibility is to raise finance via a commercial mortgage - either a business mortgage or a commercial investment mortgage. If your business is doing well and has a strong credit rating then this might be an ideal route because it could offer more protection than taking a risk by putting your home up as security on a loan. High street banks will typically offer 50% LTV mortgages while some specialist lenders might be prepared to raise that LTV to 75%.

**TIP:** *Invest only what you can afford to lose!*

Nobody wants to think about losing money. Even so, the amount you decide to invest should be an amount you can afford to lose if things go wrong. To be a successful property investor, you will need to take a calculated risk, but there is no cast-iron guarantee that the risk will pay off – and that's something we'll cover later in this book.

The price of an average house in a reasonable area in the UK is about £170,000 at the time of writing. Any less than this and either the property will be in a very poor state of repair or the area you're investing in clearly isn't very popular with people looking to rent or buy - which rather defeats the purpose!

This isn't to say you can't make money buying cheaper properties. Bargains do exist and there are always opportunities to buy a wreck and fix it up. If you go down this route you will really need to know what you're doing as buying cheap is never a guarantee of investment success.

So when you decide to invest in your first property, there is a good chance that you'll need to go to the bank to raise some financing in the form of a buy to let mortgage. You'll find hundreds of different products out there offered by lenders. As a rule of thumb, be prepared to have to put up at least 15% of the value of the property yourself as a deposit.

Although this mortgage will primarily be granted on the basis of the rental income stacking up, the banks still expect you as a buy to let investor to already have some investment money available – it gives them additional confidence that you are a risk worth taking.

If you happen to be a cash buyer, then this opens up a whole range of possibilities that will not be available to those needing finance. As well as the obvious advantage of being able to negotiate hard with vendors who need a quick sale, you'll also be able to use the money to buy at auction and not have to wait for clearance of funds from the bank.

**TIP:** *Beware of using a mortgage to buy at auction!*

The biggest risk with using a mortgage to fund the purchase of an auction property is that you may end up seriously out of pocket if your mortgage doesn't clear on time. On the day of the auction you must lodge a 10% deposit and the contracts are signed then and there, i.e. you are legally committed to the purchase. You usually then have just 28 days to complete, so if there is a problem or delay with your mortgage application and you can't complete, there will be financial penalties, including losing your deposit, and you may lose the property as well.

Another option – and this is only something you should tackle if you already have an investment track record and a clear business plan – is to do a joint venture with someone. They can provide the money and you provide the know-how and your time, or you can both put in some of each. The arrangement needs to be set out legally, but it's certainly an option and something I've done myself in expanding and diversifying my portfolio.

In short, there is nearly always a way to raise finance, you just need to have focus and a realistic plan to get there.

## How much money do you need?

It might sound like I'm stating the obvious, but it's really important you understand how much money you need in order to be able to invest. I've lost count of the number of people I've met who tell me they really want to 'get into property' but that they only have a small amount of savings and they don't think they can get much via mortgage finance. There still seems to be a perception out there that you can get something for nothing with property investment!

If you only have £10,000 to invest yourself, you're not going to be able to buy much in the UK, especially when you consider all the other things you need to pay for.

It's easy to focus purely on the property itself and ignore the other associated costs, which can really mount up. That being said, those added costs still look small compared to the £150,000 or so you will have to invest in the actual bricks and mortar (via deposit and mortgage).

Some of the costs you need to consider are:

- Stamp duty
- Solicitor's fees
- Survey
- Refurbishment and maintenance work
- Management fees
- Letting agent fees

...to name but a few.

You'll need to set aside funds for all of the above, which can run into thousands of pounds. You should work these costs into your financial plan to make sure the investment pays for itself, but you must be able to cover them, personally, if something goes wrong with your buy to let. And it doesn't stop there.

You will also need to cover any potential void periods – the term for those times where you can't find a tenant and the property stands empty.

If you own the property outright, voids will not be as much of an issue, but if your mortgage payments are covered by the rental income then you should budget for having at least 3 months' worth of emergency money set aside to cover these periods.

Let's look at the following example to help illustrate how much money you might need to finance your investment.

- Mr and Mrs Andrews hope to purchase a property for £150,000
- They manage to secure a mortgage for £120,000 (80% LTV)
- They invest £30,000 as a deposit

Now, if Mr and Mrs Andrews are just starting out, they're unlikely to buy a new property as their first investment, so they will have set aside some money to cover costs.

- 15% to cover refurbishment and any maintenance
- 5% to cover any void periods when the property is ready to rent.

This comes to a total of £30,000 extra they will need to set aside, in addition to the deposit, to make a life a bit more comfortable, and that's not including the initial purchase costs, for which they will need to budget around 2% of the purchase price, £3,000. (This percentage rises accordingly with the stamp duty thresholds.)

There are of course a number of ways to raise this additional money, although it's best if you already have the funds yourself. You could secure a bank loan, but that will set you back a lot in interest payments, depending on the term of the loan and the interest rate. You could also, as mentioned above, do a joint venture with someone who has money to invest but is short on time and expertise.

**TIP:** *Whatever route you take, you must make sure your borrowing doesn't leave you overexposed!*

Plan and budget carefully, or you run the risk of killing any property portfolio ambitions before they get started.

## Getting finance

Right now is a fantastic time to start thinking about investing in property. In fact, the best times to start thinking about investing are those times when it costs less to borrow money. Interest rates have been at historic lows since 2008, when the Bank of England Base Rate was reduced dramatically to try and stimulate the UK economy.

The Bank of England uses the powerful weapon of interest rates to control the economy. If economic growth is racing away then the chances are you'll see the Base Rate increased to control inflation. When the economic numbers are looking shaky, for example, unemployment is rising and GDP grinds to a halt or goes into the negative, then the Base Rate is reduced.

Whether it's rising or falling, the Base Rate is closely tracked by the banks, who set their own interest rates to follow suit. So if unemployment drops to a certain level, then the Bank of England policy committee may decide it's a good time to raise the rate. And if they do, then mortgages become more expensive.

And the potential highs and lows cover quite a broad spectrum. You may or may not remember mortgage interest rates running at 15% back in the early 1990s. That's in stark contrast to the 3% to 5% you can typically get today.

As I explained earlier, there are many ways to get finance. If you decide on a high street bank or building society then you will need to go through a long process of finding a bank willing to lend you the money and making sure that all your finances are in order.

A buy to let mortgage quote can be done over the phone with a few simple questions, but the process really starts when you need to produce the following:

- Proof of income
- Proof of the source of your deposit
- Details of your experience as a landlord
- A surveyor's valuation of the rental amount

While banks have become slightly more willing to lend money now that the property market is improving, you will still need a clean credit rating and be in a position to provide evidence of the above.

The good news for you as an investor is that buy to let mortgages don't currently fall under the scope of the Financial Services Authority, and therefore you won't be affected by the new, more stringent checks that have been introduced for primary residence mortgages.

For these applications for a mortgage to buy your own home, you'll need to provide much more detailed proof of income, savings, investments and pensions. The banks' scoring systems also now look at things like regular payments going out of your bank account and your lifestyle, in order to assess your financial commitments in much more detail than they used to. All this is to assess how risky you are to lend to and you should be prepared for at least two or three visits to the bank or some lengthy phone calls. You'll need to shop around to get the best deal and you may face rejection from some lenders.

However, as a buy to let investor, the main thing the bank is interested in is the potential rental income being high enough to cover the monthly mortgage repayments. Currently, most lenders ask for proof (from a surveyor) that the rental income covers at least 125% of the proposed repayment amount. Your personal financial situation and your experience as a landlord come second to that, and are really more to ensure you are a credible person to lend to.

Even though buy to let mortgage applications are far less onerous than primary residence ones, I'd still advise you to engage a mortgage broker or independent financial advisor (IFA) to do all this for you. As you become a more experienced property investor, a good mortgage broker will be an important part of your investment team and I'll go into more detail later in this chapter.

## What you need to know about buy to let mortgages

One of the most important things to understand about a buy to let mortgage is that you cannot use it to finance a property you intend to live in.

This is because the bank has assessed your buy to let mortgage using a different set of criteria than your standard mortgage, as mentioned in the last section. The latter is assessed purely on your income and your ability to pay back the loan over 25 years or so. A buy to let mortgage will be based on the income you can make from renting out the property.

Another crucial difference between the two mortgages is the loan to value or the deposit you need to put in. In the heady days prior to 2007 it was possible to get 100% or more, such was the confidence among the banks. The financial crisis changed all that, yet even now, with schemes such as Help to Buy, it's possible to get what is effectively a 95% LTV mortgage for your own home. However, if you want to take out a buy to let mortgage, the LTV is typically around 75%. It is possible to get more from a few lenders, but the interest rate won't be very competitive.

Right, that's the bad bit out of the way. Now the really good thing about a buy to let mortgage is that you can get one on an interest-only basis. This is important because paying off capital on a property you plan to exit from in the long term is not necessarily the wisest thing to do.

The more money you sink into the property through finance payments the less money you will have to build your portfolio. If we assume that the value of property always increases over the long term, then paying off the loan is not as important as paying off the mortgage on your own home when it's time to retire. In fact, if you build a property portfolio in the right way, you should make enough to pay off your mortgage and all your obligations and look forward to a comfortable retirement!

**TIP:** *Try to put in as little of your own money as possible, so that you maximise the benefit from leveraging the bank's money.*

As your property grows in value over time, assuming the figures still stack up for your investment, you may be able to re-mortgage and release all your capital, so you're left with something that makes you money, funded entirely by the bank!

## Types of buy to let mortgage

As with a standard mortgage, you will be met with a choice of different types of buy to let mortgage when you go to meet with your bank, broker or IFA. You can get either a fixed rate, variable rate or tracker mortgage. Be careful which one you choose and make sure that it fits with your investment plan.

For example, a mortgage that tracks the base rate when there is a potential increase on the horizon may not be the most sensible decision. You could end up paying more than you budgeted for if the economy starts to do well. On the other hand, you will be quids in if you fix your mortgage while interest rates are low and then the base rate rises..

The product that's right for you will depend on your plans and financial goals, which is why it's important to talk it through with a qualified, independent professional, who can look at all the rates available in the marketplace and help you make the best choice.

## Switching your standard mortgage to a buy to let

In recent years we have seen the rise of the 'accidental landlord', where people who are unable to sell their home due to market conditions decide to rent it out so they can move on. To do this, the standard mortgage on the property must be switched to a buy to let mortgage or there must be a 'consent to let' agreement with the lender.

If you can find tenants who will cover the mortgage payments and generate a monthly income for you on top, then this may turn out to be a happy accident and a route into becoming a serious buy to let investor.

However, there may be a few hoops you need to jump through prior to switching to a buy to let mortgage.

Your lender will want to know how much equity, if any, you have in your property and they will also want to know that the likely rental income will more than cover your mortgage payments before they allow you to switch.

You will need to do this even if you just want to 'tread water' with a consent to let, until the market for selling picks up. Your bank may charge one month's mortgage per annum or a higher interest rate for allowing you to go down this route, so it's advisable to raise the deposit you need and switch to a buy to let mortgage as soon as possible.

## Why a mortgage broker plays such an important role in your success

If you want to make a success of investing you need to engage someone to advise you on the financing of your investments, but what does mortgage broker actually do for you?

The two most important things a mortgage broker will do for you is save you time and money. Spending too much of your own time and money are two of the biggest threats to your success as a property investor.

Just as you might hire an electrician to do the wiring on your house or a mechanic to fix your car, a broker should be an expert in finding the best possible buy to let mortgage deal.

They will also be able to find that mortgage for you quite quickly and it will be based on the best product for your circumstances. They should also have great relationships with lenders and be able to move you through the process quickly, from application to offer.

I know a few people who tried to go it alone and used the internet to find what they thought were the cheapest products. They mistakenly thought that all a broker does is work off a list of lenders and offer the product that pays the best commission. Maybe that was the case in the old days, but now it's a much more transparent process.

You can actually find yourself much worse off in the long run by going for what appears to be the cheapest deal, only to find that buried in the small print are hefty fees and penalties you may not have picked up on.

A good broker will always show you how much money they'll make for recommending a particular mortgage to you. Even so, it's still worth doing your own research and taking recommendations from other investors. While every broker will advertise themselves as 'always on the end of the phone', you can guarantee most won't be.

You may come across young brokers in sharp suits who seem to know what they're talking about, however it may be wiser try to look for someone who has more experience. When it comes to experience, there is no substitute, particularly if you're looking to build a portfolio.

Hiring a broker is a particularly wise move for high net worth investors. The number of products available to you will be highly competitive and a broker from one of the top firms will be able to give you access to the best deals that won't necessarily be on the 'open market'.

Of course, brokers will charge a fee for their services but the amount of money they will save you in the long term, not to mention the pain and hassle, will be worth it.

If you need some guidance on finding the best broker here are my seven tips:

1. Research well and do your homework
2. Choose a recommended firm
3. Find a broker who will take your calls – even out of office hours

4. Look for someone with a proven track record
5. Present yourself as knowledgeable
6. Have an investment plan in mind to save time (good brokers are busy brokers)
7. Prepare all the information required in advance

If you follow each of these tips, your broker will take you more seriously and you should get a high quality of service.

## To pay a fee or not to pay a fee? That is the question...

When you first start searching for a broker you will come across many who will either charge you a considerable fee up front, a modest fee or no fee at all. And it can be difficult to judge which it's best to go with if you're purely searching on the internet.

The broker firms that come top on a Google search are not necessarily the best ones - they might simply have the best websites and employ an SEO company to achieve good rankings.

You need to ask the broker if they are 'whole of market' or not. If they are tied to certain lenders and not truly independent, then they will probably be cheaper than a whole of market broker, but they will make up their commission somehow.

Sometimes paying a fee up front will get you access to deals that could save you more than 20% a month on your repayments – a saving that will cover the fee many times over.

**TIP***: Make appointments with several different brokers.*

If you don't currently know any mortgage brokers yourself, nor anyone that can recommend one, then make sure you speak to several and don't just go with the first one who seems to know what they're talking about.

It shouldn't cost anything for guidance on the amount you can borrow, so have a few conversations and get a feel not only for how good they are, but also for their personality. Rapport is important in this business and you want to work with people you like and trust.

# Chapter 4

# Finding A Property

The million-dollar question in this business is: where do you find a good investment property?

On your property investment journey, you will come across a lot of people who will advise you where they think you should be buying. Being a full-time investor means that I get approached every day by all sorts of people, telling me where the next big opportunity is.

Some of these will be genuine opportunities, but often, if the opportunity seems too good to be true, it probably is. Sometimes it means that the person giving you advice stands to gain more from your investment than you do.

This is why I always recommend doing your own research and building a good relationship with an estate agent. There are plenty of online property companies around who charge what is called a 'finder's fee' for helping you find a property and they will inevitably also take a commission on the sale.

Dealing directly with a reputable estate agent is a much more transparent process and I would strongly advise forming a long-term relationship with one or two agents in the areas where you want to invest. You should be the one seeing the full benefit of any profits to be gained from your buy to let investment and not be forced to share them with a third party.

This book should be a useful tool in your research, helping guide you on what to look for in a good investment property. (What it **isn't** is a one-stop shop filled with everything you need, so you're going to have to take some more time to do all your homework!)

When you're starting out, the right property can be just down the road from where you live. Local knowledge is absolutely vital if you want to find the right investment, so talk to lettings and sales agents to find out what's available and what's in demand and get to know your own specific market. There is also a good deal of information on the internet, including land registry data telling you how much properties have been bought and sold for in the past.

Over several years as a property investor, one of the things I've learned is that property, like any other investment, is not really about what someone tells you; it's more about learning for yourself, trusting your judgement and having the right people to turn to for advice when you need it.

'Success' in property is about finding the investments that fit your plans for the future. I can't tell you what those are and neither can anyone else. Everyone's goals will be different and what makes the right kind of property investment for one person may not be right for you.

It follows, then, that the best place to invest in property for you may be somewhere very different to where I would choose. So if you have someone telling you where to invest, you run the risk of ending up disappointed and with a property that doesn't do for you what you need it to.

What every investor does have in common is a vision of what the perfect investment looks like for them. You just need to be prepared for the possibility that, once you've done the cold hard numbers, the reality might be somewhat different to your dream! The answers to two key questions are critical to your success:

- What level of rents are tenants prepared to pay to live in your property?
- Is the rental return sufficient to cover the mortgage?

The best place to invest for some people is a beaten up old property in a promising area of town. The best place for others will be a property requiring very little work or personal input. The latter generally comes at a premium unless you're very lucky. Remember, you are not the only investor out there and a lot of people are involved in the buy to let business.

Successful investors usually go with what is familiar to them. It's far better to invest in something you know than to venture into the unknown. And property is no different.

## New or old property – which is best?

Ultimately, which is best will come down to whichever fits the figures, but everyone has an inclination towards one or the other that shouldn't necessarily be disregarded.

If you're more inclined towards an older property, then you're likely to have to do some work to do to get it ready for letting. You will also be more likely to be a property developer as well as an investor - someone who likes to manage the process, from the building and refurbishment work to the point where you let the property and move on to the next one.

This type of property investment may be particularly suited to you if you're a hands-on kind of person. You might even work in the building trade or have some particular skills related to it so that you're able to keep costs down. But be warned: it used to be the case that you could do up a property to a just-about-habitable standard and tenants would happily move in, but this is certainly not the case any more.

Yes, hiring tradespeople to renovate or refurbish your property can be expensive if you don't fancy joining in yourself, but it's important that you do a good job. Lettings regulations and local council requirements are tightening all the time, so you must make sure the property you're letting is up to scratch.

I've seen tenants happily living in houses with kitchen units falling apart, boilers on the point of breakdown, and water coming in through the windows. However, this kind of tenant is certainly the exception, rather than the rule, and if you don't provide a decent standard of accommodation, you can't expect to get a decent level of rent in return.

If you happen to be investing in sought-after areas, people will have higher expectations than your average tenant and even the slightest thing can put them off.

Older properties in particular can begin to look pretty shabby if they have not been looked after. On the other hand a sensitively-restored property, or the kind of houses you might see on *Grand Designs,* not only look good, the investment in getting it right from the beginning will pay off in the property gaining more value over time.

Of course, all this depends on the kind of budget you have for the work and how long it will take to cover those costs and make a profit - something that should always be your primary focus as a buy to let investor.

If you don't fancy the hassle of renovation or refurbishment, there is always the option of buying new – either already constructed or off-plan.

The advantage of buying new property is that you won't use up any of your spare time doing work and it can be marketed after exchange for tenanting immediately on completion, so you start bringing in rental income right away. The disadvantage is you will inevitably be paying a premium for that pleasure. If the property market is picking up, developers will be inflating their prices to make as much profit as they can.

You will also almost inevitably have other hidden costs to deal with. Unlike the old days, where builders would build the property and move on, most are now part of larger companies that want to continue generating income from their build.

This income is often generated by the builder retaining the freehold and charging you ground rent. You can apply for the freehold, of course, but you may not get it. This is particularly so in the murky world of new apartment blocks, something I'll cover in more detail in Chapter 6.

**TIP:** *If you want to buy new build, offer either early, when the project is still at the planning stage, or at the end, when there are only a couple of units left.*

Developers will be keen to pick up some sales momentum at the planning stage and then will be motivated to close the project off at the end so they can move on to the next one. In both cases, you may be able to negotiate on price.

If you do decide to invest in a new development, ask yourself the following questions before you sign on the dotted line:

- Does this look like a quality development?
- Can I realistically expect tenants will want to live here, i.e. is it close to town and transport links?
- Does this developer have a strong track record?
- What are the management costs likely to be? Are they realistic?

## What makes a bad investment property?

So you have the money to invest in your first buy to let property, but you're not quite sure what makes a good one.

Hunting for an ideal investment property can be time consuming and the best advice I can give is to use a good estate agent who understands exactly what you're looking for and can introduce you to great potential investments as soon as they come to market – or even before. They will also be able to help you avoid some of the classic mistakes that people make when they buy investment property.

## Avoiding bad locations

As a buy to let investor, you should make sure you don't have any kind of emotional attachment to the property you're looking to make money out of. This is not your home, it's purely an investment vehicle.

A bad location, from an investment perspective, doesn't necessarily mean the area is run down or undesirable, it simply means it's not going to make you money. So if you buy a property simply because you think it looks really nice, or it reminds you of a house you once lived in yourself, or it seems like a quality area, you're in danger of falling into the bad location trap.

Bad buy to let locations are areas where tenant demand is weak or non-existent. That may be because they're several miles away from the nearest town or city or a decent school, or because the transport links are not good.

You need to focus on the potential of a location to generate a decent rental income and also capital growth on your investment. Properties in locations that don't look so good can be goldmines if enough people want to live in them. The two key things you need to focus on are:

- What is the history of house prices and rental values in the area?
- Is there a good rental demand that is likely to continue?

You can get the answers to both those questions online and by speaking to good local sales and lettings agents.

## Example: expensive property, average location, bad investment

Depending on your budget, it's unlikely that you'll find a perfect property that ticks all the boxes. As with anything in life, there will be elements of risk and compromise. You will need to calculate all potential risks very carefully before investing and make sure you research an area thoroughly, because getting the location wrong can be a disaster.

Mr Edwards decides to purchase a penthouse apartment for £250,000. It's in the town centre and very close to local amenities, including a shopping centre, three supermarkets and some coffee shops. On top of this, several other new homes are being built in the town as the developers move in.

The apartment is kitted out to a high standard and the development itself is the literally the talk of the town. Surely Mr Edwards has landed himself the ideal investment property?

Sadly, Mr Edwards has missed some vital clues as to how viable this investment property is from a buy to let perspective.

The first is that, unfortunately, property prices in other towns and cities nearby have always risen higher than here. Even though this town appears to be 'up and coming', it has a reputation for being unfashionable and has always lagged behind a more popular urban area just a short drive away.

The second thing is, unfashionable areas are unfashionable for a reason. They tend to be low income areas, often associated with problems such as higher than average crime rates, overcrowded schools and high unemployment.

Mr Edwards' investment is a bad one because his potential tenant pool will be extremely small to non-existent. People who want decent penthouse apartments don't tend to want them in unfashionable areas and certainly won't be prepared to pay a good price for a bad location, no matter how nice the décor. The property is simply too expensive for its setting, so capital growth will be sluggish at best - at worst, it will go into reverse.

A bad investment property won't make you money even if it could make you a good home. If you really care about making a return, ditch the emotion and take a very close look at all aspects of the area you're about to invest in, particularly average rental returns, demand for sales and lettings, likely capital growth and crime levels.

# Buy to Let Checklist

Use the following checklist as a guide to help you choose your next property. This is a simplified version of a spreadsheet I have used myself, so I'd suggest you use it as a starting point to create your own detailed spreadsheet where you can log specific data.

| | Good | Average | Poor |
|---|---|---|---|
| Location | | | |
| Price (relative to local market) | | | |
| Likely rental return | | | |
| Capital growth prospects | | | |
| Crime rate data | | | |
| Historic house price growth | | | |
| Local schools | | | |
| Perception of the area | | | |
| Employment levels | | | |
| Universities | | | |
| Hospitals | | | |

There is a huge amount of property price and local information available online - I find these websites particularly useful:

Zoopla.co.uk
Rightmove.co.uk
Mouseprice.co.uk
Crimemaps.org.uk

Use these online resources, together with your own local research 'on the ground' to arm yourself with as much knowledge as possible.

If anything, it is much easier to avoid a bad investment property than it has been in the past, simply because there is so much data available now online. The resources are there, all you need to do is use them and you will be well on the road to investment success.

# Chapter 5

# How And Where To Find A Bargain

You can always find a bargain property but there are certain times during the property market cycle when you are more likely to find one. The best times are during a prolonged slump and when a market is just beginning to take off. The window of opportunity when you can bag yourself the best bargains will be small, so it helps to look for those little signals that present themselves, often in the media and also just by looking around you.

Some people are only happy when they have some bad news to talk about and you will hear a lot more from them during a property market slump. What doom mongers have to say about the market is more likely to have a psychological effect on people's buying and selling habits than when everything looks rosy.

Likewise, when the property market is picking up, you will hear less from the doom mongers and a lot more from the people who are interested in selling property. The press often relies on those with a vested interest in selling property for their news stories (i.e. estate agents and developers), so you often get exaggerated tales about house prices soaring. The thing is, people still believe the papers and what they read online.

## In a down cycle...

In a down cycle fear tends to grip a nation. It leaves people thinking, "Will I ever be able to sell my house?", "How much will prices fall?" and the most dangerous thought of all, "If I don't sell now and quickly, I'll be stuck". It's this kind of urgent desperation that leads people into making rushed decisions. This is the time when you can come in with a 'cheeky' offer that would give you great instant equity - and you're more likely to agree a sale in your favour, as you're in a position to meet their needs.

## The start of a housing boom

If the market is beginning to 'boom' as investors call it, sellers will be panicking for an altogether different reason. They don't want to miss out on their onward purchase, so again there is urgency to agree a sale quickly before that new home they want is priced out of reach or somebody else gets there first.

## So how do you find these 'motivated sellers' and land yourself a property discount?

The answer is, your estate agent. They have access to far more properties than you could hope to find yourself and will have a relationship with their vendors. That puts them in a great position to recommend you as a solid buyer. They will also be able to offer you a wealth of knowledge about a property and its location. Good agents love good investors and are almost always very happy to give free advice on the best areas to buy or at least provide a solid starting point for you to do your own research.

In my experience, it's best to be direct and honest with estate agents about what you're looking for and, on the whole, even if the agent has a vested interest in selling the property, they will give you some hints and clues as to whether this is the right one for you. If they think you're serious about investing and you ask the right questions then you should get some honest answers in return.

## Negotiating: right property right price

To be as successful as you can be, you need to work on becoming a skilled negotiator who can drive down the asking price. Unless you happen to be investing in an area where demand is particularly high or people feel 100% confident that they can achieve their asking price, you should be able to get a discount.

Negotiating a discount is an easy way to make money at a very early stage in the process of securing your investment. You can lock in several thousand pounds' worth of equity, simply by negotiating a price reduction of 5-10%.

Unfortunately, not every vendor is prepared to drop their price. There will be some who are not in any particular hurry to sell, in which case, you'll need to have really done your research on the area, into how much similar properties have actually sold for in past 12 months or so. If there are a whole bunch of properties of a similar spec selling for a particular price, then you know that this is likely to be the vendor's bottom line, even if the asking price is inflated.

Remember, the vendor is just as keen as you to walk out of the negotiation with a few thousand pounds more than they started with. That being said, the asking price is the starting point for your negotiation and shouldn't (in most cases) be what you necessarily end up paying.

The main weapons in your armoury going into the negotiation will be time, information and cash. A buy to let investor should have more time on their hands than a typical homebuyer who probably has only a few months to move house.

The process of negotiation should start with having good knowledge of the local market, right down to what is referred to as the 'micro market'. Keep the comparables you use as close as possible in style, size and location to the property you intend to buy. This is the information you need to support your offer, i.e. justify why you're offering that amount.

If the vendor refuses to negotiate then it's best to move on. There will be plenty more opportunities to find a seller who is prepared to drop their price. There's no sense in losing money by paying more than the property is worth and, armed with your research on local prices, you should come across as a serious buyer.

Sometimes you may find that there are no real comparables and the most recent data on house sales is more than 12 months old. In this case, you need to be thinking about making that offer of 5-10% less than the asking price. The vendor may be testing the market and you might just get the discount.

When it comes to negotiating a deal, remember that time is more likely to be on your side and, therefore, the power.


## Buying at auction

I would never recommend buying at auction to anyone starting out as a property investor, even though it might seem like a great way to find a bargain.

If what you're buying is cheap, then there has to be a reason why. Generally, if it's been put up for auction, a property will have been on the market for some time and/or the owners are in a hurry to sell.

The main question to ask is why is this property up for auction? Why could it not have been sold through an estate agent?

There are several possibilities:
1.  The owner can't sell it
2.  The owner needs a quick sale
3.  The property needs a lot of modernisation
4.  There is a problem with the property
5.  The refurbishment costs outweigh the benefit of owning it
6.  The property has been repossessed
7.  The owner is deceased

If you do decide to take the risk and buy at an auction you will, in almost every case, be buying a property that needs refurbishment work, so you should always get a survey done beforehand to make sure there are no nasty surprises. (If you require a mortgage for the purchase, your lender will have insisted on at least a valuation report and possibly a more detailed survey.)

The problem is, even if you do get the survey done prior to auction, you can't guarantee that you'll have the winning bid. And this isn't the only thing that can't be guaranteed.

Take the story of one unfortunate investor, who decided to bid at auction for a Victorian property in an upmarket area with spectacular views of the sea. It sounded like the perfect investment and it was available for just £38,000.

The auction catalogue at the time mentioned that the property needed extensive modernisation. The investor no doubt thought that at such a low price it wasn't worth getting a survey done and decided to take the risk instead.

A week after he made the winning bid for the property it had disappeared. The local council had decided that the structure of the building was unsound and arranged for its demolition.

The unfortunate investor was left to pay the £38,000 PLUS the demolition bill!

This begs the question, did the seller know that they would be liable for these costs and opt to mislead the buyer? *Caveat emptor – buyer beware. Auctions are the ideal place to get rid of problem properties because the onus is on the buyer to check all the particulars before they part with their cash.*

**TIP:** *Once you're in the auction room, set the maximum you're prepared to pay and stick to it*!
It's easy to get carried away competing against another bidder. Paying over the odds for a property means it will take longer for you to realise a profit on your investment, if there is any to be had.

## Buying at auction with a mortgage

If buying at auction is risky when you have the cash, then buying at auction without any is even more of a gamble!

The minimum amount you need in cash to even consider buying at an auction is 10% of the value of the property you are hoping to buy. So if it's £100,000, then you will need to have your £10,000 ready because you will be contractually bound to pay this when the hammer falls.

If you haven't arranged a mortgage prior to the auction, you will then have a very anxious 28 days waiting for your offer – a wait that could be in vain, as most lenders will take longer than that to approve a mortgage. This leaves you at risk of losing your deposit and if anything should happen to the property in the meantime, you will be liable for any damage as well.

Ultimately, if you're serious about making a success of buy to let you would be wise to avoid anything that creates unnecessary risk and that includes auctions. Remember, there will always be plenty of properties out there that will generate the kind of returns you want.

## Buying from a property investment agent or consultancy

The birth of buy to let in the mid-1990s spawned the birth of a whole industry built around property investors. Unlike the traditional estate agent, property investment agents and consultants only deal with investors and offer select opportunities in the UK and overseas.

The investment consultancy will help developers market property investment opportunities to a wider audience. Often, a network of several agents will be marketing the same projects via websites, email and other online marketing channels.

The quality of agents varies. Virtually anyone can set up a website offering property investments and not all the people who run them are trustworthy. You should always research the company and find out whether they are members of organisations such as the AIPP. That's one step to finding out if a company is legitimate, although it's still no guarantee that you won't encounter problems. There are many, many stories of investors losing money through projects being delayed or scrapped, or simply through not getting anywhere near the returns they were told they would.

Property agents make their money through commissions paid by developers on each sale and usually help with client mortgages and paperwork. Although they're ever so friendly while the deal is being agreed, agents usually pay far less attention to investors after their money has been handed over.

Investment agents deal in all areas of residential and, increasingly, commercial property, such as fractional ownership of hotel rooms or student properties. There is usually the promise of high yields and/or high capital growth, plus 'guaranteed' rental returns.

**TIP:** *Always be wary of any rental guarantees on offer*

They're usually just funded by the inflated purchase price you paid in the first place and when the guaranteed rental period ends, you can soon find that your returns plummet.

As a new investor starting out, the offers can sound tempting and some do turn out to be good investment opportunities. However, it's vital that any investment you make has been thoroughly researched beforehand and you've done your due diligence. These companies will usually tell you there's a limited offer or put some other kind of time pressure on you, to make you think you need to act quickly. If an offer sounds too good to be true, then it is, even if a glossy brochure or website suggests otherwise, and don't ever let yourself be persuaded to short-cut your research for fear of missing the deal of a lifetime. There will always be another deal.

My personal advice is to give these companies a wide berth. With a little research, you can avoid wasting your cash on a go-between and source properties yourself or use an estate agent who only gains from the actual sale of a property rather than a complex commission structure.

# Chapter 6

# Types of Investment Property

## Apartments

Buying an apartment can either be a good investment or the worst you will ever make, depending on where it's located and, just as importantly, how the apartment building is managed.

### What's good about apartments?

Apartments are usually low maintenance compared to investing in a house. The cost of external repairs is often shared amongst the community, as are boiler repairs if the block runs off a shared boiler.

Depending on the type of development, apartments might not have a garden or other external space to manage or maintain as would be the case with most houses, so there will be less to factor into your investment forecast when it comes to overall maintenance.

If you invest in an apartment that's close to town and in a relatively good area with easy access to shops, then you're likely to find a tenant pretty quickly. Rental demand is generally good for 2-bedroom apartments that are popular with young professionals, particularly if the apartment has allocated parking, rather than communal or on-street parking.

The value of apartments also tends to lag behind houses in the same area, so the mortgage will cost less a month than it would for a house for a comparable rental return.

**What's bad about apartments?**
Investing in apartments is rarely as simple as it sounds and if you're thinking of investing in an apartment that is part of a larger dwelling, there are inevitably hidden costs.

Monthly service charges are a virtual certainty if the apartment is leasehold and, unlike buying a house with clear title that you own, you will never be fully in control of your investment. If the company that owns the development chooses to, they can set service charges higher. If the building is run and managed by a residents' committee, any decisions will be made on a majority vote and some of these decisions – which you might not personally agree with - can end up costing large sums of money.

If you decide to invest in a leasehold apartment, you will also be charged a ground rent which tends to be paid annually or every six months. You may also be required to pay money into a sinking fund which helps pay for repairs and upkeep of the building.

If you are still able to make a profit when all these costs are taken into consideration, then an apartment can make a good investment, particularly if it's in a sought-after area of a town or city.

# Hotel rooms

Hotel rooms, or fractional ownership of hotel rooms, is a type of commercial property investment that tends to have a lower entry point than a residential investment.

This works on the basis that the investor buys a hotel room or a share of the hotel room (fractional ownership) and gets a share of the profit from guests who stay in the room in return.

The term of this type of investment is typically 10 years and they often come with some form of buy-back guarantee that promises a lump sum if you hand the room back at the end of the 10-year period.

### Things to watch out for with hotel room investments

With hotel rooms, you're essentially helping the hotel company build the rooms, so there could be a significant period of time between you committing your funds and the completion of the hotel. That means your money is tied up and you're not getting any returns.

Secondly, unlike buying a conventional property, you will not be able to buy hotel rooms with a mortgage, so it's all your own cash at stake. And working out how the investment stacks up can be tricky, as the calculations of returns can be complex and there is uncertainty if occupancy rates are lower than expected. The risk here is that, unlike a straightforward residential property investment, you're relying on someone else to make a success of the business and manage it properly.

When it comes to exit time, even if the hotel company buys back the room, they're only going to buy it back for what it *was* worth a decade ago, rather than what it's likely to be worth when you want to sell it. With this investment, there is no chance of benefiting from any capital growth.

If you do decide that hotel room investments are a hassle-free way to generate a bit of income and you're willing to take the risk in the long term, then it's important to check the terms of agreement very carefully. Sometimes the returns you get are hardly worth the investment you put in and you may be better off putting your cash elsewhere.

## Houses in Multiple Occupation (HMOs)

You can read about HMOs in a lot more detail in my first book, **'HMO PROPERTY SUCCESS'**. For the purposes of this book, I'll briefly summarise what HMOs are and why they can generate more income than other types of buy to let property.

With an HMO you're essentially letting a house room by room to separate individuals, rather than having one tenant or their family occupying the whole house. The properties usually offer five or six private bedrooms and then communal cooking, living and washing facilities.

This set-up can be achieved by buying a three or four bedroom house and then converting a lounge, dining room - or even garage - into bedrooms. There is no law that says a house must have a lounge *and* a dining room, so, if the house is large enough, you should be able to divide it up more or less as you wish, subject to any building, planning and health and safety regulations.

With HMOs you can make two or three times the income you would generate from letting the same property as a single unit. The rental income you make will cover all your regular outgoings and still leave you a healthy profit on top. The other big benefit is that you rarely get badly affected by voids, as it's highly unlikely half your tenants will choose to leave at the same time. As a general rule of thumb, rooms one to four tend to cover your costs, then rooms five and above are your profit.

## Things to watch out for with HMOs

The location is a big consideration for HMOs. Not only do you need to make sure there is the right kind of rental demand, but also you will need to consider the regulations of your local council, as they differ from area to area.

This is the second major thing to be aware of – that HMOs are subject to different licensing, planning and health and safety regulations to single-let properties. If you're interested in this kind of investment, it's a good idea to go to your local council and find out exactly what their policies are, before you invest. Sometimes there are restrictions and demands that can severely impact the viability of your buy to let and you need to be clear on the rules before you commit yourself.

The other thing is to vet your tenants carefully as three to five times the number of people living in a house will usually result in more wear and tear over time, so maintenance costs will be higher. In addition, you should try to make sure, as far as you can, that there won't be any major personality clashes in the house.

The demand for HMOs typically comes from:

> Company lets
> Young professionals who work in cities
> Transient workers who need a temporary place to live
> Students
> Social housing
> Unemployed DSS

With this in mind, you need to decide which type of tenant you would prefer to be dealing with. For example, many investors prefer not to let property to people on benefits or students for fear that they may cause problems. Young professionals and other working adults are usually able to pay higher rent, but the council could give you a more guaranteed regular income stream for taking people on housing benefit. You need to research the demand in your specific area and decide the best options for you.

## Student lets

In 2012, a report from the international property agency Knight Frank revealed that there is a structural undersupply of purpose-built accommodation for students in the UK. This has prompted a huge increase in demand for this type of property.

The student property sector managed to outperform all other commercial property classes during the economic downturn. Student applicants have increased dramatically in the last decade, both domestically and from abroad. The number of full-time students in higher education is reported to have risen by 540,000 between 1999 and 2012. This has massively increased demand for accommodation, fuelling a building boom in student housing in university towns and cities across the UK.

The 'traditional student house' with five or six students sharing an old Victorian house is slowly being replaced with a new breed of purpose-built pods designed around what students need from their temporary homes.

As a result, the opportunities in this sector fall into either the traditional 'HMO' type house or the purpose-built block where you can invest in one or a number of student 'pods'. These are typically priced at around £70,000 in cities such as Leeds or Manchester - a lot less than you'd pay for a house or an apartment in the city centre. But, inevitably, there are some drawbacks.

## The problem with investing in purpose-built student accommodation

Investments in purpose built student property are set up so that investors can buy one or several student rooms in a block and gain a share of the profit from the rent. The investor buys at a low price and the developer makes their profit from the sale of each of the rooms, so it looks like a win/win.

The thing to watch out for with this type of investment is the likely resale market when you decide to exit. It's unclear what the units will be worth in 10 or 20 years' time, unlike a standard house where you own an asset that will undoubtedly have grown considerably in value over the same period.

In addition, ownership of purpose-built student housing is not as straightforward as it sounds and if you're serious about making money from property, there are probably better opportunities to explore in other sectors.

On the plus side, investing in this kind of student housing will be low maintenance, compared to running a student house, because they will be managed for you. If you're not a hands-on type of investor, this may be an attractive proposition, as you're highly unlikely to ever be bothered with having to sort out everyday repairs.

## Care homes

Care homes are a similar type of investment to hotel rooms, where you can invest in a room and take a share of the revenue generated by that room. Only they're not half as exciting or profitable as investing in traditional buy to let property!

Several companies are now marketing care homes as an alternative to traditional buy to let investing, spurred on by predictions that the number of older people in society is rising rapidly as people are living longer.

According to the Office for National Statistics, the number of people aged 65 and over is expected to rise by nearly two-thirds by 2031. This means that there should, in theory, be a greater demand for care homes.

Terra Firma, the company that bought the record label EMI for £3.2 billion in 2007, recently turned their attention to Four Seasons, the UK's biggest care home group. This action boosted the idea that care homes are an emerging investment class.

**Beware of the hype around care home investments**

There are 24,000 care homes in the UK currently and not all of them are full. In fact care homes are actually closing down in some areas of the UK, which raises the possibility that demand is not yet high enough in some locations to make this type of property a good investment.

If you're convinced by the argument that care rooms will be in high demand in the long term, make sure that you're investing in a high-quality development and that the construction company has a strong track record.

Your investment, in many cases, will be used to fund the construction of a care home, so you'll need to carry out due diligence and check that there is good demand, i.e. enough older people already living in the area or who want to spend their twilight years living there. Most older people prefer a care home out in the countryside.

Again, as with hotel rooms, if you're looking for capital growth, you'll always be far better off investing in a house that you actually own, rather than sharing ownership with other investors and companies who will also be taking a share of the profits.

## Renovation projects and older property

Buying an old house, refurbishing it and then letting it out is the most popular buy to let strategy because it works. You just need to be prepared to get stuck in and do some of the work yourself.

The good thing is, if you find a property that needs work, you're unlikely to have a huge amount of competition from other buyers and it will always be cheaper than buying new or nearly new.

The three most important things to consider with a renovation property are:

> The cost of the refurbishment
> The area the property is in
> The type of tenant you're hoping to attract

The days when you could just buy a property, make it habitable and put it on the market are now a thing of the past. This isn't the early '90s any more and even students expect a certain level of comfort.

As jobs have become more mobile these days, there is a chance that your tenant may be looking for a home from home, and they or their companies will be prepared to pay extra to guarantee comfort.

Imagine the following:

**Mr Edwards** invests £200,000 in a property but it only generates **£800 a month** in rental income because it's in poor condition.

If only he had invested an extra £20,000 in making the property look good, he could have been making £1200 a month.

So the false economy at the beginning means that Mr Edwards is only generating a 4.8% return, as opposed to the 6.5% return he could have generated by carrying out the refurbishment.

If you're not prepared to put in the time and effort to prepare your property properly for rent – and renovation and refurbishment does require effort – it's probably wiser to consider investing in something that just requires a bit of decorating and a lick of paint to get it looking right.

## Cheap terraced housing

Terraced housing is cheap for a reason: because it's usually the least desirable type of house. The rooms tend to be small, there are people on both sides and very little privacy, there's rarely any parking and the neighbourhoods are often run-down.

However, many property investors decide to go down the terraced housing route because it is far cheaper than most other property types and the gross rental returns can be high in and around some cities.

Areas where cheaper terraced housing tends to be available are often those populated by people on lower incomes or unemployment benefits. The low purchase price means the investor doesn't need much rental income to still turn a profit, and there's a high demand for cheap housing.

**Don't be fooled - cheap terraced housing can be high maintenance**

While not all terraced houses are bad investments, if you're investing in inner cities, you stand a good chance of the crime rate being higher than normal and having undesirable neighbours that will put off potential tenants.

Some of the potential pitfalls of terraced housing are:

○ Failing to achieve capital growth
○ You should expect to have to hold the property for a long time to see returns
○ The area may become a ghetto and a focus for crime over time

With the above in mind, it's extra important to find out as much as you can about the area where you intend to buy terraced housing and check that the level of rent you intend to charge reflects what's already being paid each month for other houses on the same street. Also, try to buy in areas that have a visible sense of community.

# Buying off-plan

When property prices are rising, there is often a surge in the number of people willing to put down a deposit on a property they've only seen illustrated on paper plans or in a glossy brochure.

During the last property boom in the UK, buying off-plan was seen as the ideal way to secure an investment early at a discounted price and lock in some equity. Some investors were even able to turn a profit before completion, by selling on a property that had risen in value as it was being built.

A major benefit of buying off-plan is that you get to choose your plot early and reserve the best units on a development. As many as 90% of properties may be sold off-plan before there is any visible sign of houses in high demand areas of London and the South East.

There are always 'special offers' with new builds and you may be offered some kind of discount for putting down your deposit early on a property. Just be aware that the 'discount' may not be genuine if the property's true value has not yet been established. And herein lies a big risk when you buy off-plan. If you can't guarantee what the value of the property will be when it completes, then it becomes a bit of a gamble investing your cash.

There is also the very real possibility that property prices may fall while you are waiting for the property to be built.

## Case study:

Catherine puts down a 10% deposit on an off-plan house in

a new development she has seen in a glossy brochure. She plans to pay off the remainder of what she will owe with finance.

She selects the plot she think would most appeal to tenants. She then arranges a buy to let mortgage to cover the balance, sits back and waits for her investment property to complete.

6 months later something bad happens to the economy and house prices start falling. The property Catherine bought with a discount ends up being valued at less than she agreed to pay for it.

Worse still, her buy to let mortgage was only an agreement in principle, which the bank can amend or withdraw at any time.

Catherine is left with a shortfall. The bank refuses to lend the money and the developer wants to receive the asking price set 12 months earlier.

Fortunately, the developer agrees to take back the property, but on the condition that Catherine pays the difference between what the developer can now sell it for and the original sale price that was agreed 12 months earlier.

Unless she can find a lender willing to give her a mortgage

for the agreed amount, Catherine will be left £50,000 out of pocket.

This experience is a worst-case scenario, but it's based on a true story of someone investing just prior to the last credit crunch. Agreements in principle from a lender should never be seen as a guarantee that you will get the money. Always keep an eye out for any signs in the housing market that prices may start to fall or that mortgage interest rates are set to rise – if you have a good broker, they should keep you up to date.

Finally, do be realistic and understand that the finished development itself probably won't look like it does in the brochure, so the best advice is to only buy off-plan with a reputable developer or one that you're familiar with.

But if you really want to make a success of investing in property why take a gamble on off-plan at all? I think it's far better to invest in a house you can see and touch when you agree to buy it, rather than lock in a theoretical discount on a property that may or may not look like an artist's impression.

# PART TWO:

# MAKING MONEY FROM PROPERTY

# Chapter 7

# Generating An Income

## How to calculate your rental returns

If you want to make it as a property investor, you need to understand some basic maths. There are many secret formulas and ways to calculate a return on investment and there are plenty of clever people out there who can use maths to convince you that you can get a great return on some of the worst property investments!

Don't take any notice when you see adverts promising huge double-digit net returns or guaranteed rental yields. The reality is often something quite different. Successful property investors are able to calculate returns from property themselves quite easily, using a simple net return calculation.

A gross rental return is the total amount of money your tenant pays you for the pleasure of living in your property. But this isn't what you're going to end up with. Your actual net return – or pre-tax profit – is what you're left with after all your expenses have been taken out.

Here's an example:

A pensioner is selling his flat at a heavy discount due to ill health. He's a distressed seller who needs to sell quickly so he can find more suitable accommodation.

He paid £165,000 for the flat when it was new and has now decided to reduce the price to £100,000 in order to force a quick sale.

The apartment looks like a bargain, one of those rare opportunities to buy at a heavy discount, lock in equity and generate positive cash flow as soon as it's put up for rent.

Other similar-sized apartments in the area are renting for £700 a month.

A buy to let mortgage could be secured on this £100,000 property for £400 a month.

The investor can't lose, right?

Wrong!

**Monthly Rental Income: £700**
**Monthly Mortgage: £350**
**Monthly income from rent = £350**

This is what we call the 'gross' return on this property.

To find the net return we need to look at how much this property will cost us to run.

Owning a property in this block of luxury flats means that there is a high service charge, which has just increased to £250 per month.

So if I were to invest in this apartment, the net return is suddenly looking less appealing:

**Monthly Rental Income: £700**
**Monthly Mortgage: £350**
**Monthly Service Charge: £250**

**Monthly profit from the property = £100**

£100 a month in positive cash flow isn't too bad, but you will need to put pretty much all of that aside to cover one-off repairs, which can add up to a lot on communal properties. There may also be ground rent to pay and building insurance which, again, could add around £50 a month to your on-going costs.

But this still doesn't tell you the whole story, it only gives you a cash flow figure.

Most property investors talk about yield – that's the cash return as a percentage of the current value of the property. In it's most simple form, as a gross yield figure, it only takes into account the rental income:

**Property Value: £100,000**
**Annual Rental Income: £8,400**
**Gross Yield: £8,400/£100,000 x 100 = 8.4%**

But gross yield doesn't take costs into account. To properly compare properties as investments, you need to use the net profit figure:

**Property Value: £100,000**
**Annual Net Income (profit): £100 x 12 = £1,200**
**Net Yield: £1,200/£100,000 x 100 = 1.2%**

Suddenly that yield figures has fallen dramatically and a property that only gives a net yield of 1.2% is definitely not one you should be investing in unless you've got it at a huge discount and are looking to sell on as soon as the market picks up. You really should aim for a minimum net yield of 5%, to protect yourself against interest rate rises.

While yield allows you to compare one property with another, if you want to be able to compare property with other types of investment, you need to know the return on your invested funds. To calculate the return on investment (ROI) that this £100,000 property will give, you need to factor in the amount you invested to fund the purchase.

**Deposit + Purchase Costs = £18,000**
**Annual Net Profit: £100 x 12 = £1,200**
**Return on Investment: £1,200/£18,000 x 100 = 6.66%**

As you hold your investment, you can add capital growth into your annual profit figure and you should see your ROI steadily increasing.

**TIP:** *Be clear on your projected net returns (income), yield and total return on investment figures BEFORE you buy.*

The bottom line is, to be successful in buy to let investing, always find out the total costs associated with the property you're planning to buy. That will allow you to calculate what the actual returns will be and compare investment opportunities properly.

## How long should you hang on to a property?

If we assume that the price of property in the UK doubles every 10 years, as is often quoted, then holding a property sounds like a no-brainer. Unfortunately, it is not quite as straightforward as that.

It would be more realistic to say prices *can* double every 7 to 10 years, but there is no guarantee. So whether you should buy and hold really comes down to timing. Time it wrong and you will need to hold a property a lot longer to achieve some worthwhile profits and for this you need a long-term strategy.

This is why all the property experts out there will tell you that you should look to hold a property for at least five years and not sell at all unless you really need to. Essentially, buy and hold is proven to be the best way to achieve your primary buy to let investment goal, which is to build wealth from property.

This strategy will always work for you if you can maintain positive cash flow. To do that, you need to invest in the right kinds of investment property that will allow you to generate the level of cash flow you need.

## The best kept secret in buy to let

If only everyone was familiar with the magic that can happen over time when you buy and hold a property, then everyone would be a buy to let investor! This magic starts with the way you can leverage your money by borrowing from the bank and, as the property grows in value, use it to buy more properties.

Then there is inflation. While it steadily erodes the value of the money you have borrowed via mortgage finance, property values are steadily increasing, as are rents, which tend to keep track with inflation.

That means in real terms that over time:
- The value of the money you owe the bank drops
- Your rental profits increase
- The capital value increases and you benefit from **all** the

additional equity, not just the increase on your proportion of the invested funds

Therefore your ROI gets better and better.

To give an example:

> Property Value: £160,000
> Mortgage Borrowing at 75% LTV: £120,000
> Annual Interest Only Payment (5%): £6,000
> Annual Rental Income (5% of property value): £8,000
> Year 1 Profit (before any other costs): £2,000

If inflation is running at 3% per annum, your borrowing of £120,000 effectively drops in value by £3,600. That's £3,600 you would have 'lost' if it had been your own money. As it is, it's the bank that's 'losing'.

Assuming property prices are increasing at 5% per annum, in year two of holding your investment:

> Property Value: £168,000
> Mortgage Borrowing remains: £120,000
> Annual Interest Only Payment (5%) remains: £6,000
> Annual Rental Income (5% of value): £8,400
> Year 2 Profit (before any other costs): £10,400 (£2,400 rent, plus £8,000 equity)

ROI Year 1:

 Personal Investment: £40,000

 Annual Profit: £2,000

 Annual ROI: 5%

ROI Year 2:

 Personal Investment: £40,000

 Annual Profit: £10,400

 Annual ROI: 13% (26% across the two years, averaged out)

The reason your ROI looks so healthy is because the power of leverage – which is greater for property than for any other asset class – allows you to benefit from growth on borrowed funds. And this is the magic.

Add further properties to your portfolio and your financial future begins to look very rosy indeed.

## Short-term or long-term lets?

Investing in a short-term let can be a good option for a number of reasons. Generally, you would be letting short term if you needed to rent out a property in a hurry and it happened to be in an area where there was a demand for this kind of tenancy.

On the other hand, you may have purchased a holiday property that you plan to use yourself for a few weeks each year and have short-term tenants cover the costs for the remainder. It's possible to short let any type of property, from a studio apartment to a six-bedroom house.

A short-term let will be an agreement for someone to rent a property for less than six months (the standard minimum term for a long-term let). This type of tenant may have a work assignment in the area and they won't want the hassle of finding a property and furnishing it, or paying for a hotel, which can work out as a lot more expensive over the course of a few months.

This type of short-term tenancy arrangement is more common in larger cities than it is in towns and smaller cities, where there is unlikely to be sufficient demand. It can also work well in areas of the country that are popular with tourists - in this case they're more likely to be holiday lets.

**Some advantages of short-term lets compared to long-term lets**
- You can charge 25% or more extra rent.
- The income you make can more than cover your costs while you're waiting to fill the property long term.
- If you're planning to use the property as a holiday home, short-term letting while you're not there is a great way to cover your costs.

- There is a growing demand in busy city centres, particularly in London. Large companies can supply regular short-term tenants and this can be a more stable option and reduce potential voids.
- It will be easier to raise the rent as you inevitably get more uplift with a high turnover of tenants.

## Why it's better to let long term

- The reality is that it's always harder to find tenants looking for short-term rentals. You will be targeting a much smaller sector of the market.
- The costs of running a short-term let will be higher. Tenants on work assignments working for large companies will generally expect a higher standard of accommodation than the 'usual' tenant.
- You will inevitably find that void periods are reduced with long-term lets.
- Short-term lets will take up a lot more of your time than a long-term let, simply because they require more management.
- You only need to provide the basics, such as white goods, in a long-term let.
- Planning for the future is always easier when you know what your income will be six to 12 months in advance.

## Buying property with a partner – the pros and cons

Investing in property with a partner, friends or family can sound like an ideal money-making venture. And, provided you start things off in the right way, there is certainly no problem with taking this route into buy to let investing.

If you do decide that, for financial reasons, the only possible way to invest in a property is with a partner, then you'll need to consider the long-term implications of this type of arrangement.

Here's an example to help illustrate why it's so important to get things right from the beginning:

Philip decides to enter into a partnership with his friend, Mike. They have known each other for years and trust has never been an issue between them. Neither has the money to invest in a property that will generate a good rental income, so they decide to look into pooling their money so they can buy together.

The arrangement goes well at first. They agree to split everything 50/50 – both management of the property and the income made from it. This ensures that everything is simple and fair from the outset.

It works okay for the first year. They begin to generate an income from the rent, which covers the costs and leaves them with a modest return on their investment at the end of each month.

Soon after, disagreements start to arise over who is actually in charge. What started out as a partnership soon turns into one partner taking over.

Mike reacts furiously to Philip's attempts to control everything and the arrangement soon begins to unravel. It turns out that one partner is actually more ambitious than the other when it comes to making the most out of the investment and expanding into other properties.

Each partner had their own approach and their differences were irreconcilable. What was a good friendship didn't work well when it came to business.

Sometimes differences won't surface until it is too late and one partner can be left dissatisfied or, worse still, feeling that they have been misled and out of pocket.

**Ways to make sure a property partnership works**
- Make sure that you have everything down in writing from the beginning.
- Think very carefully before entering into what amounts to a business relationship with friends or family members. The dynamics of a business relationship, will be very different and at times there will be disagreements.
- Invest in one property at a time. That way you can always keep your exposure to a minimum and invest independently.

- ○ Whoever you're investing with, make sure that they have some sense of what buy to let investing is all about. Ideally, partner with someone who has some experience.

# Chapter 8

# Letting Your Property

## How to find tenants

The easiest way to find a tenant is by using a letting agent. They will be able to advertise on popular property websites such as Rightmove and Zoopla, which is where most people will be looking for rental properties in the UK.

## Letting agent

An established letting agent will also have a shop window where passers-by may see your property advertised. The letting agent will charge you a fee for finding a tenant, however this may well be worth it when you consider the work you would need to do to find one yourself.

## Online estate agents

A variety of online estate agents services have sprung up in recent years, which cost less than the high street agency route. This can be a good idea if you want to keep fees to a minimum and get the benefit of free advertising. Beware though, the free advertising will not be on Rightmove or where most of your prospective tenants will be looking, unless you pay for extras, so it may be a false economy.

## Social media

Another growing opportunity is via social media channels, including Twitter and Facebook. If you decide to go it alone and look for a tenant yourself, it's entirely possible that with just a few posts on Facebook you'll be handling several enquiries for your property. If you intend to go down this route, bear in mind you'll need a lot of friends who actually read your social updates!

## Newspaper advert

A classified advert in the local newspaper is one of the more traditional routes to reaching a large audience and a little out of date. You'll find that newspaper advertising works better in some areas than others, so do a bit of research before you shell out for an advert.

**TIP: *Don't forget to carry out tenant checks***

You need to carry out the appropriate checks on your tenant before accepting them into your property. Referencing and credit checks may be conditions of your mortgage or property insurance.

A big advantage of using an agent is that they will take care of this responsibility for you.

# Should you engage an agent to find you a tenant or do it yourself?

Unless you really know what you're doing, you should advertise your property with an agent so that the appropriate background checks are made, with references, 3 months' bank statements and previous landlord references stating rents were paid on time.

The main benefit of using an agent to advertise the property for you is that you can keep yourself largely out of the equation when it comes to interaction with your tenants. One of the biggest mistakes landlords make is to become too friendly and fail to clamp down on problems like late payment of rent. Buy to let is a business and there is no room for sentiment when it comes to your cash flow.

The agent will be able to organise viewings and show people around – and bear in mind that they're the professionals and know what needs to be said and done.

The prospective tenant will also take an estate agent more seriously when negotiating the rent and following instructions. Estate agents will have a code of practice for dealing with different types of tenants and how to handle them, so it pays to have access to that valuable experience.

Always ensure you use an agent who is a member of ARLA or NALS, as they also have rental insurance to protect your money if anything goes wrong in the business.

## How to avoid bad tenants

A bad tenant is something no buy to let investor needs or wants. They either won't look after the property, or won't pay the rent on time - or both. This can have a significant impact on the profitability of your investment and peace of mind.

Don't think for a moment that bad tenants happen to other buy to let investors. 60% of landlords have problems with bad tenants, so the odds are that you'll get one at some point. The important thing is that you make sure all your paperwork is up to date and you know how to deal with problems if they arise.

In some of the worst reported cases, properties have been turned into cannabis farms or brothels, houses have been trashed and landlords have had to deal with lengthy evictions, with rent owed running into the thousands. Even at the tamer end of the spectrum, it was recently reported that 100,000 tenants in the UK had not paid their rent for 2 months. Just a small period of time without rent coming in can make a big impact on your cash flow and if there's damage to repair, you could end up massively out of pocket.

If you've decided to find the tenant yourself, where possible, I would strongly advise setting up a meeting with your prospective tenant, so you can get a feel for the kind of person they are. Find out as much as possible about them and their circumstances before you allow them to move into your property.

Remember, it's easier to keep someone out of your property in the first place than go through costly legal battles to remove them when things go bad, so it pays to use all the means available to help you try to ensure you let to a good tenant.

**TIP:** *Make sure you have the right insurance cover*

Buy to let investors require specialist landlord insurance, so make sure you have an appropriate policy that covers you for malicious damage by tenants. You may also want to look into rent guarantee insurance options.

# Should the property be let furnished or unfurnished?

A lot of the accepted wisdom when it comes to letting out your property these days is that it should be unfurnished. This does, however, depend on the type of tenant you're aiming to attract. Some tenants will almost always require furnished property, primarily:

- Students
- DSS
- Short-term tenants

So, depending on the area and type of properties you're investing in, furnishing a property can either work in your favour or you'll end up spending more money than you should have done. And the latter will eat into your profits!

There are advantages to letting your property furnished. If your prospective tenant sees the property furnished to a high standard, then they may find it more appealing because they'll save money on furniture and the process of moving in will be faster.

Young professionals, in particular, may not want to have to bother furnishing a place themselves if all they want is a temporary base in the city centre close to work.

If, on the other hand, your tenants happen to be a family or couple who want to rent long term, beyond six months, then most investors agree that furnishing the property will make no difference. In fact, it may even put them off if they were hoping to make the property more of their own home.

If you do decide to go down the furnished route, then make sure you do it properly, as tenants are far more discerning than they used to be and landlords are upping their game to make sure they stay competitive. Student properties may not demand the latest in stylish furniture, but it will be easier to attract them if everything is in good repair.

## Part furnishing

Part furnishing your buy to let property is a good compromise between spending far too much money and satisfying most tenant types. Putting in white goods and some basics – beds, wardrobes, a sofa, etc. – will mean tenants can move in right away at very little cost, but there's still room for them to bring in their own furniture and furnishings if they want to.

I have heard stories of landlords having to put furniture in storage just because they found a fussy tenant who didn't like their taste. Make sure you're very clear with tenants about what's staying in the property, because storage is expensive and will eat into your profits, unless you can find another home for any unwanted furniture.

## What furnishings you should provide in a property

| Furniture & appliances | short term tenants/ students | Long term tenants / families |
|---|---|---|
| beds | √ | X (with some exceptions) |
| sofa & chair(s) | √ | X |
| table | √ | X |
| wardrobes | √ | √ |
| TV | √ | X |
| DVD/CD player | √ (luxury only) | X |
| cooker | √ | √ |
| dishwasher | √ (luxury) | X |
| fridge freezer | √ | √ |
| washing machine | √ | √ |
| curtains/ blinds | √ | X |
| microwave | √ | X |

**As a rule of thumb, apartments in city centres will usually require some kind of furnishing while you can probably get away with providing the minimum in larger family houses.**

The more equipment you supply your tenant with, the more chance there is that something will get broken. So save yourself a lot of hassle by only providing the minimum amount required. What your tenant doesn't have, they won't miss!

## Setting the rent

The easiest way to set the rent on your property is to look at what people are paying for comparable properties in the same area.

There is plenty of information available online these days and it should take less than a few minutes to gauge rental demand by looking at websites such as Rightmove or Zoopla, because nearly every property up for rent in your area will be on these websites. If you're investing in HMOs, you'll find most people look for rooms on SpareRoom.co.uk and EasyRoommate.com.

There isn't much point in guesswork at this stage, because you may end up either setting the rent too high and getting no interest or setting it too low and regretting it later.

If you find yourself struggling to let the property or the phone hasn't been ringing for weeks on end, it could be a sign that you have a lot of competition, even if you think the rent you have set is competitive with other properties in the area. Like any investment, the market can be brutally efficient and will dictate rent levels.

If you own a property that doesn't seem to be attracting tenants, it may be the wrong type of property for a particular area or it may be too far away from local amenities, in which case you'll need to adjust your rent accordingly to avoid lengthy voids. This is why it's so important you take time in the beginning to thoroughly research the area and the demand. Voids are the death-knoll for cash flow and if it turns out you can't charge as much rent as you thought you could, over a sustained period it could seriously impact the viability of your investment plan.

Bear in mind that as long as you're giving tenants what they want, most will happily pay a little more for things like:

- A nice view
- A garden (young families)
- Modern fixtures and fittings
- Good storage
- Extra space
- Higher floors (if apartments)

The goal is to let the property, even if it means taking off that extra profit you were hoping for.

## Why setting the right rent is critical to your profit

Before you get to the stage where you're setting the rent, you will hopefully have taken the advice I gave earlier on generating a profit from your investment. Rental income is absolutely critical to this.

The absolutely minimum rental income you should consider when budgeting for your investment is an amount that at least covers your running costs, with money left over to also cover any void periods (the times when you don't have a tenant). It's critical that in your initial planning stages, before you buy, you're satisfied you have an accurate and realistic picture of the rent levels in your area for your specific type of property and that you've calculated the running costs correctly. Getting these figures wrong could be disastrous for your profits.

In the vast majority of cases, renting is not a long-term choice for people and they will leave eventually due to changes in their circumstances. You will be faced with re-setting the rent on your properties every now and then, even if it's just to keep up with inflation.

Of course, the longer you hold a property, the less pressure there is on the rental income, as the effect of inflation slowly works its magic and the capital value rises.

# Types of tenancy agreements

Don't get so carried away with your buy to let adventure that you overlook some of the legalities. Lettings regulations are changing and tightening all the time, so making sure you're legally watertight is extremely important. One of the big things to get right is the legal agreement between you and your tenant.

Both you and your tenant have certain rights and responsibilities, whether you have put the tenancy agreement in writing or not, so it makes sense to do the paperwork properly and make sure everyone is clear on the terms.

A tenancy can either be fixed term or short term (week by week, month by month).

The most common tenancy agreement is known as an assured shorthold tenancy agreement or AST. Unless you have been letting out a property since the 1980s or your tenant is paying you over £100,000 a year, the chances are your tenancy agreement will be an AST.

If you use a letting agent, they will take care of all the paperwork as part of the service they provide, including protecting the tenant's deposit and handling all the related administration, but if you've decided to do it yourself, you can find standard ASTs online to download and in larger stationers.

If you are simply using an 'off the shelf' AST, it may be worthwhile speaking to a legal lettings specialist, to make sure all the terms are present and correct for your particular type of property, let and tenant.

# Chapter 9

# Investing Overseas

Properties by the beach in a warm climate or in some of the world's most attractive cities can be very tempting, but if you're a UK-based investor, how do they stack up as investments against properties closer to home?

A lot of overseas properties look unbelievably cheap compared to what you would pay for the equivalent in the UK. They may come with incentives, such as a rental guarantee, or there might be an appealing extra, such as a pool.

If you're buying a holiday home for yourself, then by all means get carried away, but if you're a serious investor, these considerations are secondary to the question: will I make money out of this property in the long term?

## Never invest in a property market you don't understand

Warren Buffett said, "Never invest in a business you can't understand", and that certainly applies to investing in overseas property. Becoming a buy to let investor means that you absolutely have to think like a business owner.

If you don't understand a country or have never even visited it, how can you be sure that you can actually make more of a profit from a property you will rarely get to see, thousands of miles away? You don't know the area, the currency, the economy, even the language may be foreign to you. And then there's the legal system. Buying, owning and operating a buy to let could be very different to doing the same here in the UK.

You will need to arrange a specialist mortgage to invest overseas and if you don't know the country yourself, you'll need to have a trusted professional who does and who can give you good, independent information and advice. This is critical when it comes to all paperwork and financial arrangements.

**TIP:** *Use your own independent professionals*

If you're buying new or off-plan from a developer or agent, they will have their own team of mortgage brokers, lawyers and surveyors. Whether they're UK based or overseas, always insist on getting a second opinion from an independent professional in each case, to make sure your own interests are being properly taken care of.

On the positive side, investing overseas can certainly pay off in terms of the price you pay for property. In some European countries you could by a small shopping mall for the price of a single property in the UK. Just be very careful to find out why the property seems like such a bargain. Remember, you are going to need to rent it immediately and then sell it at some point in the future, so it's vital you have good evidence that there is – and will continue to be – strong rental and resale markets.

The big wins tend to come from investing early in emerging markets, where the economy and living standards of a population are rising and pushing up prices. In these locations, you might see some spectacular growth in the value of your investment – much higher than can be achieved in the UK.

Just be aware that the investors who really reap the benefits of investing overseas tend to be people who have spent a lot of time and put a lot of effort into analysing the market. They are the ones who know about opportunities at the earliest stages and it's likely that by the time you get to hear about them – certainly by the time there's a glossy brochure – the window for making the best profits has been and gone.

## Potential pitfalls of investing overseas

No matter how smooth the salesman or agent has been, don't for a minute expect the process to be plain sailing, if you're dealing with builders, you may need to make frequent trips abroad and if the property is being bought off-plan, delays regularly occur, so you'll need to have a backup plan in case things go wrong.

You could fill a library with stories of people who have lost thousands of pounds or even their life savings through buying property abroad. Whether you're planning to invest in EU countries or beyond its borders, one of the biggest issues you'll face is that of transparency.

**The story of the British investors who lost £600,000 in Turkey**
One of the most alarming stories I've come across involves a group of investors who lost £600,000 attempting to buy property in a Turkish holiday resort.

The resort was already popular with Brits and this particular group of investors thought they were buying some property as an investment. They were sold the idea that they could invest in the resort for as little as £38,000 per property and benefit from some high returns.

The fraudster, who was actually a UK national, conned her victims by convincing them to invest in a deal that she promised would make them a return in a matter of weeks.

She convinced one investor to lend her £50,000, which she said would generate a 50 per cent profit, i.e. it would come back to them as £75,000 in less than 6 months. The promised returns never arrived. Fortunately, the fraudster was caught and convicted, but it still left the investors significantly out of pocket.

This is an extreme case, however it does highlight the danger of deals that look too good to be true and of presuming that when you're abroad, somehow there's less need for diligence. Far too many investors still think, "Oh, that's just how they do it out here…" and accept what they're told by whoever's flogging the deal, because they don't know what they're doing. And that brings me back to my earlier point: never invest in a market you don't understand. You need to be extra vigilant when investing overseas and if you invest outside the EU there are even more potential pitfalls.

Travelling to and from a property overseas, the costs can certainly add up. It can also be time-consuming, particularly if you need to obtaining residents permits (outside the EU), where you may be required to pay a fee for staying longer than a few weeks.

In terms of your profits, have you investigated and understood currency exchange rates and the tax implications both of making money in another country and of bringing your profits back to the UK? You may think you're doubling your rental profits or capital growth by investing overseas, but those profits can easily be wiped out if the exchange rates go against you and you're required to give a large chunk of money over to HMRC.

Another important thing to consider is the long-term potential and the security of your investment. How much protection do you have in place in the event that things go wrong?

Political and economic stability in your chosen country is of vital importance. As we have seen in recent years, even Europe is not immune to conflicts and civil wars - as the near-economic collapse of Greece and Cyprus recently demonstrated. If you're thinking of extending your adventure beyond Western Europe these are legitimate concerns and you don't want to be having sleepless nights thinking about them.

While the UK economy will fluctuate, it is a reasonably stable and safe market, unlikely to ever experience the volatility you see in some other countries. You'll never get the huge price rises of emerging markets, but then you'll never get the crashing lows either.

# PART THREE:
# MANAGING YOUR INVESTMENT PROPERTY

# Chapter 10

# Being A Landlord

It's a great feeling when you invest in your first property. But now comes the hard bit: being a landlord. You've got to decide how the property will be let and managed and how to deal with tenants who may not always be the kind of people you imagined.

## Should you manage the property yourself or use an agent?

If you want to grow a buy to let business, you have to learn to delegate. One of the things I learned when starting out in business was that there are always certain tasks that are better given to someone else, either to save you time now or money in the long term. You're in this business to make money, so you need to balance cutting out any unnecessary costs that might negatively impact on your monthly profits, while recognising that paying for a good service is likely to reap rewards over the longer term.

Trying to do everything yourself can actually end up costing you more and hold you back from what you're trying to achieve in property investment. How many successful entrepreneurs do you know who do their own accounts, cleaning and administration?

There is lot more to running a buy to let property than simply arranging a mortgage and getting a tenant in. There's the marketing of the property and tenant referencing, lettings regulations you must comply with, legal processes and paperwork that must be administered correctly, maintenance requirements, a variety of issues and complaints that might need to be handled…the list goes on. And all these various tasks that are best handled by an experienced professional, not to mention the advantage that a lot of the legal liability for paperwork, deposit protection, etc. falls to them, not you.

There are, of course, both pros and cons to hiring an agent and I think that when you're starting out, it's helpful to work with someone who knows what they're doing.

As I've built my portfolio, I've gradually employed a team of people to let and manage my properties for me, so I no longer use a letting agent. However, what works for me may not necessarily work for you, and if you only have one or two properties and/or don't have the time to focus on the administration of your investments, then an agent is probably the right route for you. Either way, I know that I, personally, would not have made it this far or been as successful as I have without help from trained professionals.

# Advantages of doing it yourself

## You save money on letting agent fees.

There is no question that a letting agent will take a significant chunk of the money you make from letting your property – usually somewhere between 10% and 15% of the monthly rental income for a full letting and management service.

So if your property is renting for £800 a month, you will only see £680 to £720 of that money – and remember that some agents will also charge set-up fees, inventory fees and tenant checking fees when there is a change of tenancy.

## You choose the tenants.

If you like to be hands on, then at least you can choose your own tenants. Remember that you will need to do background checks, immigration status checks and ask for reliable references. Appearances can be deceptive, as the old saying goes, so make sure that you are completely happy before you allow someone to live in your property. Do bear in mind that credit checking and referencing may be a condition of your mortgage or insurance.

## You will be more involved in what's happening.

It won't be physically possible for your letting agent to regularly check every property on their books, so none of them will be able to do it as often as you can. You may also be able to build a better relationship with your tenant than they might have with an agent and respond faster and more efficiently to any problems the tenant might have.

## Disadvantages of doing it yourself

**You will end up committing far too much of your valuable time.**
You may still have a job or your rental property could be some distance from your home, so managing it yourself could mean spending lots of time travelling around.

Things can go wrong at any time and you will have to drop whatever you're doing to deal with issues. And while the property is being marketed, there's all the to-ing and fro-ing for viewings – for which prospective tenants sometimes don't even show up! – not to mention the time you'll need to spend on administration.

The lettings agent, on the other hand, will have a reliable set of tradespeople to take care of things like the gas, electrics, plumbing, repairs and decorating. If you're a DIY expert yourself, you may feel able to tackle a lot of maintenance yourself, but what happens when you have a large portfolio of properties?

**You're liable for complying with all the lettings regulations**
One of the biggest benefits of using an agent who is a member of

ARLA or NALS is that they are kept up to date by their regulatory body or association on all changes to lettings regulations. They have insurance and legal advice on tap.

Unless you're absolutely confident that you have the time and know-how to keep on top of legislation and understand how to make sure you and your properties remain compliant, I'd say this is a big argument for not doing it yourself.

**You don't have the benefit of training and experience.**
Agents let and manage properties all day long. They know the local market inside out, they're up to date with what tenants need and want and they've handled pretty much every problem that could come up. They know how to resolve issues and carry out evictions. If you try to handle everything yourself from the outset, you're going to end up learning some hard and possibly expensive lessons.

Every time you need professional advice you'll have to pay for it, whereas if you use a reputable agent, most will happily give you free advice, about your let, the market and buy to let in general. Don't underestimate the value of experience.

**...and a final advantage of using an agent**
You can reduce your tax liability! Your letting agent fees can be offset against your rental income, which means HMRC will

effectively help pay for the management of your properties. So the more properties you have, the more money you can put to better use.

## Dealing with problem tenants

Problem tenants can be a real nightmare. The more properties you have, the greater the risk of finding one, so it's very important that you have a plan in place to deal with the most common problems.

## Dealing with late rent or non-payment

One of the biggest headaches you will encounter is tenants not paying their rent on time – and there are more of them doing this than you might think. 100,000 tenants in the UK had not paid their rent for 2 months, according to a recent study - and they're only the cases that were reported; there are no doubt plenty more on top of that.

Sometimes tenants genuinely simply fall on hard times and unemployment is a major factor, particularly in tough economic times. But much of the time, when tenants are late paying rent or stop paying entirely, it's because they're either bad at managing their money, or they think they can get away with it.

Regardless of the reason, when tenants fall behind with their rent, you need to act quickly. If you use an agent, they will chase the tenant up for you and issue notices and demands as necessary. However, if you're managing the property yourself and have a relationship with the tenant, you may be tempted to go easy on them and give them more of a chance than perhaps an agent would.

My advice is don't. If they think it's okay to be late paying rent, then they'll keep doing it. The constant hassle for you of chasing them up every month will begin to outweigh the benefit of letting the property, so it would be wise to begin proceedings to evict the tenant and claim the money owing.

## How to take action

You don't want your tenant to think you or your letting agent are a soft touch, so it is vital to start proceedings as soon as possible when the rent goes into arrears.

If you have a tenancy agreement in place your tenant should be paying at least a month in advance and you need to stick to this agreement, otherwise you can end up with all sorts of problems, i.e. the tenant might think they can miss a month while they're waiting for their wages to come in, or they promise to pay double in the future.

Experience has taught me that the moment you start feeling sorry for your tenant and accept their reasons for needing more time to pay, the more likely you are to end up out of pocket. There will be genuine cases, however most of the time it eventually becomes clear that delayed payments are simply an attempt at avoiding paying altogether.

So when should you start taking action on your bad tenant?

- A day or two late. There is no harm in making a phone call to ask what's happening with the rent, if only to make sure that everything is ok.

- A week late. You or your letting agent should already be sending the tenant a polite letter reminding them that the rent is overdue. At this stage it could be an oversight and you don't want to accuse or antagonise your tenant.

- Two weeks late. By now the tenant has had plenty of time to pay. They may come back with excuses, but now is the time for you to appoint a solicitor or eviction specialist to begin the process of recovering the rent arrears.

**TIP:** *Act quickly!*

The longer you or your agent delays the process of taking action on late payment, the longer you'll be waiting for your cash. If you're relying on the income you make from rent, this can be a big problem for you.

## What to do if your tenant is damaging your property

Rent arrears are one thing, damaging your property is another and if the damage is caused by carelessness or neglect, you should act swiftly to recover the cost of the repair.

Some people will advise you to simply deduct the money from the tenant's deposit but if they stay in the property and continue to cause damage, the repair costs can soon stack up until you end up with a shortfall.

It's far better to insist that they pay up immediately for any damage, rather than have them sitting in the property for another two months, possibly causing more. (I say two months because that's the minimum notice a landlord must give the tenant on an assured shorthold tenancy agreement.)

## How to get rid of a bad tenant

Getting rid of your tenant isn't as easy as simply kicking them out when things go wrong or sending in the heavies! The law in this country protects tenants very well and they have the right to be left to live in peace in your property. Anything you do that appears remotely threatening can leave you in hot water, rather than the tenant, regardless of whether they owe you rent or have caused upset or damage.

So when you decide enough is enough and you want to get rid of a troublesome tenant, you need to act not only with speed but with clear knowledge of how the law works.

If you want to evict a tenant before the agreement is up, you will need to go to court. You must make sure that all your paperwork is in order and you have followed the correct procedures, issuing notices in the right order and at the right time.

Two months is the minimum period you need in most cases and it can take a month or so for the case to go to court – then you will need to wait for the court to order the tenant to vacate the property.

The most common reasons for evicting a tenant are rent arrears, persistent late payment of rent, damage to the property and antisocial behaviour.

In most cases you will need a Section 21 notice. It is worth checking with your agent or an eviction specialist, or even websites such as Shelter, to see the latest rules regarding particular types of tenancy agreements, because advice will be pro-tenant and there may be some loopholes you hadn't thought about.

For your Section 21 notice to be valid, it needs to be in writing and give the tenant two months to leave and it **must** be served in the correct manner. After this notice period expires, the court can evict a tenant at any time. If you have a change of heart and decide to let your tenant stay, then they misbehave again and you want to evict them, you will need to issue another notice as the first one will no longer be valid.

For more information on the rights of tenants visit england.shelter. org.uk

## Putting up the rent

Raising rents can mean a mixture of pleasure and pain for the typical buy to let landlord. Naturally you don't want to upset your loyal tenant by raising their rent but, at the same time, knowing you can increase your profits every now and then simply by charging someone more for the accommodation you're providing is one of the many perks of investing in property.

That doesn't mean you can simply put the rent up whenever you like. If the rental period is fixed for six or 12 months, then you can't increase the rent during this period - unless you insert a clause that allows for it.

You may want to do that, but amending tenancy agreements in this way is likely to result in your tenants viewing you as a bit of a chancer who's going to take advantage of them, and they'll simply go and rent somewhere else instead. The most reasonable thing for you to do is set the rent according to local market comparables and at a rate you're comfortable with.

Most landlords will let property on a six or 12-month term,

therefore it won't be long before you can either raise the rent or find a new tenant willing to pay it.

**TIP:** *Don't be too greedy with rent.*

Be careful if you intend to raise the rent to a level that might be seen as unreasonable by the tenant. It could result in the tenant delaying payment while they appeal against the increase. They're unlikely to pay if the amount is in dispute because doing so would be regarded as acceptance of the increase. Being too greedy could put a dent in your cash flow and lose you a tenant.

**Real life example:**

A penthouse owner decided to let his apartment for £1200 a month in an area where there wasn't a great deal of demand for properties of that type. Even so, he managed to find a tenant willing to pay the high monthly rent. The tenant moved in and things went well until the owner decided to pass on a large chunk of his monthly service charge to the tenant.

The tenant moved out due to the landlord failing to disclose the extra costs up front and the property remained empty for several months. You will get far more respect from your tenants if you're transparent and clear about the amount they will be expected to pay. Losing a tenant over technicalities is a false economy.

## How to prepare for when a tenancy comes to an end

Long-term tenants are nice to have and some can be with you for years but the average rental period for someone on an Assured Shorthold Tenancy is around nine months.

This nine months can whizz by quickly. Ending a tenancy comes with its own set of tasks for landlords or estate agents as it involves administration, inspection of the property, calculating how much of the deposit you need to retain to cover cleaning and (or) repairs, and then carrying out any maintenance in preparation for the new tenant.

You will also need to set aside time to make sure you market the property well in advance of the current tenant moving out and have a new one lined up to move in, so you don't suffer any void periods.

### Check for damage and wear and tear

You should arrange a visit to your tenant's property a week or two before they move out so that you have time to assess how much work needs to be done to tidy up the property and obtain quotes, if there's anything you feel the tenant should pay for.

If there is wear and tear and you're confident that you can prove any damage is as a direct result of the tenant's neglect or lack of care, then you should be able to deduct the cost from their deposit. If there is a dispute over whether the tenant is liable for any damage, cleaning costs, replacement of items, etc., then you will need to approach the tenancy deposit scheme provider where you lodged their deposit. They will mediate and make a ruling.

**TIP:** *Keep all furniture, fixtures and fittings receipts and note all communications*

This will help date and value the items in your property, so that if there is a dispute over damage, you have evidence to support the cost of replacement or repair. Also make sure you keep clear records of when damage was noticed, reported and brought to the tenant's attention, and copies of any letters you sent asking them to pay for it.

**Things to do to prepare for the next tenant**
- Make sure your current tenant(s) vacates the property on time.
- Ask the tenant to leave the property in good order. Having them clean the property can save you a lot of work.
- If there are carpets, make sure you or the tenant gets them professionally cleaned. (If they were professionally cleaned when the tenant moved in, they should pay for the same to be done when they move out.)
- Make sure the kitchen is clean. Dirty ovens and broken

kitchen units can put prospective tenants off or reduce the amount of rent they're willing to pay.

○ Fling open the windows and install some air fresheners. There's nothing worse than a property that still smells of its previous owners!

# Chapter 11

# A Landlord's Responsibilities

Becoming a landlord places all kinds of demands on you. The more properties you accumulate, the more these responsibilities grow and you'll need to exercise good judgement in a variety of areas to be successful. Some responsibilities you can delegate while others will require more of your personal input.

## Your legal responsibilities as a landlord

It is your responsibility to ensure that the property you are letting is safe for your tenant and maintained to a decent standard.

We hear far less about neglectful landlords these days than was once the case. There used to be a lot of stories on the news about 'rogue' landlords who were careless with gas boilers or gas fires before safety checks and certification were a legal requirement.

A lot of legislation has now been brought in to protect tenants from careless landlords. Your letting agent will be able to provide you with a list of everything you should be aware of and all the checks that need to be carried out before you can safely let your property.

The following are of particular importance:

| Key areas | Responsibilities |
| --- | --- |
| Gas safety | Equipment must be safely installed by a Gas Safe engineer. You must give a copy of the safety certificate to the tenant and carry out checks annually. |
| Electrical safety | A 'Part P' registered electrician should check that all electrical fittings and appliances are safe. |
| Fire safety | Provide fire alarms and extinguishers and if providing furniture, make sure it's fire safe. |
| Maintenance | You will be responsible for repairs to the property. |

In addition to the above areas related to the inside of the property, if there is a garden, garage or other outbuilding, you may be responsible for some maintenance, depending on your agreement with the tenant.

## Protecting your tenant's deposit

Since April 2007, it has been a legal requirement for all tenant deposits to be protected in one of the Government's approved schemes. The deposit can't be treated as some extra cash to spend or used to help cash flow during the tenancy.

The reason this was introduced was to protect tenants against unethical landlords making up spurious excuses to keep hold of the whole deposit at the end of the tenancy. Now you need to have a good reason to withhold or deduct any of this deposit when the tenancy agreement comes to an end.

You can legally make reasonable deductions for:

- Damage to the property
- Missing items
- Cleaning
- Unpaid rent

You won't be able to claim for things like wear and tear on carpets, however if someone burns a hole in it, then this would fall under damage, and you should be able to use the deposit money to buy a new one.

If there is any dispute, the tenancy deposit scheme provider will ask both you and the tenant to put forward your cases to them, along with all supporting evidence. They may also visit the property themselves. Their decision is final and the authorised amount will be returned to each party – or the whole deposit to one party, if that is their conclusion.

## Why you shouldn't 'bother' your tenants

You may have already concluded that the less 'hands on' you are, the better time you will have in buy to let investing. This includes keeping your relationship with tenants professional.

The last thing a tenant needs is for you to be popping round every couple of weeks checking on things. Tenants like to make a place a home even if they're only staying for a few months. And it's important for you to remember that your tenants have a legal right to 'peaceful enjoyment' of the property while they live there.

Tenants have been known to change the locks to stop the landlord entering the property when they're not around. Being locked out of a property you own is not ideal, so make the tenant aware in the tenancy agreement of how much notice you will give them for a visit.

## It's a crime to withhold your details from the tenant

As much as you might want to check on your tenant and contact them, they have a similar right and are legally entitled to know your name and your UK contact address. Either you or your letting agent needs to give them this information and if you refuse you can be prosecuted, so be warned.

# Chapter 12

# Tax And Property Investment

The most onerous side of property investment is calculating your tax liability and it certainly pays to have an accountant who is familiar with buy to let portfolios, to help you pay as little tax as possible on your buy to let income.

I'm not going to tell you ways to avoid paying tax or advise you on your tax affairs (a) because I'm not qualified to do so and (b) because everyone's tax affairs are different.

There are ways to keep tax down, but if you don't pay what you owe, you will end up with a fine or a court appearance and could possibly even face jail time for tax avoidance.

Entire books are written on tax and property investment but for the purposes of this one, I'll simply give you an outline of your liabilities as a buy to let investor and ways it is possible to offset the amount the HMRC will inevitably take away.

Information on tax can, of course, change with each passing Budget. At the time of writing, buy to let investors are firmly on the radar of the HMRC, particularly when it comes to holiday rentals.

Powerful lobby groups are also putting pressure on the Government to end some of the tax advantages that have resulted in an explosion in the popularity of buy to let over the past couple of decades.

According to data reported in the Telegraph newspaper in 2013, landlords claimed £13bn in allowable expenses to offset against rent. This is said to have taken between £3bn and £5bn from the Government's coffers which, historically, is something that doesn't go down too well with the administration.

A lot of people think that landlords are responsible for things like unsustainable house price inflation and that it's all down to the tax relief landlords get. A lobby group called PricedOut discovered that 17% of sitting MPs were landlords, compared with just 4% of the population as a whole, and argued that they therefore had a clear incentive to keep the status quo!

So if we assume that nothing will change too much in the next few years, there are four ways the tax man can take money from you:

## Capital Gains Tax

Capital gains tax (CGT) is what you may need to pay if you sell your investment property for a profit. You won't be asked to pay this tax if you make a loss and sometimes you may even be able to reduce your CGT liability by including some of the expenses you will have incurred in letting and preparing a property for rent.

As of 2014/15 you automatically get a tax-free allowance of £11,000 on the gains you make through the course of the tax year. If you decide to sell your investment property you should declare that you have done so on your self-assessment tax return.

Capital gains is charged at either 18% or 28%, depending on the amount of capital gain you have made in the tax year. Some of the expenses you can deduct from your capital gain include:

- Estate/letting agent fees
- Solicitor's fees
- Costs of advertising the property for sale
- Stamp Duty
- Refurbishment costs (but not general maintenance)

## Stamp Duty Land Tax

Stamp Duty is one of those areas the Government likes to play with. It is the tax you pay when you buy any property in the UK costing £125,001 or more.

| | |
|---|---|
| £0 - £125,000 | 0% |
| £125,001 - £250,000 | 1% |
| £250,001 - £500,000 | 3% |
| £500,001 - £1,000,000 | 4% |
| £1,000,001 - £2,000,000 | 5% |
| Over £2,000,000 | 7% |

The same stamp duty rate is payable whether you are a buy to let investor or a homebuyer.

If you're buying some of the cheaper housing in cities in the North of the UK, you can save yourself paying this tax if you buy below the £125,001 threshold.

## Income Tax

If you're generating an income from renting out a property, you will of course be liable to pay some income tax on it. As with all tax liabilities, if you don't declare the money you're making you may get a penalty from the tax office.

According to current income tax rules, you must report any income you make in the tax year over £2,500 on your Self-Assessment tax return.

If it's less than £2,500 a year, the advice is to ring the Self-Assessment Helpline and ask for a P810 form.

The good news with income tax is, you can claim a lot of costs and offset them against your income to lower your tax bill. There are different rules for the following:

- Residential properties
- Furnished holiday lettings

## What you can claim for

| Residential Property | Furnished Holiday Lettings* |
|---|---|
| Letting agents fees | 10% of net rent as a 'wear and tear allowance' |
| Legal fees for lets of one year or less | Plant machinery and capital allowances |
| Accountancy fees | Equipment used outside the property such as vans and tools |
| Buildings and contents insurance | Capital gains tax relief |
| Interest on property loans | |
| Maintenance and repairs | |
| Utility bills | |
| Rent, ground rent, service charges | |
| Council tax | |
| Cleaning/ gardening | |
| Direct letting costs e.g. advertising | |

## Inheritance Tax (IHT)

A lot of people decide to get into buy to let investing not only to make money but also to leave something behind for their families. So if you're planning to leave your family some cash behind and make sure they get to see the benefit of the work you're putting into property investment, then you need to plan ahead.

Inheritance tax is what the government takes from your estate after you die and they will assess your entire estate so that they can redistribute a large percentage of the wealth you have accumulated during your lifetime.

If you don't have very much, then IHT won't be a concern, but I assume that as you're reading this book you will already be planning to make a million or more from property investment.

If you're already making a million, then you will be over the current threshold, which stands at £325,000. Anything over this threshold is taxable at 40%. It does seem unfair, considering that you have already paid your fair share of tax, only to have the Government take another big chunk away when you're gone, but that's just the way it is.

### IHT calculation example:

> Julian leaves his children a portfolio of properties worth £800,000.

His children will not see anything taken away on the first £325,000. Unfortunately, the remaining £475,000 will be liable for 40% tax.

Julian's family lose £190,000 of their inheritance to IHT.

**But things are rarely this straightforward when it comes to inheritance:**

If Julian is married and has no children, his wife is not required to pay any inheritance tax on the £800,000 he leaves behind.

If, on the other hand, Julian is married with children then things get a little more complicated – or a little more interesting, depending on how you view it.

Julian dies with a portfolio of properties worth £800,000. He leaves £200,000 of the value of his estate to his children in his Will.

Because he didn't use up the full tax-free allowance of £325,000, the remaining £125,000 passes on to his wife and her allowance is increased to £450,000

Eventually, when she passes away with assets of £600,000, 40% IHT will be due on anything over the £450,000.

40% of £150,000 is £60,000, leaving the children with £540,000.

By leaving the full £800,000 to his children in his Will, the family lost £190,000 to IHT, but by splitting his estate, they only lost £60,000. So, rather than £610,000 inheritance, the children would have £740,000, saving £130,000 from disappearing into Government coffers.

As you can see, it's well worth speaking to a solicitor and an accountant to find the best way for you to pass on your wealth.

**But what if I'm not married?**
If you're not married or in a civil partnership, then the above tax breaks don't apply and inheritance tax will need to be paid on anything over the £325,000 threshold.

**How else can I reduce IHT liability?**
One way to reduce IHT is to gift part of your buy to let property or portfolio as an undivided share to another member of your family. You will need to survive for seven years for this to take effect but,

even if you leave it late, three years will be enough to see some reduction in what your estate is liable to pay.

The biggest single thing you can do to reduce inheritance tax is to make a Will and get an expert to advise you on all the various tax issues. This may cost a bit of money, but spending a few thousand on advice can save the ones you leave behind hundreds of thousands of pounds.

# PART FOUR:
# CONSOLIDATION

# Chapter 13

# Portfolio Building

Building a portfolio of buy to let properties is where the returns start to get really interesting, but you do need cash to achieve this. There is no such thing as a 'no money down' deal any more so you need to be prepared and able to borrow or fund the purchase of more properties using the income from your day job or the profit you generate from your other properties.

You could fund purchases through re-mortgaging and releasing capital, depending on how much equity you have in your existing properties and how willing the banks are to lend you money for a buy to let mortgage.

Let's say you manage to raise £100,000 or you receive it as a pension lump sum. What do you do? Is it enough to invest?

Even if you do invest it, it sounds like a lot of money to lose, doesn't it? This is until you see what happens when you build a portfolio.

The important thing to appreciate – and it's one of the most fundamental reasons why property is such an incredible investment vehicle – is just how far that £100,000 can be stretched.

One of the worst-kept secrets in property investment is that the more you stretch the money you have, the more money you can make in property and here's why.

If you invest all that cash in one property that costs you £100,000 and the market is growing at 5% a year, you could sell that property and make £5,000.

If, once you buy that property, you rent it out for £750 a month and your costs are, say £100 a month, then you will be left with £7,800 a year to add to that £5,000 capital increase. Do bear in mind, though, that you will have tax to pay on your income and on the profits from any sale.

If you keep the property long term and don't sell, then your rent will rise steadily but your return on capital will be making less than a 2.5% return on your property unless you put the rent up in year two.

**Now let's consider how leveraging using the bank's money and buying more than one property can make a big difference to your bottom line.**

With £100,000 cash at your disposal, the bank should be in a position to give you more than one buy to let mortgage, so you can start building a portfolio of properties by leveraging your money, instead of spending it all on one property.

If we assume that the LTV is a conservative 75% then buying three properties with a mortgage will use up £75,000 of your money. You still have the remaining £25,000 to cover your costs and expenses.

You now have three investment properties worth £300,000 in total. If each of the three investment properties rises in value by 5% a year, then instead of getting a 5% return on your whole £100,000, you're getting a 20% return on your investment of £75,000. You've made an extra £10,000 and still have £25,000 in the bank!

So you've made £15,000 in a year on the value of the portfolio alone. You could decide to sell the properties and realise a little bit of profit, but the smart property investors don't sell their properties – they use them for ongoing income.

The actual income you make while you're building your portfolio will come from the rent your tenants pay. So, looking at your investment: the bank invests the lion's share of money in your portfolio, while the tenant gives you the income you need to continue investing in more properties. Now you're starting to make Other People's Money work for you!

The trick is to make sure that the properties you're investing in are available at or below market value and local rents will cover your mortgage payments and any bills, so that at no point do you have to subsidise the investment.

The mortgage costs of running 3 properties valued at £100,000 will be around £18,000 or £1500 a month.

If you can let all three properties for £750 a month then your rental income will be £2,250 a month.

This leaves you with £750 a month or £9,000 a year before any costs are deducted. (Remember, you can offset some of your tax liability against the running costs of each of your properties.)

If we assume that you stop at three properties and the price you originally paid doubles in 10 years, then you will hold three assets worth a total of £600,000. Now you can see, the bigger your portfolio the more money you can make. The only real hurdle you face is getting finance to make this possible.

There are some people who tell you that putting in a larger deposit is better because you will have more equity. If it's your own home, on which you have to pay the mortgage out of your own earnings, it might make you feel more secure to have an equity 'cushion'. But in buy to let, as long as the portfolio is comfortably covering its own running costs and turning a good profit, the LTV doesn't really matter.

When you're investing in property, you need to keep as much of your cash as possible available to reinvest. The less money you have tied up, the more possibilities you have to eventually build that million pound property portfolio!

## Spreading your risk

How successful you are at building a property portfolio depends on how much you spread your risk. You could quite happily invest in UK property and spread your risk with different types of property investment in different towns and cities.

Some investors might be tempted by the enticing returns to be found in more exotic locations around the world. Spreading risk, however, shouldn't be about taking uncalculated ones in markets you don't know a lot about. Investing in one bad property or losing money in an investment that turns out to be too good to be true can easily wipe out other profits and have a negative impact on your ability to grow your portfolio.

In property investment it's better to be the tortoise than the hare. You need to generate returns smartly over time, rather than get carried away by clever headlines in property brochures promising amazing returns.

If, on the other hand, you really want to go for it and you're certain that you can absorb any losses from investing in high growth markets, then this is a strategy that can certainly generate wealth faster than investing in the UK – if you get involved early enough in the market growth cycle and things go according to plan.

Property experts used to recommend dividing your property portfolio as follows:

> 60% in safe markets
> 30% in high-growth markets
> 10% in speculative markets

The financial crisis changed this way of thinking. There are fewer high-growth markets left in the world after the great global property boom burnt itself out in 2008. There are still some opportunities in emerging markets, but emerging market investing is far more risky now than it was 10 years ago.

Property bubbles are commonplace and as recovery returns to more familiar markets like the UK, France, Germany and so on, it's wiser to look closer to home if you want to take a risk.

What are the risks of investing in UK property?

| | Low Risk | Medium Risk | High Risk | |
|---|---|---|---|---|
| Property prices falling | √ | | | The UK is at the beginning of a new growth cycle |
| Risk of a property 'bubble' | | √ | | Outside London this is unlikely. Mortgage lending remains tight |
| Risk of oversupply | | √ | | Oversupply is an issue in some parts of the UK but not in and around London and the South East |
| Oversupply of rental properties | √ | | | Rental demand remains high in most part of the UK |
| Falling property sales | | √ | | Property sales are set to be affected by tighter rules on mortgages |

A lot of the above will depend on the area you decide to invest in but, as a rule of thumb, this can be applied to any property market and if you're investing abroad you might also add currency fluctuations into this table.

Turkey, for example, saw a dramatic decline in the value of its currency against Sterling and the Dollar in early 2014. This effectively meant that property bought in Turkey was cheaper in currency terms.

An example of spreading risk within the UK might be to invest in a diverse portfolio of residential properties, from high-yielding HMOS to student lets and family homes.

## How to insulate yourself from housing market bubbles and crashes

We've already established that property markets move in cycles, so another crash (or adjustment) is inevitable in the future. Many people were fooled into thinking that property prices would rise forever in the heady days of 2005, until market forces once again conspired to end one of the biggest property booms in history.

So how do you insulate your portfolio from the worst that a downturn can throw at you?

The best way to insulate yourself against a future property market crash is to plan to hold your property long term. If you take the short-term view, you will always run the risk of getting caught out by future property market fluctuations.

*"You don't know who's swimming naked until the tide goes out."*

In this quote, the world's greatest investor, Warren Buffett, was referring to the business side of investing but it applies equally to property investment too. If you think of the water as your liquidity then if you don't have enough liquidity - i.e. cash flow - to see you through market downturns, the results can be catastrophic not only for your portfolio, but also for your future as an investor.

So insulating yourself from a future crash is about bringing in a level of income that will not be disrupted by what the market happens to be doing. If you can maintain your rental income and it covers your costs from the beginning then you will have nothing to worry about.

If, on the other hand, you take risks with negative cash flow or you buy properties in the hope that they will rise in value by 10% or more, you will get caught out sooner or later.

Property investing is a long-term game, it isn't meant to be a gamble. If you do place a bet on the future you're much more likely to find yourself exposed and swimming naked.

# Chapter 14

# Your Exit Strategy

An exit strategy is your plan for swapping your asset, which in the case of a buy to let investor is your property or properties, in exchange for some money.

It's all very well having millions of pounds tied up in property, but when the time comes when you want to get out of buy to let, you need to have some kind of strategy in place, and that strategy should be in place from your early days of investing. You should also have some idea of when your exit will be.

People invest and build wealth so that they can 'exit' usually for one or more of the following reasons:

- Property is your pension
- You want to achieve financial freedom
- You want to hand things over to your children

To achieve all of the above, it really comes down to how much money you need and by when. Cash flow generating portfolios are not built overnight. They are built over the course of several years.

A buy and hold strategy should be generating you enough income through rent to make it worthwhile. It's rarely the case that you will make a good rental income when it's easier for people to buy their own property and, likewise, you're unlikely to see high capital growth when property values are falling.

This is why a diverse and balanced portfolio will help you achieve your aims of a retirement income or financial freedom. Nobody can tell you exactly what your exit strategy should be without knowing how much money you need to make from the sale of your properties. In some cases it may be easier just to hang on to them if you have enough income.

If you have invested in the right types of properties, your ownership costs will fall over time. Regular checks on your mortgage rates and the length of time you have left on them will help you set a firm date for your exit.

However, if you have invested in the wrong type of properties, for example, you have too many apartments with hefty service charges that rise every year, then you may be in trouble when it comes to your exit strategy.

If the value of the apartment hasn't increased for several years - and this is the case in many of the UK's apartment-saturated towns and cities - then selling may not be an option. In addition, the income you make from rent will always be affected by things like rising service charges and communal maintenance bills if the block is older.

## When property is your pension

Statistics show that one in three people are using property as their pension, to varying degrees. That's a lot of people banking on property to provide them with vital income when they retire.

## So how does property stack up against a pension?

If we look at the last decade or so, the story of pensions has not been a happy one. When you put money away into a pension you are essentially giving away control of it to a fund manager who will invest it in a variety of places to generate you a return in the long term.

The idea is that when you retire, you will have a sum of money to maintain your lifestyle. The problem with a pension is that unless you're in a very generous pension scheme that maintains your earnings as in the public sector, you will more than likely be disappointed after collecting your gold clock and waving your work colleagues goodbye.

Have pensions ever lived up to their promises?

They may have done in the past, with the exception of those who got caught out by with Robert Maxwell and Enron.

But the great global downturn of the 2000s changed all that. Suddenly, eye-watering amounts of cash ended up being lost on the stock markets. Annuity rates hit their lowest levels for decades when quantitative easing began to impact on their value.

There was a time at their lowest point in 2012 when £300,000 in our pension pot provided you with an annual income of just £18,000. Not a lot even by today's standards. Now I'm not suggesting that you abandon pensions altogether. It is prudent to diversify your investments for the future to spread your risk. So why not have the best of both worlds?

The last thing you need when you reach retirement is to have to continue working in a menial job to try and make ends meet. Property investment is so popular because it can help you avoid ending up a 'checkout pensioner', working on the tills in a supermarket to make ends meet, and can provide you with a much better standard of living when you're too old to be part of the rat race.

The great thing about becoming a property investor is that you are in control of your investment. As long as the tenant pays the bills and covers all your costs with some left over to generate a profit, then you will be well on the road to generating enough income to sustain your lifestyle in the future.

# Chapter 15

# Summary

Planning for a future where there will be more older people chasing a dwindling amount of state pension payments means that the need has never been greater to plan your financial future.

Becoming a buy to let investor is a positive step towards securing that financial future. The only surprise is that more people are not doing it. Not everyone has the means or the cash to begin, but if you do, then investing in the right property in the right location is one of the safest investments you can make.

Best of all, property is a tangible investment, something secure that you can fall back on in an increasingly virtual world where nothing is certain and the gap between rich and poor is rising.

If you own a property portfolio, you will be able to insulate yourself from the worst that economic downturns can throw at you because:

Property is an appreciating asset. It is virtually guaranteed to grow in value over time.

Your tenants will cover the cost of ownership and generate a profit for you.

You can borrow and leverage the bank's money to buy more properties that will increase your profits dramatically.

Compared to other investments, such as the stock market, you will not be risking 100% of your money. This simply can't happen with property. Yes there will be downturns and economic cycles, but in the long term, property anywhere will rise in value simply with inflation.

People talk of buying property as 'getting on the ladder'. I like to think of it as getting on an escalator because your investment rises the longer you hold on to it.

Long term, property prices only tend to ever go in one direction and that's up.

The number of properties you can own when you step onto our theoretical escalator is only limited by three things: time, energy and resources. If you can manage all three then you will be well on the way to financial freedom!

I wish you the best of luck on your journey!

Nick

# HMO PROPERTY SUCCESS

## THE PROVEN STRATEGY FOR FINANCIAL FREEDOM FROM MULTI-LET PROPERTY INVESTING

# Foreword

This book is about cash-positive investing in Houses in Multiple Occupation and is aimed at those of you looking to generate on-going monthly income. It won't tell you everything you need to know – this is not intended to be an exhaustive manual! – I'm simply trying to give you a picture of what's involved in building an efficient HMO business and becoming a successful investor.*

Financial freedom means different things to different people; to me it means having the reassurance that, even if I stopped working tomorrow, the level of income generated by my HMO portfolio is sufficient to not only pay the bills, but also provide my family with a good quality of life for the foreseeable future. Everyone's financial requirements are different, so when I say I'm giving you a proven strategy for achieving financial freedom, what I'm doing is showing you how to secure excellent returns from buy to let and you can take that to whatever level you want and/or need. For some people, three or four properties will mean financial freedom; others may need a portfolio of ten or more.

Lastly, just before we get started, something that I don't hear property investors talking about enough is the importance of having supportive family and friends, so that's something I want to stress to you. It will be nigh-on impossible for you to succeed in this business if the people around you aren't understanding and encouraging, because becoming a professional property investor is like any other start-up business - there are peaks, troughs, exciting times and times when you just need to get your head down and push through. But I promise you, and you can promise them: it's worth it.

As my most wise and successful mentor once told me:

*Leap and the net will appear.*
*Take action now...*

*The caveat to the blueprint for HMO success that I talk about is that it's very hard to make the model work in London, where the property price / rental income ratio is generally much higher than in the rest of the country.

*"Never allow yourself to become one of those people who, when they are old, tell you how they missed their chance."*
**Claire Ortega, Author**

# PART ONE:

# UNDERSTANDING YOUR INVESTMENT

# Chapter 1

# Why do you want to invest?

When I first began investing, I was pretty sure property was a sensible choice because I knew it was an asset class that could provide me with on-going income while appreciating in value to make a nice pension pot for the future. That was in the 'noughties', when the market was booming and buying property was easy, so I simply went out and bought what I knew would rent profitably. What I didn't do until a year or so later was take those vague notions of 'income' and 'pension' and start to make some real sense of them.

It's impossible to make the right investment decisions unless you have sat down and clearly established the financial and lifestyle motivators behind your desire to invest. Property is only 'a sensible choice' if it delivers on your objectives, suits your attitude to risk and personality, works for your lifestyle and – importantly – you understand that it is a business. Far too many people have ploughed their capital into bricks and mortar with barely a second thought and ended up with something that simply makes their lives a misery.

If you don't go about it in the right way, investing in HMOs can be incredibly challenging, time-consuming and labour-intensive. The potential financial rewards certainly make it worthwhile, but only if you're able to set up and manage a system to effectively run your portfolio as a real and profitable business.

I was lucky that when I bought my first few properties the market was rising and it was so easy to essentially buy 'no money down' – I don't think I would have got away with being so relatively unprepared today. In the current economic climate, and at a time when regulation and availability of financing and refinancing is so much tighter, investing in property is a very different thing and, to be truly successful, there's a great deal of work to be done before you even peer in an estate agent's window. And it all begins with *why* you want to invest.

## Your goals

What effect do you want property investment to have on your life? A lot of people talk about becoming 'financially free' through property, but the exact definition of that is different for everyone, depending on their current situation, expectations and desires. You need to make a clear list of exactly what you need and want your investment to give you – financially and in terms of lifestyle – and make each item time-specific. It's been proven that the more detailed you can make your goals, the more likely you will be to achieve them, so it really is worth spending time on this.

*"Setting goals is the first step in turning the
invisible into the visible."*
**Tony Robbins**

If you want income, the key questions you need to ask and
answer are: how much and by when? I'm sure you've heard of
SMART as a tool for setting goals, and it's certainly a good way
to check you're thinking in the right way. Look at each item on
your list and make sure it's Specific, Measurable, Attainable,
Relevant/Rewarding and Time-bound. So, in the case of income,
you might put: 'I will be generating £5,000 monthly income
from property within the next 2 years, so I can send my child to
private school.' It's important that you're realistic (you're not
going to make a million in a year!), but at the same time, don't
be afraid to dream big.

*"A vision is a clearly-articulated, results-oriented
picture of a future you intend to create. It is
a dream with direction."*
**Jesse Stoner Zemel**

And people always achieve their goals more quickly if they're
motivated by emotion, rather than purely by money, so try to attach
some kind of personal element to each one.

Some people make the mistake of leaving out some lifestyle
goals, because they think their ideas sound a bit silly or aren't that
important, but this is about you, nobody else, and if you want it,

write it down. And write it as though you've already achieved it – don't allow for the possibility of failure! For example:

*In 6 months' time…*
I spend the whole of every Sunday with my family
I have a massage once a week
My wife has the 4x4 she wants

…and then you can work out the income and time freedom you'll need to generate in order to realise those goals.

Once you know where you want/need to be in the next 6 months, year, 3 and 5 years, you can start to break that down into shorter periods of time and set the weekly (or even daily) targets you need to hit in order to stay on track to achieve your goals.

A good device for illustrating your goals and staying motivated is a vision board – and not just one. My home is full of them, ranging in size from A4 magnetic ones stuck to the fridge door to huge 8x4 foot boards that cover entire walls! I'm a big believer in the power of visualisation and I and my family sees the results and benefits of it every day.

> *"The future you see is the future you get."*
> **Robert G Allen**

# Why property?

I've already said that I chose to invest in property because it gives me an income and a pension pot, but it's more than that. It suits my lifestyle, work ethic, skills, risk profile, personality, tax situation and inheritance plans for my children – and these are all things you need to consider carefully.

I'm not a wealth or financial advisor and couldn't even begin to start breaking down the pros and cons of property for every possible circumstance. You need to find financial professionals who can advise you properly and I'll talk more about that in Chapter 6. For now, I would simply say that you will need some significant capital behind you if you're serious about building a portfolio (I'd suggest at least £50,000 for each property you intend to buy) and I'd stress the importance of speaking to a wealth advisor. They can look at all your financial interests and plans for the future and help you decide the best way to invest in property to suit your own, personal situation – and whether property is even the right investment vehicle for you.

What I *can* do is explain why *I* chose property. Quite simply, it offers the most reliable, tangible, flexible, profitable form of investment I've been able to find, and I can break that down into six key aspects:

1.  **Leverage:** No other asset class offers the opportunity to leverage in the way that property does. Banks

and building societies lend against property at the level they do because property is seen as having a fundamental 'bricks & mortar' value. Markets peak and trough but a property will almost always hold a certain level of value, so while maximum Loan to Value rates may fluctuate (in the past 8 years, I've seen them fall from 125% to 60% and go back to 85%), you can still leverage other people's money to make a better return on capital than you might otherwise – i.e. you can make your money go further. For example, if there was a 15% rise across all markets:

£100k invested in stocks = £15k growth
£100k invested in £25k deposits on 4 properties, each worth
£100k = £60k growth

2. **Refinancing:** The ability to refinance a property, as an extension to leverage, means you can end up with an income-producing asset that has none of your own capital tied up in it. You can't achieve this as quickly and easily as you once could, but if you manage to buy a property at a good price and that particular sector of the market rises sufficiently, you should be able to remortgage in time and release the money you originally invested. By reinvesting that money in another income-producing property, you're expanding your portfolio and maximising the return on your capital.

3. **Income:** With all other asset classes, you mainly profit from growth on the capital. Although there may be interest payments on other types of investment, I haven't found any that offer the same income potential as property.

4. **Control:** Unlike most other forms of investment, such as stocks or bonds, you have a high degree of control over the investment returns a property provides. While you can't control either the property market as a whole or mortgage rates, you do have the power to decide:

   - the type of property you buy
   - what mortgage product you have
   - how you let the property
   - the type of tenants you accept
   - the rent you charge (to a certain extent)
   - how much you spend on managing and maintaining the property

   Essentially, you have a high degree of control over income and expenditure, and, therefore, profitability.

5. **Opportunity:** The diversity of opportunity to make money from property is really exciting to me, and one of the reasons it's used by so many people as a wealth creation tool. Whether you want on-going income,

short/medium-term gain, a pension plan, a home for your children in years to come or a lump sum return in the future, property can work for you. You can buy to let single or multiple occupancy units; renovate a property and then sell or remortgage; self build or develop yourself; strike a deal to sell property or land to a developer; get paid for sourcing property; do everything yourself and make it your career, or work with other people to make it a more passive investment... It really does offer a huge variety of options – even one property can allow you to realise different returns at different times in your life, depending on what you need and when.

6. **Systemisation:** This is a big part of why property works as an investment vehicle for me. If you can put the right systems and team in place to effectively source, acquire, refurbish, let and manage a portfolio, you can reap considerable financial rewards for relatively little of your own time. That frees you up to either focus on high-value aspects of your business, or simply to enjoy some of your lifestyle activities. I said earlier that property is a business, and you need to have the ability to establish and manage a 'head office' in a way that works for you. But as long as you can do that, your systemised business should be able to function as a money-earner whether you're there or not.

I have over 20 people working for me, including a PA, a bookkeeper, a property manager, two lettings negotiators and a maintenance team of more than ten contractors. They take care of my income-generating portfolio, while I spend my time looking for new HMO deals and work on other property-related opportunities. It's good systemisation that's accelerated the growth of my property business and allowed me to pursue other interests – lifestyle and business - in a way that would otherwise be impossible.

> *"90% of all millionaires become so through owning real estate (property)."*
> **Andrew Carnegie**

## Is property right for *you*?

As well as speaking to wealth and tax specialists to help decide whether property is an appropriate investment vehicle from a financial perspective, there are a number of things you need to consider on a more personal level. Investing in high income-generating properties – i.e. HMOs – may suit your financial plans, but…

…are you equipped with the skills to either run an HMO portfolio yourself or effectively manage the outsourcing?

Are you:

- Computer & internet savvy?
- A good administrator?
- Organised?
- Motivated?
- Good at time management?
- Able to employ and manage a team of staff?
- Surrounded by a good personal support network?

...is your attitude to risk in line with the fact that property is considered a medium to high-risk investment? Can you accept having millions of pounds of mortgage debt?

...do you have the people skills to build relationships with other property professionals?

...do you have the appropriate general business skills to succeed?

...do you understand financing and how to put together a business plan?

...will the demands on your time – which are considerable in the first two or three years of building a portfolio – suit your lifestyle?

...can you project manage? You can outsource renovation and refurbishment management to a certain extent, but you still need to understand all the elements and be able to manage the overall project.

If this is the first time you've run your own business, you must understand and be prepared for the highs and lows you'll experience in the first few years. Read as many books as you can about start-up businesses and entrepreneurs - Seth Godin's 'The Dip' is a good one to start with - and you'll see that most of them share the same pattern of successes and challenges, and most have failed at some point. To give yourself the best chance of success, I'd recommend that you keep finding out about people who've already succeeded and learn from their mistakes.

*"Anyone who stops learning is old, whether at twenty or eighty. Anyone who keeps learning stays young."*
**Henry Ford**

I read at least one book a week to help keep my mind and business on track – and they're by no means all related to property. Some of the books that are broadly considered 'personal and professional development' tools are exceptionally good; some are, frankly, pretty bad, but there's always something that you can learn from even the poorer ones. You can find a list of the ones that I've found particularly helpful – quite a few of which I've read several times - at the end of this book and also on hmopropertysuccess.co.uk.

But I'd say that the best measure of whether you're suited to property investment is the feedback you get from other investors. Spend some time with other people who are already doing what you want to do, talk to them about their property business, see for yourself what's involved in making a success of it and ask yourself whether you can see elements of yourself in them. People have different approaches and not every investor has the same temperament, personal manner, background or goals, but all of them will probably be:

- self-confident
- committed
- hard-working
- self-motivated
- self-improvers
- people who enjoy business
- good listeners
- good negotiators
- well-supported by friends and family

You'll probably have to pay for their time – and almost certainly to access the best – but it'll be money well spent, I promise you.

*"Business and making money are not so much about what happens to you, or the rules that are out there, but your attitude, perseverance, and desire to succeed."*
**Dolf de Roos**

# Checklist

# Is property investment right for you?

Have you done all these things?

## Goals

- ☐ Listed financial and lifestyle goals
- ☐ Checked goals have SMART attributes
- ☐ Made some kind of visual illustration to keep you focused and motivated

## Investment options

- ☐ Spoken to a wealth manager / financial advisor
- ☐ Considered which type of property investment will suit your goals
- ☐ Identified capital you can access to fund acquisition and refurbishment

## Property as a business

- ☐ Understood the potential risks and rewards
- ☐ Considered skills required to run a business
- ☐ Compiled and committed to a reading list
- ☐ Spent a day with more than one successful investor

Once you've clarified exactly why you want to invest and established that property is the right investment choice to help to realise your goals, you need to look at HMO property investment in more detail.

# Chapter 2

# The HMO model

**HMO** (āch'ĕm-ō') n. Abbreviation for House in Multiple Occupation: a property shared by at least 3 tenants, forming more than 1 household*, where the tenants share toilet, bathroom or kitchen facilities.
*(as defined by www.gov.uk )*

(*A household consists of either a single person or members of the same family who live together. It includes people who are married or living together and people in same-sex relationships.)

Investing in HMOs is by far the best way to maximise rental income and monthly profit from buy to let. There are some exceptions – such as luxury homes and corporate lets in capital cities – but, by and large, buying properties in areas where rental accommodation is in high demand (see Chapter 5) and letting the rooms to individual tenants will generate two to three times the amount of rental income that you could achieve by letting it as a single unit. Yes, the associated costs are higher and it takes more work to manage, but the rental income certainly makes the extra effort worthwhile.

To give you an example... By the start of 2007, I had a decent-sized portfolio of properties, but all were let as single units and, while the portfolio as a whole was profitable, one four-bedroom detached house was losing me money each month. It was a lovely property, so, rather than simply cutting my losses and selling, I decided to create two extra bedrooms and turn it into a six-bedroom HMO. The rental income jumped from £1,200 to £2,500 a month and the liability in the portfolio suddenly become its most profitable asset. That was my 'light-bulb' moment, when I realised how much more profitable my portfolio could be.

Just a little word of warning: if you're now thinking of doing the same to an existing portfolio, stagger the conversions. While it was, ultimately, undoubtedly the right move to turn 20 of my properties into HMOs, what I didn't quite think through was the practicality of doing all 20 at the same time! I think I was so overcome with excitement that I'd 'discovered' this brilliant new business model, that I didn't properly think through the logistical or financial implications. Having all those properties not generating any income for nearly two months, on top of the cost of the necessary refurbishment, meant things were very tight – not to mention hectic - for quite a few months. I'd certainly take my time if I did it again!

A lot of people still think of HMOs as 'student housing', but the model has come a long way in the last ten years and the vast majority of both already successful and new investors I meet are letting rooms to young adults in full-time employment. Some fall into the 'young career professionals' category; others are working in bars, restaurants and shops. Many are on short-term contracts and find it much more convenient to rent a room than a flat for a few months, as landlords usually request a 12-month rental commitment; some tenants will rent a room in the same property for years.

As the landlord of an HMO, you are typically responsible for:

- providing and maintaining all fixtures, fittings and white goods
- fully furnishing the property – including kitchen/ dining  equipment, but not linen
- paying council tax and utility bills (excluding telephone)
- providing and paying for broadband
- providing a regular cleaning service for the communal areas

…in other words, you're providing the kind of accommodation your tenants might expect if they were living at home with their parents – in some cases, better accommodation! The tenants seem to like the ease of all-inclusive rent and, because many of them are of a similar age, it's often a good social environment for them. (See Chapter 9 for more detailed information on refurbishment and getting a property 'ready to rent'.)

## The cons

I'm going to start with the downsides, or the more challenging aspects of operating HMOs, because there's no getting away from them and if you're going to get into this business, you need to understand exactly what lies ahead.

**Bad press.** One of the things you'll always come up against is the preconception that multi-let houses mean cheap and nasty accommodation, run by landlords who care more about making money than the wellbeing of their tenants – packing as many people as they can into one house for the sake of profit. Like it or not, there's a popular feeling out there that 'decent' landlords let properties as one unit, rather than room by room, and choosing to go down the HMO route is rather unsavoury.

Unfortunately, yes, there are some landlords who don't comply with either property regulations or their legal and moral obligations to their tenants, don't look after their investments, and, as the standard of accommodation goes down, so does the quality of tenants. And, because of the media's love of a good horror story, it's these tales of 'slum landlords' and tenants treating properties like 'doss houses' and running cannabis factories that people hear about.

So, although the kind of HMOs I'm talking about running are nothing like that, nor the old stereotype of 'student accommodation' and, thankfully, the number of good, professional landlords is increasing, you need to be prepared for a less-than-enthusiastic reaction when you tell people what you're doing. My advice is to talk as little as possible about it until you're up and running, because it's very easy to be put off by 'advice' from people who have very little relevant understanding or experience.

**Heavy management demands.** Ask any investor not currently investing in HMOs why they're not, and the first thing out of their mouth will probably be, "It's far too much hassle dealing with all the tenant problems." A group of unrelated people living in a house together can sometimes result in more disagreements and more (often petty) complaints, and you'll undoubtedly get far more maintenance issues than you would renting an unfurnished property to a family. You need tact, diplomacy, strength of character, a good team of tradesmen and the willingness and ability to respond quickly to issues.

**Admin.** With multiple tenants come multiple sets of paperwork and an increased number of phone calls, viewings, move-ins and move-outs.

**Tighter legal requirements.** HMOs fall under very specific licensing, planning, health and safety, building and letting regulations and laws. There has been a lot of change in policy over recent years, so you need to make sure that you not only adhere to the policies and requirements in force at the time you acquire and let your HMO, but that you stay up to date and compliant. (See Chapter 3 for more details.)

**Staff.** If you want to build a significant portfolio of HMOs, there's no question you'll need to employ a team of people to help you run it. You could probably manage between two and five houses on your own, but after that, it can quickly become a full-time job. And going back to why you want to invest, I bet, 'because I want to be a property manager' wasn't anywhere on your list! So you'll need to be prepared and able to hire and manage staff of your own.

The good news is that, while all this is time-consuming and requires organisation and attention to detail, it can all be systemised and outsourced to a small team, under your control. I'll stress again that you must understand this is a property **business** and you'll need business skills to run it.

## The pros

The upsides of investing via the HMO model echo the key reasons I gave in the last chapter for why I invest in property as an asset class. To reiterate, HMOs offer the most reliable, tangible and profitable form of investment I've been able to find.

**CASH FLOW!** I haven't met a single investor who's operating HMOs for any reason other than cash flow and profit! HMOs involve far more work and the running costs are higher than for single lets, but the rental income is up to three times as much as you would get from letting the property as a single unit. That means both your yield and profitability tend to be significantly higher than average buy to let figures. Two reasons why the cash flow is so good are:

**a. Voids don't have the same impact as with single lets.** As a general rule of thumb, in an average 6-bedroom HMO, rooms 1 to 4 cover your costs and rooms 5 and 6 are your profit. The likelihood of having more than one room empty at a time is extremely low, so even if you lose a tenant, you're still profitable, compared to losing a tenant in a single let, which results in you having to cover the property costs yourself – every time.

**b. Virtually recession-proof rental income.** When times are hard, people cut costs and an all-inclusive room rental makes it easy for people to budget and much cheaper and less hassle than renting a whole flat. I haven't suffered any drop in tenant demand since the credit crunch hit and have consistently operated at 98% occupancy.

**Flexibility of investment.** Because HMOs tend to be larger properties, the building usually offers the potential to be reconfigured as/when the demand (for rental or sale) changes. Most of the HMOs I've bought have been family houses that I've then reconfigured, by way of stud walls and adding bathroom facilities, so they could easily be turned back into family homes if there was a high demand for those. Similarly, there may be the option to separate the house into separate flats or adapt it to accomodate those with disabilities or the elderly. Buying things that offer a good degree of flexibility means you give yourself the best chance of maximising profitability into the future.

**Helping with the housing shortage.** Most investors I know have an element of philanthropy in their overall life plan and, while I'm not for a minute claiming to be investing purely for the good of others, the simple fact is that by providing good quality accommodation and maximising the occupancy potential of some of the existing housing stock, we're helping. The Government needs more good, private sector landlords offering decent, affordable housing.

## Key Performance Indicators (KPIs) for HMOs

I'll cover KPIs further in Chapter 13, but here are the headlines, for now. Whether you're running a portfolio of HMOs or single-let properties, you have to be able to monitor and measure your investment against itself, other similar properties in the market and other investment options. You need to set up a system – I do it on Excel spreadsheets - to track income and expenditure, rental and capital values and occupancy figures. Those will allow you to assess your returns and see whether you're maximising those returns.

You need to be absolutely precise about the costs and rental income for each property. While that's something your bookkeeper should take care of for you on an on-going basis, you must be able to calculate for yourself - with a high degree of accuracy - how profitable a property is likely to be, BEFORE you buy it. There are a lot of costs associated with buying and operating an HMO and you need a spreadsheet that breaks those down in detail so you can quickly calculate whether the monthly cash flow stacks up and how good a return you'll be getting on the capital you'll need to invest.

Returns can be measured in a number of ways, but I focus on three in my business: profit, return on investment (ROI) and yield.

## Profit

Fundamentally, this is what keeps me, my lifestyle and my portfolio going – and I presume it's your main reason for going down the HMO route. In addition to monthly bills, you'll need to plough some of the rental income back into your investment, in the shape of maintenance and updates to fixtures, furnishings and the fabric of the property itself, but you should be building those costs into your budget, so that your 'profit' figure is, or could be, personal income.

Remember to include tax in your costings and revisit all the items on your income and expenditure spreadsheet on at least a monthly basis. Even small reductions in utility bills, a quarter of a percent reduction in mortgage interest and minor increases in rent can add up to a significant increase in profit across a portfolio of properties.

# ROI

$$\text{Annual Profit} \div \text{Total Capital Invested}$$
$$= \text{Annual Return On Investment}$$

As a professional investor, ROI should be right up there with profit as a key measure. If your main investment goal is monthly income, you may be tempted to put more capital into your HMO in order to reduce your mortgage payments, but I don't think that's a smart move. I've already said that one of the main benefits of investing in property (versus other assets) is that you can leverage the bank's money and benefit from capital growth on not just your own money, but theirs as well. Investing as little of your own money as possible means that you'll be maximising the return on your own capital – essentially making your money work harder for you.

One of the main benefits of renting out rooms is that the rental income (and therefore profit) is maximised, so you can afford to gear highly. In time, you may be able to refinance so that there is less of your own capital left tied up in the property. If you're able to take all of the original capital out, you'll have an 'infinite' ROI: all the profit for no financial investment.

**Example:**

| | |
|---|---|
| Annual rental income | £30,000 |
| Annual costs | £18,000 |
| Annual profit | £12,000 |

Total capital invested        £75,000
(deposit, buying costs, refurbishment, furnishing, etc.)
Annual ROI        16% (£12k ÷ £75k)

*Refinance after 5 years, withdrawing £50,000, to leave only £25,000 capital invested:*
Annual ROI        48% (£12k ÷ £25k)

You can also add capital growth figures to rental income to gain an ROI figure for a period of time, e.g.

| | |
|---|---|
| Original purchase price | £200,000 |
| Capital invested | £75,000 |
| Value after 5 years | £250,000 |
| Capital growth | £50,000 |
| Rental profit | £60,000 (£12k x 5 years) |
| Total profit over 5 years | £110,000 |
| Annual ROI over life of investment | 29.3% ((£110k ÷ 5) ÷ £75k) |

Once you have your ROI figure/s, you can compare it/them to other investment returns and see how your HMOs are performing for you.

## Yield

This is talked about as a headline figure by the media and many investors but, for me, it comes behind profit and ROI, and is simply an indication of how 'good' my investment choice is for the area.

There are two key reasons why I don't rate it as highly as the other two as a measure of success:

a. National yield figures are usually either gross or don't even state whether they're gross or net – i.e. costs are often not factored in. And sometimes a figure stated as 'net' actually only takes into account the mortgage repayment, none of the other associated costs.

b. Yield doesn't take into account how much of your own capital has been invested, i.e. whether you're highly geared or own the property outright, your yield figure could be the same.

People calculate yield in slightly different ways, but the most common calculations are: rental income divided by the property's value (gross yield), and profit divided by the property's value (net yield).

To use the figures from the last example:

| | |
|---|---|
| Purchase price | £200,000 |
| Rental income | £30,000 |
| Profit (income – costs) | £12,000 (£30k - £18k) |
| Gross yield | 15% (£30k ÷ £200k) |
| Net yield | 6% (£12k ÷ £200k) |

The national average yield figure quoted tends to fluctuate between 4% and 5% - this is mainly based on single lets and is usually a gross figure. As a general rule, HMOs gross between two and three times the national average yield and your net yield percentage should still outstrip the national gross.

Although a lot of the KPI data can be compiled by your property manager and bookkeeper as your business grows, you will have to be able to do it all yourself in the early days. I'd suggest that if you're not already familiar with this kind of data compiling and tracking, that you read some basic business administration books and make sure you understand how spreadsheet programs such as Excel can help you.

The most important thing with analysis and tracking tools is that you understand them and they're user-friendly for you; what's perfect for one investor isn't necessarily the right format for another. Work out a system that suits you, so you can keep it up to date and won't waste time completing information that's not useful to you.

## Make it personal

Remember that this is *your* business. The key KPIs listed above are, in my opinion, the most important ones that will enable you to monitor and compare your investment, but there may be others that you'd like to add, according to your fundamental goals and objectives. KPIs don't have to simply be financial, so if spending more time with your children is something you'd like property investment to facilitate, then make that measurable and put it on your spreadsheet. Because if you're succeeding financially, but not in terms of lifestyle goals, it needs to be flagged up and put right as soon as possible. Regular KPI analysis will keep not only your business, but also YOU on track.

# Checklist

# Understanding the HMO model

Have you done all these things?

- [ ] Understood the difference between student HMOs and renting rooms to working adults
- [ ] Appreciated the downsides and really considered whether you're able and prepared to deal with them
- [ ] Considered again whether the 'pros' will satisfy your goals and objectives
- [ ] Read business administration books/guides and researched KPIs
- [ ] Become familiar with Excel, or a similar spreadsheet program
- [ ] Thought about the type of KPIs you'll need to track in YOUR business

# Chapter 3

# The financials

Choosing how to finance your HMO investments is a major decision. There are various different options that you'll hear people talking about – great mortgage deals, joint ventures, lease options, etc. – but, fundamentally, which route you take will depend on four key factors:

1. How much capital you have
2. The bank's willingness to lend to you
3. Your attitude to risk
4. Your ability to find the right people and build good relationships with them

Before I go any further, I need to make one thing very clear: 'No money down' (NMD) deals **do not exist**. They used to, but regulations have tightened since the credit crunch hit and I haven't found a single NMD scheme since that is considered legal.

*You cannot buy a property solely in your name without putting some of your own capital in and, if you don't fully disclose to a lender where the deposit funds are coming from, you are committing mortgage fraud.*

It's also mortgage fraud to not advise the lender of the **actual price** you're paying for the property (which is what some NMD schemes rely on), so if anyone suggests that to you, walk away from them. I'm amazed at how many people I meet who still think they can invest in property without any personal investment of money or time. Thankfully, the number of companies and self-proclaimed 'gurus' out there suggesting it's possible seems to have fallen over recent years, but there are still quite a few rogues looking to take what little money people do have and give them little or nothing in return.

You need money behind you to invest in buy to let. As a rule of thumb, for every HMO you buy, you should budget for:

- a 25% deposit
- purchase costs of around £2,500 (solicitor's fees, disbursements, surveyor, etc.)
- Stamp duty of 1% of the purchase price (if purchase price is £250,000 or less; it's 3% if over £250,000 and 4% if over £500,000)
- somewhere between £5,000 and £30,000 for refurbishment (if required) and getting it ready to rent
- A 'contingency fund' to cover up to 2 months' initial mortgage payments and any other unexpected costs

So, if you're buying at £200,000 (a pretty average purchase price), you're going to need somewhere between £50k and £70k.

This is not a business for the under-funded; it is a major investment and carries risk. The rewards are potentially very good, but it's certainly not something you should enter into lightly and that's why you need to work with a great team of professional advisors. Whoever you choose to help and advise you with financing (broker or IFA), should work together with your legal representative and wealth manager to make sure that what you buy and how you buy it is appropriate for your circumstances and in line with your objectives.

## Risk

Property is considered a medium-risk investment, with the risk reducing the longer you plan to hold the investment for. HMO investing in particular offers the potential for great rewards, but with that comes greater risk.

> *"Progress always involves risks. You can't steal second base and keep your foot on first."*
> **Frederick B. Wilcox**

Getting a good ROI means taking on a lot of mortgage debt; having the right business structure in place to run your HMO portfolio involves employing and being responsible for other people; you stake your reputation on every deal you make and, if you choose to partner with another investor on joint ventures, you're not only risking your own money, but theirs as well. It all amounts to a lot of financial and emotional pressure and you need to seriously think about whether you're happy to accept that level of risk and responsibility.

The ultimate level of risk is massively reduced if you approach everything in a professional way, research and execute all your choices properly and become an excellent business manager. In short, it's up to you and dependent on the kind of person you are. If you're confident in your own abilities and are prepared to work hard at this business, you shouldn't need to worry unduly about the risks you're taking, because you'll know that you're doing everything possible to mitigate those risks.

> *"Risk comes from not knowing what you're doing."*
> **Warren Buffett**

**Key financial risk factors and how you can insulate yourself against them:**

Risk: capital values (house prices) going down.
Mitigate by: buying property at 10%+ below its 'true market'/ surveyed value and considering it a long-term investment.

Risk: rents falling.
Mitigate by: buying in areas where demand is currently high and likely to be high into the future.

Risk: void periods.

Mitigate by: providing good quality, well-maintained accommodation at a fair market rent.

Risk: tenants causing damage to property.

Mitigate by: referencing tenants properly and insuring against malicious damage.

Risk: costs rising.

Mitigate by: testing your initial figures against a number of different cost base scenarios to make sure your investment still stacks up BEFORE you buy.

All of these factors can be tackled once you start researching your local property market, but the first risk you'll need to address is the risk that a lender takes in lending you mortgage finance.

## Buy to let mortgages

Buy to let mortgages are different to residential mortgages in two main ways: the loan-to-value ratio is lower and is based primarily on the rental income potential of the property. I say 'primarily' because most (if not all) lenders will require you to have a personal income of at least £25,000 p/a before they'll consider you for a buy to let mortgage.

There are two steps you should take before approaching your financial advisor or mortgage broker:

1. Put together a personal financial statement: a document that lists all your assets, liabilities, income and expenditure, and that calculates your monthly cash flow and personal net worth. You can find templates if you do an online search.

2. Check your own credit score, via Experian or Equifax. As with any mortgage application, the lender will carry out a credit check on you, so make sure you're in the best possible position and if there is anything adversely affecting your score, contact the companies directly and see what you can do to sort the problem out – something like a missed payment is sometimes simply a misunderstanding that can be rectified. It also helps your score if you've lived at the same address for more than three years, have been employed for a number of years and are on the electoral roll.

Once a lender has established you're credit-worthy, how much they'll lend is usually calculated on the basis of the rental income (as verified by a surveyor) being at least 120%-130% of the monthly repayment amount. And, as things currently stand, you will probably be looking at a 75% LTV ratio.

**Example, assuming a requirement of 125% x monthly repayment**:

| | |
|---|---|
| Property value | £200,000 |
| Borrowing required at 75% | £150,000 |
| Monthly mortgage repayment | £625   (£150,000 x 5% ÷ 12) |

(at 5% mortgage interest rate, interest only)
Required rental valuation          £781 pcm (£625 x 125%)

Although the monthly rental income for an HMO is usually around £2,500+ pcm, most lenders won't accept a 'room rental' valuation, as they're always considering a worst-case scenario and will err on the side of safety – i.e. you only being able to rent the property as a single unit.

So you need to look for the kind of property that would not only make a good HMO but also rent well as a single unit let – otherwise you may have to be prepared to accept a lower LTV and put in more of your own capital, and that's not going to give you as good a return as if you gear highly.

A caveat to the above is that you might need a specialist HMO mortgage – which you almost certainly will with a licensable HMO – so you'll need to discuss it thoroughly with your broker or IFA. Lenders will look at whether you're buying something that's already classed as an HMO and will also need full disclosure on how you intend to rent the property, so you must make sure that you – and your financial representative – are declaring what's legally required.

One final thing you need to bear in mind is that lenders limit the number of buy to let mortgages an individual can have, so make sure that you thoroughly plan with your wealth manager, IFA and legal representative how to grow your portfolio legally and efficiently.

## More creative ways of funding your investment...

I said at the start of the chapter that how you're able to finance your investments is dependent partly on finding the right people to work with and on your ability to build good relationships with those people. You'll only be able to embark on the more creative options if people trust you and you can prove to them that you know what you're doing, so there's no point in trying to approach investors for joint ventures (JVs) or put together a lease option or other 'creative purchase' proposition until you've got at least a couple of successful HMOs under your belt. In other words, there's no getting away from needing capital when you start out!

I've done many JVs and partnering with other people has allowed me to grow my portfolio far more quickly and easily than I would otherwise have been able to. And every one of those JVs is a true partnership – we share the risk and the reward equally – which is how you need to approach these deals. Finding the right people to partner with, whose investment goals you can satisfy and vice versa, isn't a quick process and it's not something you can really put a timescale on. People buy into people, so make sure the buzz surrounding you is that you're a) good at what you do and, b) ethical and decent in all your business dealings.

*Always do what you've said you'll do,*
*when you've said you'll do it.*

# Tax & wealth planning

This is an incredibly important area of investment in general, and property tax is its own world. You may already have a tax advisor, but do they have experience of working specifically with buy to let investors? How you're taxed on your property investments will depend on a number of factors, such as how they are legally owned, how you take income from them and what other businesses and income you have, and everyone's situation is different.

As I've already said, you need to make sure that your HMO portfolio sits properly within the context of your existing financial/tax affairs and that property is, in fact, the right investment vehicle for you. So - if you haven't already - start looking into getting specialist, tailored advice now.

# Checklist

# Getting to grips with the financials

Have you done all these things?

- [ ] Put together a personal financial statement
- [ ] Discussed investment objectives with a financial advisor and assessed potential returns from property versus potential returns from other investments
- [ ] Sought out a specialist tax advisor and taken the time to really understand their advice
- [ ] Checked your credit score and taken steps to remedy any issues
- [ ] Fully considered key financial risk factors attached to HMO investments
- [ ] Investigated with your IFA the implications of needing an HMO-specific mortgage
- [ ] Put together an investment plan and clearly established how your investments will/can be financed
- [ ] Begun to think about what JVs might be appropriate for you in the future

# Chapter 4

# The legals

Buying, owning and letting investment property is very different to buying and owning your own home and, especially in the case of HMOs, there are numerous legal considerations you need to become familiar with.

One of the challenges of being an HMO investor is keeping on top of and up to date with all the legal requirements associated with your investment, so you'll need outside help and advice on an on-going basis. Some of this comes from engaging legal and financial professionals; some relies on you building relationships with local council departments and landlord associations; all of it demands that you, personally, understand the legal implications of every aspect of your property business.

Getting things right from the start will make life a lot easier and cheaper as you grow your portfolio. Too many investors 'dip their toe in the water' at the start by buying one HMO to see if they fancy it as an investment strategy. They take very little advice before they make their first investment, on the basis that they can 'sort it out later', if they decide to press on. What they don't realise is that there are on-going implications for the way some tax and legal matters are entered into and arranged at the outset.

Falling foul of your legal obligations can result in anything from a simple demand that you rectify a situation, to a criminal conviction, a hefty fine and prison time. In short, this is not an area you can afford to get wrong!

Although I'm not a qualified legal expert, I do have a great deal of hands-on experience as a 'consumer' in the field of HMO legals, so am going to highlight the key points I think you need to be aware of and regulations you need to comply with. I'm not going to go into a lot of detail because, a) I'm not a property lawyer, b) many of the precise legal requirements vary from council to council and, c) detail is what I pay experts for! You can spend an awful lot of time getting bogged down in research into specialist areas that others have spent years training for, so save yourself the time and effort and engage those experts to advise you.

## The legal set-up and administration of your business

As I said in Chapter 1, it's important to speak to a wealth manager or independent financial advisor about your investment plans, so that they can look at property in the context of your other financial affairs. That will have an implication on the way you legally own your properties and structure your property business. Many buy to let investors own properties personally, then let and manage them through a Limited Company; some set up a new company, others use an existing one. For some people, having a company own a property portfolio is more suitable – everyone's situation is different and you need to work with financial and legal advisors to decide on the right set-up for you.

Having a Limited Company or Limited Liability Partnership brings its own associated legal requirements, including filing returns with Companies House and making declarations and filings with HMRC, and there can be heavy penalties for non-compliance. You will need to make sure your books are kept up to date and all legal and financial paperwork is filed properly.

Because HMO investing involves more certification, compliance and general paperwork than other types of property investment, I'd highly recommend you don't try to do it all yourself. I'll talk more about the team you should have around you later in the book, but three key members of that team should be:

1. a very good accountant who's a property tax expert
2. a legal representative with specific experience in buy to let investing
3. a bookkeeper experienced in buy to let – and preferably HMOs

You may be concerned with keeping costs down when you're starting out but, trust me, the cost of getting the right advice to make sure your business is correctly set up from the start is not a cost you should be cutting. Good professional advisors will end up saving you many times over what you pay them.

## Conveyancing

Getting a good buy to let deal often relies on you being able to complete quickly, so your legal representative must be willing and able to move things along and look for solutions, not excuses! Look for a legal/conveyancing firm that has experience specifically in the acquisition of properties for buy to let portfolios and try to make sure that the person dealing with your purchase is a buy to let investor themselves. They'll understand the things that are really important to you and know how to approach any problems that might come up.

As an HMO investor, it's more than likely you'll want – and usually need - to make alterations to the properties you buy, in order to make them fit for purpose. Extensions, movement or erection of walls and converting garages into bedrooms or living rooms are all very common, so whoever's carrying out your conveyancing needs to know these things are important to check in the property deeds – and/or lease, in the case of leasehold properties. New build deeds often prohibit the conversion of garages and leases often state that you can't alter any internal walls, and if a conveyancer fails to highlight any such clauses to you, you could end up with a property you can't let in the way you planned - and that could be disastrous for your investment strategy.

Similarly, they need to know to particularly check for any previous planning applications/issues and any upcoming changes in the law (such as the 'garden grabbing' legislation in 2010 that made it easier for local councils to refuse development requests) that might affect your plans for the property.

If you're buying with a spouse or business partner, you'll also need to decide whether to own the property as 'joint tenants' or 'tenants in common' for inheritance purposes (as joint tenants the property automatically passes to the other owner/s, whereas as tenants in common you can leave your share to any beneficiary in your will). A good legal representative should be able to help you with regard to your will and be willing and able to liaise with your wealth manager and mortgage broker to make sure you take ownership of the property in the right way, as quickly and efficiently as possible.

## Planning

I don't think I'm over-exaggerating when I say that planning can be a minefield. You need to be aware that your investment is likely to be subject to certain planning laws and those laws vary from council to council – not only with regard to building works, but also change of use. Ignoring the issue of planning is not an option.

National legislation currently states that you don't need planning permission to change a property's use class from C3 (standard single household home) to C4 (HMO of up to 6 people), BUT local councils can adopt an Article 4 Direction requiring that you DO apply for planning permission. The main issue with this is that the planning application process is likely to take longer than the conveyancing process, so you might end up completing on your purchase before a decision on whether to grant planning permission has been made!

You need to think very carefully about this, as entering into an investment that may turn out not to be fit for purpose could have serious financial implications for you. I've heard several horror stories about people who have bought properties without doing the necessary research – usually they've simply heard someone talk about the profitability of HMOs and have decided 'it doesn't sound that difficult to me…' – and they've ended up with a house in the wrong location that they can only let as a single unit, which doesn't cover their costs. They only have two choices: to let it out and keep subsidising the costs out of their own pockets, in the hope that the market will rise enough for them to sell and at least break even; or, to sell right away and take the financial hit.

The best you can do is talk to your local council planning department to find out what their policy is and approach your local landlords association to find out what other investors' experiences have been.

There's also a lot of useful information on the Government's site: planningportal.gov.uk.

If you want your HMO to house more than six people, you will definitely need to gain planning permission, and I would always recommend you hire a local Chartered Town Planner to advise you and complete the application on your behalf. If you can build a good relationship with a planning expert, sometimes they're happy to give you a verbal idea as to whether a particular property would be likely to be granted planning permission (for change of use and also for any extensions or conversions you might want to carry out), although this would be in no way binding on their part.

## Licensing

First things first: not all HMOs need to be licensed. National regulations (as per The Housing Act, 2004) state that HMOs only require a licence if:

- the property has three or more storeys
  AND
- it is occupied by five or more people, forming two or more households.

But local councils have the power to impose additional licensing in certain areas so, as with planning, you need to speak to them to find out their policy.

Licences are issued for five years and tend to cost between £100 and £200 a year, depending on where you live and how your local council calculates the charge – some charge per unit (i.e. per bedroom) and some per property. In my local area, the current charge is £885 for 5 years. I hear a lot of landlords talking about how expensive licensing is, but I don't think somewhere between £8 and £17 a month is worth getting heated up over – especially when you consider the benefit of being able to tell your tenants that your HMO is registered with the council and meets approved living and health & safety standards.

If your property is subject to licensing, your local authority will check it to make sure there's enough space for all the tenants and that it's being managed properly. You'll also need to comply with gas and electrical safety, health & safety and fire safety requirements – which, no surprise, tend to vary from council to council!

## Building regulations (an extension of Planning)
Another area where you need to make sure you're compliant. People sometimes make the mistake of thinking that if they're not actually 'building' anything – i.e. extending or converting lofts etc. – then building regulations don't concern them. Wrong.

The main thing to know here is that if you're undertaking *any* work to the property, you must speak to the council about their building regulations policy BEFORE you start works, otherwise you can get in a mess, with regard to both their assessment and potentially having to redo work.

As well as having to comply with general building regulations, your HMO may need soundproofing. The planning department can advise you of this – usually it's only an issue with licensable HMOs – but it's not something you want to come as a surprise, because it can cost tens of thousands to soundproof a whole house.

## Health & Safety

If your HMO is licensable, then the council will advise you of everything you need to do health and safety-wise to make sure your licence is granted. But even if you don't need one, it's a really good idea – certainly on the first one or two properties you buy – to have someone from the housing department visit (Housing Standards Officer, or similar) to check you're doing things properly.

As a landlord, you have a legal duty of care to your tenants and must carry out a fire safety risk assessment, to show that you've identified and considered all potential risks and taken steps to mitigate them. You could do this yourself, but for around £200 a qualified Fire Risk Assessor will carry out the assessment for you and not only make sure you're doing everything legally required (such as ensuring your furnishings and furniture comply with fire regulations), but also make recommendations for additional sensible steps to take – for example, installing smoke detectors in all rooms (heat sensors in the kitchen) and fitting fire doors to all bedrooms and kitchens.

As far as how many of the 'additional recommendations' you should implement is concerned, a good rule of thumb is: are you satisfied that if anything happened to one of your tenants and you ended up in court, you could honestly say – and prove - you'd taken all reasonable steps to ensure their safety? That's why instructing a professional to carry out the risk assessment and going over and above the basic legal requirements are both advisable…I like to sleep at night!

## Certification required

HMOs, where tenants are sharing kitchens and bathrooms, don't currently legally need a valid Energy Performance Certificate (EPC), but I'm sure that will change in the future and so suggest you make one available to your tenants anyway.

What you absolutely DO need is:

1. An annual gas safety check, carried out by a Gas Safe registered engineer, and that record must be made available to the tenants (and copied to the local council if the property is licensed).

2. An Electrical Installation Condition Report certificate. All fixed electrical installations must be inspected and tested by a qualified electrician at least every five years and the local authority can require

the certificate to be produced in 7 days – for any HMO, not just a licensed one.

As you've probably gathered, because so much of the legislation around HMOs is defined by local councils, it's absolutely imperative you speak to the various departments – and don't presume they speak to each other! – to find out their overall attitude to HMOs and exactly where you stand with regard to:

- Planning
- Licensing
- Building regulations (including soundproofing)
- Electrical safety certification
- Fire safety (and speak to your local Fire Safety or Community Safety Officer)

Your local landlords association should also be a great source of information - I've found most other landlords are only too happy to share their experiences and steer you in the right direction.

## The legal agreement between you and your house sharers

The document you should be using to form the legal contract between you and your tenants is an Assured Shorthold Tenancy Agreement (AST). In student properties, where it's usually a group of friends moving in together, it's common for there to be just one AST, which makes all the tenants jointly and severally liable for the total rent. But with HMOs for working adults, who usually don't know each other and don't want to assume responsibility for the rent in this way, landlords tend to issue separate ASTs for each room.

The key thing is that you understand and comply with your rights and responsibilities as a landlord. In simple terms, you are obliged to:
- provide suitable, secure accommodation
- properly maintain all fixtures, fittings and furnishings you've provided, in addition to the fabric of the property itself
- ensure the health and safety of your tenants
- allow your tenants peaceful occupation of the property
- give adequate written notice to terminate the agreement

You can buy an AST 'off the shelf', from a stationers or online, but most landlords tend to want to customise it. DON'T simply do this yourself! You could end up in a legal mess if any additional clauses were to be challenged, so always use a legal letting specialist to ensure that, a) the agreement is appropriate for letting to a tenant of an HMO and, b) all terms are legally enforceable. It's worth spending a few hundred pounds getting the contract right in the beginning, because you're going to be issuing a lot of them and need to be confident that your adapted AST will stand up in court.

# Checklist

# The legals

Have you done all these things?

## Legal advice

☐ Spoken to a wealth advisor, property tax expert and legal representative with specific experience in buy to let investing

☐ Researched local legal firms to find a good buy to let expert

## Planning

☐ Spoken to local council planning department to find out local policy:

☐ Is planning permission required for change of use?

☐ What is the general policy with regard to development?

☐ Spoken to local landlords association about planning regulations and recent decisions

☐ Checked on www.planningportal.gov.uk/buildingregulations

## Licensing

☐ Looked at www.gov.uk/house-in-multiple-occupation-licence

☐ Spoken to local council about its HMO licensing policy

- ☐ Spoken to local landlords association about specific local requirements

## Health & Safety

- ☐ Spoken to local council & landlords association
- ☐ Looked at www.firesafe.org.uk/houses-in-multiple-occupation/
- ☐ Obtained a Fire Risk Assessment form (freely available online)

## Tenancy agreement

- ☐ Read through a standard AST and understood rights and responsibilities
- ☐ Spoken to a legal lettings specialist

# PART TWO:

# SECURING YOUR INVESTMENT AND PREPARING TO LET

# Chapter 5

# Become your own local expert

As you're probably gathering, there aren't any short cuts to becoming a successful HMO investor – either financially or in terms of time and effort! You'll get the best results from buying a property with built-in equity that's in high demand – i.e. the right property, in the right location, at the right price – and doing that requires expertise.

While you can 'outsource' legal, financial, trades and management expertise, the best person to source property on an on-going basis is you. You can tap into the knowledge and services of local estate and letting agents who know the area well, but they're highly unlikely to be experts in sourcing HMOs, so you're going to have to be able to quickly assess yourself what's going to work and what isn't.

Don't make the mistake of chasing after deals around the country, or let yourself be persuaded by investment companies and people selling leads that they've discovered the 'new hot spot' and can let you share in the good fortune of 'an incredible deal – but hurry, or you'll miss out…' Almost every town and city in the UK has a shortage of multi-let accommodation and you can always find some kind of good deal locally, provided you know where and how to look, and how to negotiate.

## Why doing it yourself is better than buying leads

Whoever's selling leads will tell you how well they know the area and how great their contacts are. They'll say they're either not in a position to buy the properties themselves or aren't interested in expanding their own portfolio any further, so are looking to gain some financial reward in another way: the fee they charge you for benefiting from their expertise.

The main issue with buying leads where you simply pay a fee is that the 'expert' selling to you has no on-going interest in the property you buy. They get their fee whether or not you ultimately make money from the property, and when you're looking at investing as much capital as you are in an HMO, that's an awful lot of faith to be putting in someone else. I've come across far too many people who've bought leads that have turned out to be bad investments – at best, they just about break even; at worst, they're left with a property that's not worth what they paid for it and which nobody wants to rent at anything like a reasonable market rate. Yes, you can – and should – do your own research on any property you're considering buying, to satisfy yourself that it's a good deal and meets your objectives, but then what are you paying the sourcer for?

Look at how much they want to charge and work out how much of your own time that could buy – time you could spend getting to know your area really well – and you'll see that working on becoming your own local expert is a far better long-term investment.


## Why invest locally?

The question is, really, why not? If you happen to live in an area that doesn't have sufficient demand for HMOs (often the case with rural locations), you might need to look as far as an hour away, maybe more. But, as a rule, you will be able to find solid investment properties within easy striking distance – 15 to 30 minutes - of your home.


Benefits of basing your portfolio locally:

1. **You can focus your efforts.** You can't possibly become an expert in all the various micro-markets in the UK, so why not focus on a place you already know something about? By concentrating on just one area, you give yourself the best chance of success in that area.

2. **You can be where you need to be quickly.** Good deals often need acting on right away so there's a real advantage in being able to look at a property as soon as you hear about it and meet with vendors and agents. Even if you have someone else fully managing your portfolio, there will be times you'll want or need to visit your properties or deal in person with some issue,

which is a lot easier – saving you time and expense - when you're close-by.

3. **It'll be easier to build good relationships.** You'll be on hand to liaise regularly with estate and letting agents, attend local property and networking events and can tap into existing contacts to find good tradespeople and suppliers Also, there's often a natural resistance to property investors from homeowners, but if you're a local yourself, you may find it easier to overcome that and also to negotiate with vendors.

4. **You can build your profile locally.** Become known for doing what you say you'll do and for running an ethical, reputable business. I have ***never*** shaken hands on a deal and then backed out, even when it's turned out not to be quite as good as I first believed. Your reputation is everything, so make sure people want to do business with you and talk about you for the right reasons. Get involved with local events and give back to your community, whether it's offering your time and expertise for free or helping financially, such as sponsoring a local sports team. Just make sure you do it for the right reasons and choose things that mean something to you – I'm talking about good PR, not shameless self-promotion!

*"It takes many good deeds to build a good reputation and only one bad deed to lose it."*
**Benjamin Franklyn**

And as your business and reputation grows, you'll find that other successful people will gravitate towards you and more and more opportunities will come your way – and not just in the property sphere. Through building my HMO portfolio I've been invited to lots of different business and social events and have now become a huge fan of motor racing and horseracing! I've built friendships with people I've met at those events and have already partnered with several of them on different projects.

## The expertise you'll need to gain

You need to immerse yourself in the property market so that you know exactly which properties, in which streets, at what price, will make good HMOs. And to make sure they're a good investment not only today but also into the future, you need to understand market trends and be able to spot local economic indicators.

## The ability to value a property

Valuing a property is not an exact science – ultimately you can say that a property is only worth what someone will pay for it on a given day – but you need to get to the point where you have an instinctive feel for a fair price. You can only do that by building a bank of knowledge about what's recently been sold and looking at market trends, then putting that knowledge together with the current supply and demand situation: how much of what you're looking for is currently on the market and how many people are competing for that type of property?

You can find sold property prices online – **rightmove.co.uk** and **landregistry.gov.uk** are two of the best sources – but it's also worth spending time talking to estate agents. They'll be able to speak about specific areas with more knowledge, give you details of potential HMOs that have recently sold, and it's also a good way of testing which agents might be the best ones to try and work with going forward. You'll quickly see the ones that understand buy to let and are interested in building longer-term relationships with investors/landlords.

A couple of good online tools for seeing what's currently happening to prices in your local area are:

- **propertysnake.co.uk**, where you can put in a postcode and it will show you how long a property's been listed online and when and by how much each property was reduced in price
- **the Property-Bee toolbar** for Firefox, which will bring up all changes to the price and details made since the property was listed, for any property you look at on Rightmove and PrimeLocation, as well as a few other sites.

Using these tools, together with the information you get from agents, and your own additional research, should give you a very good idea of values.

Buying at the right price is so important for an investor. When it's your own home, you're often prepared to pay a little more than you really wanted to because of the emotional investment, but this is strictly business, so make sure you have 'number-crunched' thoroughly and are as sure as you can be that the property will not only deliver the cash flow you need, but also be a good long-term investment. Look at how average house prices in the region have performed over the past 20 years and then compare how the kind of properties you've identified as good potential HMOs have performed against that average. You should aim to buy property that has consistently outperformed - or, at the very least, kept up with – the local average, because that's a very good indicator that it will continue to do the same.

## Recognising economic drivers

These are key to supply and demand in an area, affecting both the capital value of your investment and on-going income potential. HMOs are most successful in areas where there are good transport links, decent local amenities, employment opportunities and a shortage of quality accommodation.

A lot of people simply look at what's going on in the area at the moment and whether it's 'regenerating', and that's a fair indication that there may be good current demand. But where's the investment coming from and what's the future plan? Wine bars and restaurants come and go; you need to know what the local plans are for the next 5-20 years, because you're in this business for the long term. You have to be as certain as you can that the demand for rooms isn't going to suddenly fall because either businesses are closing down in the area or a whole load of new multi-let accommodation has suddenly been granted planning permission.

Information about future plans for the area is freely available from your local council, but you can usually get more in-depth information from speaking to local businesspeople, other investors, good estate agents and surveyors who have lived and worked in the area for a while. And revisit this research every six months or so to make sure you're always aware of what's coming up and can adjust your investment (by changing how you let and who to, or selling and reinvesting in another property), if necessary.

## The local council's attitude to HMOs

Given that pretty much every council will have a slightly different policy and attitude towards HMOs, you need to become an expert in yours. You must know exactly where their boundaries fall, because neighbouring councils can have different regulations, for example, one might have adopted the Article 4 Direction requiring you to seek planning permission for any HMO, while the other might be happy for up to 6 people to share a house without planning. A common issue is parking: some councils will only permit an HMO if there is a certain amount of off-road parking with the property; others don't mind whether there is or not. Another consideration is how 'C3' they view an area, i.e. are there certain pockets that are considered 'family home-friendly', where the council would refuse permission for a property to be rented out as an HMO? Depending on a council's attitude (and taking into account all your other research), you may decide not to invest in a certain ward if there are too many requirements and restrictions.

## Tenant preferences

Different types of tenants often have certain areas - even particular streets - that they like to live in, so you need to research where the kind of people you want to rent to are requesting rooms. Sites such as **spareroom.co.uk** and **uk.easyroommate.com** have 'wanted' adverts and you can usually see their employment status. Letting agents, even though they might not rent rooms out themselves, often know the particularly popular and not so popular areas. Working adults, for example, tend not to like living in a particularly student-oriented area and want somewhere they can park, so narrower streets without off-road parking, within walking distance of a university won't be suitable.

And find out what they're looking for, in particular. All house sharers prefer refurbished properties with decent kitchens and bathrooms and many expect wireless broadband, but what else does your target market expect – and are they happy to pay more for it? Is a cleaner expected, or satellite TV? You want to provide whatever there is a demand for, and a shortage of.

# Rental values

While average property prices tend to peak and trough, rents are usually fairly consistent, so their performance over time isn't so relevant. What you need to focus on is how much tenants are prepared to pay for what level of accommodation. HMOs vary wildly in quality, so the average room rent for your area might actually be significantly lower than you could charge for what you're offering. Where I invest, double rooms vary between £350 and £500 a month.

As with the above, look online at what people are prepared to pay for an all-inclusive room rent – SpareRoom puts out a monthly index of room rental prices, which you can access from the website for free - and then go and look at some of your competitors' properties. Get to know exactly what standard you need to provide so that you can charge the highest reasonable rent and still keep the property full.

You must also make sure you know the rental values for letting a property like yours as a single unit because, as I mentioned in Chapter 3, lenders may be basing their mortgage calculations on that single let value. An area might stack up well on purchase price and on-going cash flow potential, but if it's an area that tends to attract low-income families, the monthly rental value for letting the property as a family home might be too low to make the purchase worthwhile, because of the amount of deposit you'd have to put in. Talk to local letting agents about your plans and ask their professional advice on which areas might be best to consider, then back it up with your own online research.

All the elements above combine to give you a detailed picture of the local HMO market. As you build your knowledge of values and analyse them together with costs and income to calculate potential returns, you'll start to see which areas/streets are most viable, with the right balance between accommodation potential, affordability, demand and capital growth potential.

*There is no secret to success; it is the result of preparation, hard work and sheer determination.*

# Checklist

## Becoming your own local expert

Have you done all these things?

### Property prices and trends

☐ Researched sold price data on rightmove.co.uk and landregistry.gov.uk

☐ Looked at how 'for sale' prices are currently shifting, via propertysnake.co.uk and Property-Bee

☐ Compared the performance of 'HMO type' properties with the market average over the last 20 years

☐ Spoken to local agents about the current local market and trends

### HMO-specific research

☐ Established local council's attitude to HMOs

☐ Checked the areas in which planning and licensing are needed

☐ Researched rental values for letting both rooms and the property as a single unit

☐ Looked at the rental index data on spareroom.co.uk/rentalindex

☐ Researched tenant demand: exactly what do they want, and where?

☐ Been to visit existing HMOs for competitor research

☐ Tested purchase and rental figures on an HMO viability spreadsheet

# Chapter 6

# Your team

Once you've researched your local HMO market thoroughly, you should have a level of expertise that very few other people will have. Most of the professionals you'll deal with as you source, buy, refurbish, let and manage your portfolio won't know as much as you do about the market as a whole – and that puts you in a great position for being able to ask the right questions and pick the best people to work with.

There are some very good reasons why you should surround yourself with advisors, suppliers and associates:

1. You can't be an expert in everything, so the very best thing you can do for your business is tap into the knowledge, skills and resources of the people who *are* experts in their own specific area of property investment.
2. By outsourcing as much as possible, you're freeing up your own time. And, as you become better at finding and negotiating great deals and running your business, your time will be worth many times more than the cost of paying someone else to do various jobs.

3. Property can be a lonely business if you do most of the work yourself – you'll find it much more enjoyable with a good team and network around you.

I use the services of more than 20 different people on a regular basis. They're all very good at what they do, which enables me to acquire properties efficiently and for the business to run with minimal daily input from me. I think of these people as my 'team':

- Wealth manager
- Buy to let specialist property lawyers
- Independent mortgage broker
- Accountant
- Bookkeeper
- Estate agents
- PA
- Property manager
- Lettings negotiators
- Project manager for refurbishments
- Maintenance team and specialist contractors

Since I began investing, there have been some changes to my team, and you may find you don't get the perfect people first time around. But I've worked with all my current advisors, suppliers and employees for a number of years now and am happy that it's a very strong line-up.

## Your key players

***All professionals giving you financial advice MUST be properly
qualified and regulated by the Financial Services Authority (FSA)
and anyone giving you legal advice should be suitably qualified
and regulated by The Law Society and the Solicitors Regulation
Authority (SRA) (or the Council of Licensed Conveyancers (CLC)).*

## Wealth Manager

As I've already said, property investment needs to fit properly
alongside your other financial interests. Whether you choose to
engage a wealth management firm or take advantage of your bank's
wealth management service, try to work with someone who either
invests in property themselves or already has a number of property
investor clients. It'll short-cut your discussions and they're likely
to have researched the subject very well indeed.

Take your investment objectives and personal financial statement
along to your meeting, so that the wealth manager can get a clear
picture of your current situation and where you want to get to. They
can then help you decide the best way to structure your investments.

Importantly, they can also help you with inheritance planning. Too
many people invest in property so they have something to leave to
their children, without realising that it can be one of the least tax-
efficient ways to pass on money. You'll need to amend your will
and may need to set up Trusts – it's a complex area, and demands
specialist advice.

*As well as being FSA regulated, ideally they will also have the CISI Masters in Wealth Management (MCSI after their name).*

## Property tax specialist / accountant

Wealth management firms are usually able to give you tax advice and handle your accounts, but you must make sure that you've had a proper discussion with someone who is a property tax expert. As I said earlier in the book, your investment plans will impact your current tax situation - and vice versa, - and a specialist will be able to advise you how to set up and run your HMO business in the most tax-efficient way.

## Mortgage broker / IFA

Your mortgage broker can make or break a deal. You're looking for someone who understands exactly what you're aiming for and appreciates that things often need to happen quickly. Make sure they're independent (i.e. can access all mortgage products in the market) and have worked in buy to let for a number of years, as they're likely to have established relationships with buy to let and HMO specialist lenders.

I'd never attempt to find a mortgage myself by going direct to different lenders, for three key reasons:

1. It can be incredibly time-consuming and I'm not a mortgage expert.

2. Good brokers usually have access to mortgage products that aren't publicised – you only know they're there if you ask about them, and if you don't know they're there…!

3. As an individual, trying to contact lenders to progress an application can be an incredibly frustrating experience and you're unlikely to have any luck moving it along quickly. An effective broker will be able to access the right people and push your application through.

Never underestimate the value a good broker can add to your business. Being well-financed will mean you'll not only be able to act quickly on deals, but also get better deals and be more profitable.

*Any person acting as a broker or making recommendations for your mortgage finance must have one or more of these qualifications: Certificate in Mortgage Advice (Cert MA); Certificate in Mortgage Advice and Practice (CeMAP) from the ifa School of Finance; Mortgage Advice and Practice Certificate (MAPC) from the CIB in Scotland.*

## Specialist property lawyer

Ideally, they should be buy to let specialists and have experience of dealing with HMO investors. As with your broker, your legal representative can make the difference between a smooth and speedy transaction and a complete nightmare! You can instruct either a solicitor or a licensed conveyancer – both are qualified to handle property transactions – but one of the benefits of engaging a solicitor is that you can choose a firm that also has solicitors specialising in other areas of law. That means your legal representative can tap into the knowledge of colleagues for advice on things like tax planning, wills, litigation, etc. and you may be able to keep all your legal affairs under one roof.

Some firms have specific case-progression departments; some solicitors/conveyancers will progress things themselves. Both have pros and cons - the important thing for you to establish is:

1. Are they happy to work to a timescale established at the start (unforeseen circumstances aside)?
2. Will they update you regularly?
3. Will you be able to easily speak to the person directly dealing with your transaction?

You also need to make sure that whoever you choose is happy to liaise and work closely with your broker/IFA and wealth manager to keep your business on track with your objectives.

I realise I'm painting a picture of perfection here, but these legal representatives do exist! Take personal recommendations from other investors and meet in person with all those on your 'shortlist'. Homebuyers usually engage solicitors over the phone, or online, but when it's someone who's going to be so crucial to the success of your business over a number of years, you need to make sure there's a good personal relationship and understanding from the start.

The other person who can really help you stay on the right side of the law is a local planning expert. Planning regulations have a tendency to change rather quietly, so if you can build a relationship with a Chartered Town Planner, they can guide you and help you minimize the risk of falling foul of regulations.

## Estate agents

You might be lucky enough to have local estate agents who already understand about investing in HMOs, but it's more likely that you'll have to 'train' them. Avoid agents who want to take your contact details before they've even asked what you're looking for – focus on the ones who actually want to have a conversation with you. You also want someone who knows the area and market well, so try to deal with senior negotiators or the branch manager, as they're more likely to be able to have a productive discussion.

Independent agents are usually owned and/or managed by people who have lived and worked in the area for quite some time. They're often on local boards and well-connected, so can be a very useful source of information about planning, upcoming developments, people who might be interested in JVs, etc.

Talk to the agents about your plans, show them you have your finances and legal representation in place, then view a few properties and explain exactly what's right and wrong, so they build up a picture of your ideal HMO. Contact and feedback are key; always do what you say you'll do, view properties they recommend right away and keep them posted on what stage you're at in any transactions so they don't need to 'chase' you.

You want to get to a position where you have three or four agents that understand exactly what you're looking for, know you'll act quickly and make sensible offers, so will call you as soon as they see a property that might be suitable. The quicker a sale can be agreed and completed, the sooner the agents get their money – you're an agent's dream! – so don't give them any reason not to want to have you at the top of their buyer list.

*Agents MUST be members of The Property Ombudsman. Ideally, deal with agents who are Fellows of the National Association of Estate Agents (FNAEA) and/or the Royal Institution of Chartered Surveyors (FRICS).*

## Reliable contractors

Reliable contractors are worth their weight in gold – and then some. You need a team for your refurbishment projects and then a team that can handle on-going maintenance. While you'll probably be able to use many of the same people, some contractors prefer to only handle larger projects and some only smaller ones, which is often the case with electricians and plumbers. The most important thing is that you hire the right people for each job.

**Refurbishment core team:**

- Builder (ideally who can also project manage – otherwise you may need someone else to manage it), preferably a member of the Federation of Master Builders
- Plasterer
- Painter/decorator
- Glazier, FENSA regulated
- Locksmith, ideally from the Master Locksmiths Association
- Carpet fitter
- Plumber, Gas Safe registered
- Electrician, 'Part P' registered
- Cleaner

You may be tempted to project manage the refurbishment yourself, but I'd highly recommend you employ someone else to do it. The refurb contractors need to be able to work together – if they all have their own agendas, you can find projects stall or take longer than necessary because they're all blaming each other for not being able to get on to the next stage. A project manager (often a builder) will have a regular team that he knows will work efficiently together and you pay him to make sure everything stays on track. It also means you only have one person to liaise with.

**Maintenance core team:**
- General handyman
- Plumber, Gas Safe registered
- Electrician, 'Part P' registered (for general maintenance and safety checks)
- Portable Appliance Tester
- Gardener (the handyman may do this for you)
- Emergency locksmith, ideally from the Master Locksmiths Association
- Cleaner

You'll need to call on most of these people at short notice, so do everything you can to make sure they respond to you quickly. A very good way of ensuring they do is to make sure you pay them quickly when they invoice. Most – if not all – of these people will be self-employed and/or running small businesses and really can't afford to wait several weeks for payment, so will greatly appreciate you settling their bills right away.

## The cost of your team
Cost is something that always comes up when I speak to investors who are just starting out and it's a significant concern for those who only have the funds to finance one property initially. They're worried that they're going to end up spending too high a proportion of their money on good advice, particularly with financial and legal professionals, and that's entirely

understandable, but legal and financial advice isn't something you should scrimp on.

It's hard to say how much is 'reasonable' for someone to charge you for advice; what I'd say is that you should most definitely feel you're getting value for money. In your initial preparation and research, you should have worked out how much your own time is worth, looked at the risks and associated potential costs of getting things wrong, and therefore be able to work out whether the costs you're being quoted for mitigating those risks and greatly reducing the chance of succumbing to the potential pitfalls of investing are fair.

## "Where do I find good contractors?"

What people are usually asking with that question, is whether I can give them a list of reliable people to use! As with so much of this business, you get the best results if you do your own homework, which means networking locally with other landlords and asking friends to recommend contractors they've used. You can also look on websites such as RatedPeople.com and mybuilder.com, where tradespeople have been rated on their work.

Two important things to check are: 1) that any contractor you use has their own insurance and, 2) whether they have some formal accreditation or membership of a relevant industry body, so a good place to start is **trustmark.org.uk**, which has a database of tradespeople that operate to government-endorsed standards. If someone you're considering isn't listed on there, that doesn't mean you shouldn't use them, but do check their credentials thoroughly to make sure they're properly qualified for the job you need them to do, and insured against any damage they might cause.

And when you speak to contractors about what you need them to do, be honest and clear about your future plans. You want to try from the start to use people who will be willing and able to work for you as your portfolio grows.

Building good relationships with all the people on your team is vital to your success. You're going be dealing with them on a fairly regular basis – some more often than others – so it's important that they're not only very good at what they do and understand your business, but that you actually get on with them. When you like the people you do business with, and they like you, things get done more efficiently and everyone wins.

> *"Pretend that every single person you meet*
> *has a sign around his or her neck that says,*
> *'Make me feel important'. Not only will you*
> *succeed in sales, you will succeed in life."*
> **Mary Kay Ash, Entrepreneur**

As well as my professional team, I also get a lot of good ideas and advice from other investors and businesspeople that I choose to spend time with. When I started out, I went to every 'property meet' and seminar I could find, but I honestly didn't find them very helpful, mainly because they weren't focused enough on what I wanted to do and there were too many people simply trying to sell to me. That's not to say you might not get something from going along to some, but I'd suggest you're selective.

Visit one or two of the larger national property investment and landlord shows/exhibitions and listen to as many relevant seminars as you can. If what they say makes sense to you, talk to the speakers afterwards and ask them their opinion on which meets and events are worth attending. And talk to other visitors – you'll find that most people can't wait to discuss their portfolio! Make sure you've already done a lot of your objective planning and market research before you go, so you'll really be able to focus on the people you think it might be worth meeting with again.

# Summary

## Putting together and changing your team…

You need to have some of your team in place before you start looking for properties and others you can pick up along the way. I would certainly recommend that you don't take any investment action without having consulted the key financial and legal professionals:

- ☐ A wealth adviser/manager
- ☐ An independent financial adviser (IFA)
- ☐ A property tax specialist
- ☐ A buy to let specialist mortgage broker (your IFA may fulfil this role)
- ☐ An experienced buy to let solicitor or licensed conveyancer

As you start searching for properties, you will identify:
- ☐ Estate & letting agents
- ☐ A project manager
- ☐ Renovation/refurbishment tradespeople
- ☐ Maintenance contractors

And, as your portfolio grows, you will need to recruit:
- ☐ A bookkeeper and accountant (your tax adviser may take care of this for you)

☐  A property manager

☐  A PA/administrator

Your team will, undoubtedly, change over time. Some will move jobs or retire, and you'll probably find that others are just not a good fit for you and your business. And, while it's certainly inconvenient to have to source new professional specialists and contractors, it's something that simply comes with the turf, so make sure you're always aware of good local people that may be able to help you in the future.

# Chapter 7

# Researching properties

If you've already done everything I've outlined so far, you'll be in a very good position to research properties. Just to recap, by this point you should be able to tick off the following:

- Established financial and lifestyle objectives and created some kind of visual reminders of these
- Put together a personal financial statement
- Looked into what's involved in running a small business
- Researched and considered the risks and downsides of investing in HMOs
- Met with a wealth manager (or at the very least an IFA) and put in place an investment plan
- Dealt with business set-up, inheritance issues and your will
- Established available financing options with a mortgage broker/IFA
- Engaged (or at least identified) a suitable legal representative
- Done some initial local area research into supply and demand and sales and rental values
- Investigated good local contractors

The first thing you have to be clear on is who's going to rent your rooms and what they're looking for, because demand is the driver for your business. You can then start looking at the best way to satisfy that demand in a way that meets your financial objectives.

## Your target market

I'd say that working adults between the ages of 20 and 35 will make up the vast majority of your tenants and they'll have all kinds of different requirements, depending on their job and personal situations. There might be a shortage of rooms in certain specific locations, for example, for NHS staff near a hospital or for commuting professionals close to a station, but, as a general rule, you need to cast your net wide and make sure your property appeals to as many people as possible.

**General wants and needs of people renting rooms:**
- A good-sized double room
- Reliable shower/bath
- Plenty of space in the kitchen
- On a bus / train / tram / tube route
- Easy walking distance to shops
- Parking
- Warmth!
- Broadband
- *In certain, usually high-value areas in and around London, working professionals will expect an en-suite

Some of the things we tend to be very concerned about when we're looking for a home to buy - such as a garden and sitting room – simply aren't that important when you're talking about an HMO. Fundamentally, people want a good private space and decent washing and cooking facilities; how well you satisfy the other requirements will make the difference between you letting your rooms more quickly than your competitors and being able to charge the top rents in the area. See Chapter 9 for more details.

## Online research

These days you can find a huge amount of very up-to-date information, about prices, room-seekers and properties, quickly and easily online. You will need to talk to agents to get some more specific local information, but start with the internet so that you're well-prepared for your discussions in person and can get used to analysing figures. The more online research you do, the better a feel you'll get for which properties in which areas would be worth viewing.

## Tenant demand/s

You need to research what the demand *is* and what the demand is *for*. The top three sites I'd suggest you use are: spareroom.co.uk, uk.easyroommate.com and gumtree.com. Go to the 'rooms wanted' section, put in your town or city name and see how many people are looking for rooms. Then do the same search for rooms advertised, and if there are at least twice as many 'wanted' adverts as there are rooms available, it's worth taking your research further.

Go back to the 'rooms wanted' section and see which specific areas the people who are prepared to pay most want to live in. Again, put that area name or postcode into the 'rooms available' search and look at the supply/demand ratio. Once you've identified the areas where demand is outstripping supply by at least 100%, you can start to focus in on exactly what people are looking for, in terms of room size, communal facilities, parking/bike storage and broadband/satellite TV, so you can start making a list of refurbishment requirements and associated budget.

Remember to use this research alongside your general area research for future demand. For instance, an area might have quite an average supply/demand balance at the moment, but if inward investment has already been allocated for transport or facilities, or businesses have confirmed plans to move into the area, they're strong indicators that buying into the area now could actually be a very good investment.

## Property values

Rightmove.co.uk and landregistry.gov.uk are two of the most useful sites for checking past and current property values. You can search for properties by postcode and make comparisons over time, even breaking it down into types of housing stock (detached houses, semi-detached houses, flats, etc.). The thing you won't usually be able to see is the condition of each property, but if you look at enough data, you should be able to get a pretty good idea of how much each type of property in each area is worth.

I'd suggest that you base most of your initial research on properties - in areas of high room rental demand - that could provide a minimum of:

- 5 double bedrooms and one single
- Two bathrooms (one of which could be a shower room)
- A large kitchen/dining room
  or
- Good-sized kitchen and a separate living room

Those are the basics of a fairly average HMO, which usually comes from reconfiguring/converting/extending a property that's currently being used as a family home. That might be something that:

- Already has all the required rooms if you simply reconfigure a current sitting room and dining room as bedrooms
- Offers the potential for conversion of a garage or conservatory into a bedroom or living area
- Has one or two large rooms that could be split into two – or more rooms

…hopefully you get the idea. Most of the properties that offer enough space will be detached or semi-detached houses with three or four bedrooms, so start searching with those criteria.

You can easily spend several days looking at prices and comparing areas in terms of how much space you get for your money, which areas are holding their values well, and which have suffered badly during the recession. Don't get too bogged down – all you need is to identify a reasonably accurate price range that you can use to work the investment viability numbers, and an idea of which areas are likely to hold their capital values.

While you're looking at the property prices, also try to note how long properties have been on the market and by how much the original asking price has been reduced. As mentioned in Chapter 5, Propertysnake.co.uk tracks properties for sale nationwide and details when and by how much the property has been reduced, and the Property-Bee toolbar for Firefox gives much the same information. This will help you build up an idea of the demand for each kind of property, as well as a realistic value, and also support your reasoning for future offers.

(And don't forget to check the rental values for letting this kind of property as a single unit, as that figure may be used by your lender in calculating your mortgage amount.)

# Narrowing it down...

You'll need to look at a **lot** of property details – probably over 100 - in order to end up with a shortlist of ten or so that are worth viewing. Most online details include a floor plan, which makes your life a lot easier, as you can quickly see whether the layout is going to work for you.

Once you find a potentially suitable property that's in the right location, at the right sort of value, you can really start number-crunching, using different purchase price scenarios, maximum and minimum expected rental prices and approximate refurbishment costs. Your spreadsheet should be set up with formulae to auto-calculate yield, ROI and profit so that you can easily compare the KPIs for each property. (This can and will be refined if you actually decide to proceed to offer, but for now you just need to know that it's financially worth pursuing.)

Armed with the printed details of the properties on your shortlist, you can now leave the house!

# Doing the legwork

Before you go and see any of the selling agents, have a drive past the properties, to get an impression of the location. Some things to consider:

- If there are loads of 'room to rent' signs around, you

may not have done your research properly

- If there are lots of 'for sale' boards, that's a sign supply is exceeding demand and you may be able to get a good deal on the price
- Look at the general state of the neighbourhood – does it appear relatively safe and reasonably well maintained?
- What's the parking situation?
- Are there any off-putting things not mentioned on the online details, such as derelict buildings or electrical substations?

And do you like the look of the property? Although you're not going to be living in it yourself, you may need or want to sell at some point and you're certainly looking for something that will keep up with or exceed average capital values for the area. I always trust my gut when I look at a property and if I don't really like the look of it, regardless of what the figures say, I won't buy it.

Once you're happy with your drive-bys, book viewings. If you've already met with the agents when you were doing your initial area/agent research, you can make telephone appointments, but if you haven't, make sure you go into the branch, introduce yourself and explain what you're doing. Ask the agents for their opinions on the properties you've shortlisted – including ones that are on with other agents - and don't forget to check whether they have any new instructions that might be suitable, even if they haven't yet got hard-copy details. You need to build an open, trusting relationship with the people who will probably be your main source of new acquisitions.

## Viewing properties

When you're viewing a potential HMO for the first time, try to simply think of it as a box and don't get distracted by how it looks at the moment. Any wall that's not supporting can be removed; stud walls can be put up; garages and conservatories can be converted; bathrooms and kitchens can be refitted and/or new ones created. What you really need to look out for are the things that can add significant expense to a refurbishment project and/or that may make the property unsuitable, such as:

- Can all prospective bedrooms be easily accessed from communal areas?
- Are there any wall cracks wider than a 10p coin? That often indicates significant movement, possibly subsidence.
- Which side/end of the house is the plumbing currently on? Extending an existing plumbing system or installing a completely new one can be major works.
- Does the roof look in reasonable condition and is the chimney stack straight?
- Are many of the windows single-glazed?
- Is there a connection to a telephone exchange?

Have a good look round outside, checking for anything you couldn't see when you did your drive-by and look at any potential for building or extension – even if you're not planning anything at the moment, you might want to in the future.

A bit of advice for when you're looking at all this on your first visit is not to say too much about your plans to the vendor. Most of the properties you'll be looking at will be someone's home that they've loved and raised a family in, and the last thing they want to hear is that you're planning on ripping out walls and fixtures, painting over all their lovely décor and installing fire doors. Some vendors can get very offended and if they think you're only interested in how much profit you can make, it will only make negotiations harder down the line. Less is more in this case.

If you think you might be interested, have a brief chat to the vendor to find out their situation – why they're moving and their ideal timescale – as that'll give you an idea of whether it'll fit with your plans and, more importantly, how far you might be able to negotiate on the price.

## Second viewing

If a property stood up to your initial financial analysis, you liked the look of it on the first viewing and it compares favourably with the other contenders, book a second viewing. When you call to book, confirm with the agent that you've understood the vendor's situation correctly and tell them you'd like to take your time on this viewing. Call your builder and ask if he'll go along with you to highlight any potential issues he sees and also recommend and estimate the cost of any works. If your builder isn't able to go with you, try to take someone else who can be a second pair of eyes – you can research approximate costs later.

Go through each room carefully and make a list of all the refurbishment work you'll need to do. If the vendor's there, ask them when the plumbing and heating systems were installed and last serviced and how old the electrics are. Essentially, by the time you leave this second viewing, you should have a very good idea of how much you're going to have to do to get the property ready to rent.

## Detailed financial analysis

This is the last step before you decide whether to make an offer and is really about confirming the price at which the deal stacks up for you.

Double-check you've factored in all the refurbishment items and got realistic estimates/costs for carrying out the work, then triple-check you've included all the other costs associated with the purchase and getting the property ready to rent. Check the ongoing monthly cost estimates, work the numbers on an average income situation (although you should be confident you can achieve well above average income!) and then also make sure you know what your 'break even' point would be as well as the maximum you can afford to pay.

You're almost ready to put together your offer…

# Checklist

## Researching and identifying properties

Have you done all these things?

### Online research

- ☐ Established which local areas have the best demand v supply ratio for rooms
- ☐ Revisited local area research for future plans
- ☐ Confirmed specific tenant preferences for location and facilities
- ☐ Understand local market house price performance and established 'fair' purchase prices
- ☐ Have a good idea of current supply and demand for properties for sale
- ☐ Created a detailed spreadsheet to analyse costs, income and expenditure and KPIs
- ☐ Shortlisted at least 10 properties

### Viewings

- ☐ Driven past before booking viewing
- ☐ Met with agent before viewing, to discuss requirements in detail
- ☐ Viewed once, checking for overall suitability and any major issues

- [ ] Established vendor's situation and timescale
- [ ] Discarded unsuitable properties and given agents feedback
- [ ] Viewed for a second time, preferably with a builder, and made detailed notes

## Decision making

- [ ] 'Stress-tested' figures

# Chapter 8

# Making an offer

Before you make an offer, you need to make sure everything's in place, ready to proceed, and that you put together your offer in such a way that it has the best chance of being accepted.

Take the details of the property or properties you're satisfied will make good investments, along with your financial analysis figures, to your broker. They won't be able to make any promises, but should be confident you'll be able to secure financing for the purchase. People talk about 'agreements in principle', but the reality is that until you put in a formal application and the mortgage valuation has been carried out, there's no cast-iron guarantee that you'll get a mortgage. This is just one instance when you'll really see the benefit of having a specialist broker who has excellent relationships with lenders.

Instruct your solicitor (if you haven't already) and make sure you give them everything they need to be able to act for you – including documents that confirm your identity and any other instruction paperwork they require you to sign.

The other professional you'll need to source is a chartered surveyor who's accredited by the Royal Institution of Chartered Surveyors (RICS). Your mortgage lender will carry out a valuation, but you may need to instruct a Homebuyer's Report or Building Survey to get a more detailed report on the fabric of the property.

## What should your offer be?

By now you'll have a very good idea of: a) what you think the property is really worth, b) the figure at which it works best for you without being a 'silly offer' and, c) how flexible the vendor is likely to be - and now it's a case of juggling those things and putting together a reasonable offer.

Yes, every property has a value, but there's also a value to time. You need to be able to judge your vendor, understand their position and then negotiate a price that means you feel you have a good deal, and so do they. If their time pressure is greater than their need to hold out for more money, and you can help them move on without ripping them off, that's a win/win situation. Similarly, if the vendors want to wait until they've found somewhere to move on to, and you decide you can work to a longer timescale, that also has a value.

When you put forward your offer, it's best to do it in person, either to the vendor or to the agent:

- Explain why you're making the offer that you are (local research on sold prices, level at which your business

model works, etc.)
- Confirm your position: that your broker and legal representative are ready to act for you
- Suggest a timescale
- Confirm everything in writing

If the offer is significantly lower than the asking price, you don't want the vendors to be offended, so do make it clear to them that you're basing your offer on the price that works business-wise – you're not suggesting their home is vastly overpriced!

And one very important piece of advice: be sure you're prepared to proceed with this purchase, because once your offer has been accepted – regardless of the fact that you're not under any legal obligation – you've made a verbal agreement. In my opinion, that morally obliges you to see the deal through (unless, of course, you get an adverse survey that significantly affects the property's value). I said it earlier: your reputation is everything and you certainly don't want to become known as someone who makes casual offers or pulls out of deals, especially in the area where you live and socialise.

*A good reputation can open doors;*
*a bad reputation will close many more.*

## If your offer's rejected...

...never go back to the agent immediately – take some time to reconsider the figures and your options. This is why it's a good idea to view ten properties initially: assuming you researched them properly before viewing, you should end up with two or three you'd be happy to proceed on. Always know your limit and be prepared to walk away from a deal if it gets too expensive or the vendors get too vague on the timescale. Your investment business plan will be based on a certain number of acquisitions a year and it's rare that you're able to be completely flexible on completion dates.

The first thing to consider is whether you're prepared to increase your offer. If so, you might choose to make it conditional, such as offering X amount more, provided completion takes place on or before X date.

If you're not prepared to pay any more, then explain why not and say you'll leave the offer on the table for a certain length of time (I usually give them a week), in case the vendor decides to reconsider.

## If your offer's accepted...

Have a small celebration! Then you'll need to be like the conductor of an orchestra for the next few months, making sure your ducks stay in line.

Get things moving with your mortgage broker, who will make sure the lender instructs the valuation as soon as possible, and have your solicitor confirm to you that they've agreed the timescale with the vendor's solicitor. Most solicitors will be resistant to agreeing exchange and completion dates at such an early stage in the process, which is why you need to work with a buy to let specialist who understands the importance of keeping your plans on track. It's also worth checking out whether you can gain access to the property to start refurbishment work before completion. Most of the time this won't be possible, but there are exceptions and it's worth asking, as every day the property is untenanted, you're funding the mortgage repayment yourself.

You may think the property is completely sound, especially if you've had your builder give it the once-over, but for the sake of around £500, I'd rather instruct a Building Survey and find out about any hidden problems before my refurbishment team find them or – even worse – serious problems emerge once the property's tenanted.

You also need to meet with your project manager, go through the refurbishment plan (see the next chapter) and ask him to make sure his team will be available to start as soon as the purchase completes.

Speak to your local council planning department about your plans for refurbishing the property so you can make sure you're compliant with building regulations before work starts (your project manager may do this for you). Also, if you've been told you don't need either planning permission or a licence to let this property as an HMO, ask them to confirm it in writing. If you do need to apply for either one, then make sure you do that as soon as possible.

Complete, sign and return all paperwork you receive from your broker and legal representative right away and make sure deposit funds and fee and disbursement payments are all where they're supposed to be in good time. Although the estate agent (or their sales progression department) will be contacting your legal representative for updates on a regular basis, it's a good idea to speak to them yourself every now and then. Ideally, liaise with the vendor directly, so you can reassure them that everything's going smoothly and arrange any extra visits to the property you might need.

And, importantly, speak to a buy to let landlord insurance specialist – your mortgage broker will probably have a recommendation – to make sure you'll have the right insurance in place not only when you take ownership of the property, but when your tenants move in.

While every purchase is different, and the timescales can vary wildly, depending on the vendor's position and your own situation, you should expect the process, from offer to completion, to take around three months. Your conveyancer will be able to provide you with information about each step involved – familiarize yourself with it, so that you can not only make sure you're doing everything you need to, but also know where the other parties involved should be with their paperwork.

# Checklist

# Making an offer and buying a property

Have you done all these things?

## Preparation
- ☐ Established vendor's position
- ☐ Met with broker and gained assurance you'll be able to finance the purchase
- ☐ Instructed solicitor to act for you
- ☐ Understood the steps involved in the conveyancing process
- ☐ Found a good local chartered surveyor

## Making the offer
- ☐ Put it forward in person – to vendor or agent
- ☐ Confirmed in writing: offer amount, your position, suggested timescale

## Offer accepted
- ☐ Make sure mortgage broker moves things along as quickly as possible
- ☐ Confirm timescales with solicitors
- ☐ Ask about gaining access before completion
- ☐ Instruct Building Survey

☐ Consult with project manager

☐ Speak with planning department of local council

☐ Sign all mortgage paperwork

☐ Sign purchase contract

☐ Get buildings insurance in place

☐ Transfer completion monies to solicitor

☐ Secure quotes for comprehensive landlord insurance

# Chapter 9

# Refurbishment

Assuming everything goes smoothly with the purchase, you should be able to collect the keys around lunchtime on day of completion. You now need to do everything you can to get paying tenants happily settled in their rooms as soon as possible, and that relies on meticulous planning. If you plan well and there are no unforeseen delays, I'd say you should be able to complete a fairly comprehensive refurbishment (gutting, updating plumbing and electrics, refitting bathrooms and kitchen, then decorating) in around four to six weeks.

Before you do anything else, go and introduce yourself to the neighbours and let them know that there will be work going on for roughly the next 4 weeks (or however long). Reassure them about what you're doing, and give them your contact details, so they can get in touch if they have any issues or concerns. Again, this business is all about relationships and taking the initiative in this way will be much appreciated.

# Your refurbishment plan

Meet your project manager and his team on site to confirm exactly what needs to be done, map out floor plans and agree an achievable timescale. Ask them to supply written quotes and you might want to put together some kind of incentive scheme – perhaps that you withhold a percentage of the invoice until you're satisfied there aren't any 'snagging' issues after completion of the project, or a bonus for bringing it in on time and to standard.

All the contractors you engage MUST have the correct liability insurance and they should also be suitably accredited and/or members of relevant trade associations or bodies (see Chapter 6).

You then need to sit down and create a detailed written plan (I find a spreadsheet is best) that includes:

- every job required, broken down by room
- the contractor required for each job
- a schedule of works, showing the length of time each job will take
- all health and safety elements
- dates and times of deliveries of supplies/materials from external suppliers/contractors, e.g. carpet fitter
- Dates/stages when you'll need to adjust your insurance, depending on when the property's furnished and occupied

Go through it carefully with your project manager to make sure you haven't missed anything, and that he's also happy his team can work to the final schedule.

It takes a fair amount of work the first time you put one together, but if you take time to get it right, you'll have a great template for all future projects. I share mine on a cloud-based system so that everyone involved in the project can see exactly what stage we're at and I liaise regularly with my project manager in case any of the plans need revising as we go along. Also remember to update your financial analysis spreadsheet if any of the refurbishment costs change.

## Health & Safety

Before you start any renovation or refurbishment, you must make sure your planned work is going to comply with Building Regulations. You should already have checked this out with the local council; if you haven't, then don't start any works until you have, or there may be penalties.

Then, even though you may be happy that you understand your health and safety responsibilities, it's a good idea to ask the local council Housing Standards Officer and Community Safety Adviser (or similar from the Fire Service) to come to the property while you're refurbishing it. You can explain to them exactly what you're doing, and make sure they're happy with your plans. You don't have to pay for this, and it avoids you having to possibly make changes at a later date. Particular points to query with them are:

## Housing Standards Officer

- Are the kitchen (particularly cooking) facilities suitable for the number of people?
- Are the room sizes acceptable (especially important if you're creating new rooms by putting up stud walls)?
- Are the proposed bathroom facilities sufficient?
- Are there any other facilities I should provide that I've missed?

## Community Safety Adviser

- Is the fire alarm system (or smoke detectors) I'm intending to install acceptable?
- Do I need to put up fire exit signs?
- Are the fire escapes (which can simply be ground-floor windows that open wide enough and at the right height) acceptable?
- Where do I need fire doors?
- What fire safety equipment do I need in the kitchen? (usually extinguisher and blanket)
- Do I need any other fire extinguishers?
- What lock systems do I need on fire escape routes? (Your front and all other door/s must be able to be opened from the inside without a key.)

In terms of fire regulations, even if you're not licensable, it's sensible to ask a professional for their opinion on what's a reasonable level of safety.

Personally, I choose to err on the side of caution with health and safety. As I said earlier in the book, you have a duty of care to the people living in your HMO and need to take all reasonable steps to ensure they don't come to any harm.

Ask both the Housing Standards Officer and Community Safety Adviser if they'll come back once the refurbishment is complete and confirm their findings in writing. They may not – sometimes verbal advice is all they're prepared to give – but you should also ask one of them if they'd be happy to go through the fire risk assessment form for you. Again, they may not, but it's something that a suitably qualified professional should carry out, as they're better placed than you are to assess levels of risk. You may have to pay a Fire Risk Assessor to complete it for you, which can cost anywhere between £100 and £300 – not a great deal, in the grand scheme of things – and you can easily find a local assessor online.

Security options for room doors vary greatly, from Yale locks to code entry panels; you can also reduce the number of different keys you and/or your property manager have to hold. It's entirely up to you, but bear in mind that tenants will occasionally lose keys, lock themselves out and sometimes move out of the property without returning their keys, so you need to be able to gain entry and re-secure the property easily. Ask around at your local landlords association, and see what other people find works best, but if you do use keys, particularly for the main front door, I'd recommend you pick a system that gives you full control over who can duplicate them.

## 'Interior design'

This is where you need to strike the right balance between finish and budget. Your décor, fixtures, fittings and furnishings need to be hard wearing, modern and visually appealing, while staying within budget. An average of six people coming and going all the time means that, no matter how well you start out, your property is going to suffer quite a high level of wear and tear, so make sure carpets don't show dirt and stains easily, pick paint colours that will always be readily available, so that walls and paintwork will be easy to touch up, and make sure the kitchen and bathrooms are easy to keep clean. Most of this is common sense!

It's impossible to be prescriptive on cost, but I'd suggest you shouldn't spend more than £600 on furnishing each bedroom and make sure the furniture you buy for the communal areas is built to last...on the understanding that you'll probably have to replace most items every five years or so.

In terms of where you get the furniture from, it's a bit like finding good local contractors – there'll be somewhere in your area that deals in low-cost, sturdy furnishings, so ask around your team and other landlords. I have a great supplier, who now knows exactly what I need and can kit out whole houses for me, as well as replace individual pieces of furniture very quickly.

**Minimum furnishing requirements:**

| | |
|---|---|
| Bedrooms: | Bed with mattress, wardrobe, chest of drawers, curtain/blind |
| Living room: | Sofa/s and/or chairs (seating for at least 4 people), table, television & DVD player |
| Kitchen/utility: | Large fridge (6 shelves min), large freezer (6 drawers min), good-sized oven and hob, washing machine, adequate drying facilities (either a coin-operated tumble dryer or space for drying racks). Some landlords also install a dishwasher, but it's not essential. |

You then need to stock the kitchen with everything you'd expect to find there - crockery, cutlery, glassware, cookware, utensils, kettle, toaster, microwave, etc. - and have an iron, ironing board and vacuum cleaner stored somewhere in the property. Essentially, all the tenants should need to provide for themselves is bedding and towels.

# Finishing off and getting 'ready to rent'

Once the property is completely refurbished and furnished:

- Make sure your gas & electric checks have been carried out and display the certificates in the property – the kitchen is usually the best place
- Have the Fire Risk Assessment carried out by a suitably qualified professional, and take any recommended steps
- Install wireless broadband, making sure there's sufficient bandwidth allowance to handle six people online at the same time
- Get the property thoroughly cleaned and arrange for an on-going cleaning service to take care of the communal areas – I'd suggest at least once a week
- Have a pinboard in the hallway or other communal area that clearly displays:
  - fire escape information
  - the property manager's information
  - what to do / who to call in case of an emergency
  - refuse & recycling calendar
  - issue log, for your manager to see
- Make sure you have enough keys cut. As well as supplying the tenants with keys for the front door(s) and their rooms, if necessary, both you and your property manager should hold a full set and you're likely to need additional copies of at least the front door(s) for your cleaner and handyman, plus a set to give out to contractors.

- Ensure you've documented everything that's been done, and carefully filed all your receipts, as a lot of the work may be tax deductible
- Go back to the neighbours to let them know that work's finished, and thank them for their patience

Then stand back and see what finishing touches you need. Put up a few pictures in the communal areas, and also a couple of mirrors, which can really lighten up a dark hallway or landing. Remember that the doors to the bedrooms will be shut all the time, and, particularly downstairs, where you've used what used to be reception rooms as bedrooms, that this can make the house quite gloomy. A mirror will reflect what light there is, and add a bit of depth to narrower areas.

And, lastly, while it's still looking brand new and perfect, try to choose a sunny day and take as many pictures as you can to use in your advertising – at least one of each room, including the bathrooms. More and more landlords are also making video 'tours' of their properties, so, if you can, do that as well. Take a few props to the house (bedding, lamps, plants, flowers, fruit bowls, etc.) to make it look homely, and make sure you get all the shots you need, because once tenants have moved in, it'll never look quite like that again!

# Checklist

# The refurbishment process

Have you done all these things?

## Preparation

- ☐ Licensing secured (if required)
- ☐ Planning secured (if required)
- ☐ Compliance with Building Regulations established
- ☐ Informed neighbours about planned work / timescale
- ☐ Got written quotes from contractors
- ☐ Appointed a Project Manager
- ☐ Agreed an incentive / bonus scheme
- ☐ Created a detailed refurbishment plan

## Health & Safety

- ☐ Met with Housing Standards Officer at the property
- ☐ Met with Community Safety Advisor from the fire service at the property
- ☐ Carried out Fire Risk Assessment
- ☐ Got all gas & electric checks and certification
- ☐ Chosen key system

## Decorating & furnishing

- ☐ Planned a neutral décor

- ☐ Found hard wearing fixtures & fittings supplier/s
- ☐ Found a good local furniture supplier

## Finishing off...

- ☐ Installed wireless broadband
- ☐ Found cost-effective energy supplier/s
- ☐ Had the property thoroughly cleaned
- ☐ Clearly displayed house, safety and local information for tenants
- ☐ Cut enough keys
- ☐ Put in 'finishing touches'
- ☐ Taken photos (and video)

# Chapter 10

# Getting tenants into your rooms

## Part one: marketing your property

This is only a short section, because it's really not that complicated! There's the advertising and then the viewings and, provided your advert is good, and you 'vet' your enquiries properly, it shouldn't take very long to fill your rooms, particularly when the property is newly refurbished.

One bit of advice I'd particularly highlight is that there's no reason why you can't start marketing the property while the refurbishment is still going on. Obviously, wait until the walls have been plastered and there aren't wires dangling everywhere, so that it's completely safe, but taking enquiries a week or so before you're actually ready to rent can sometimes mean you already have tenants ready to move in on the day the work's finished. The downside is that you won't be able to post any internal photos on the advert, but don't underestimate the attraction of the prospect of fresh paint and a brand-new boiler!

# Where to advertise

The vast majority of your target audience - young professionals - will certainly be searching online on SpareRoom, EasyRoommate and Gumtree. It's not cheap to keep adverts running and well-promoted, so while you're starting out, I'd suggest only advertising on one of those sites and doing it properly. Go back to your research, and see if one site shows a greater demand than the other, in terms of 'room wanted' adverts for your area, but SpareRoom is probably the best in your option currently. Put up as many pictures as you can, and, if you've been able to take video footage, put that up as well. The more of your property prospective tenants can see in the advertising, the more likely they are to feel positive about viewing.

You might decide to also try the local newspaper, but that can be quite expensive, so make sure you carefully track how many enquiries you get, and the quality of them, to see if it's really worthwhile continuing. I've certainly found that I get a high number of unsuitable tenants calling from newspaper adverts – unemployed, on benefits or with a child – and it wastes time having to deal with these enquiries.

If you have a hospital close by, see if the HR department will take your details and put an advert up on their intranet – sometimes larger businesses will also do this – but they may only work with you if you are a locally accredited landlord. If you haven't done so already, look into accreditation schemes, and see if you can enrol.

# Handling enquiries

When you're first starting out, it's important to track where your enquiries are coming from, how many turn into viewings and how many of those turn into lets. You need to know which adverts are generating the right quality of responses so that you can focus on those in future.

Make sure you always take a full name and number, ask where they saw the advert, establish that they're in employment, and find out when they need a room, and for how long. You can then offer to show them the property.

# 'Selling' your rooms

You're not just marketing the property when you conduct a viewing as a landlord; you're marketing yourself. I've heard of people deciding not to take a room, not because there was anything wrong with the accommodation, but because they were put off by how the landlord behaved with them, so be aware of how you're coming across!

If they're keen to take one of the rooms and you're happy to accept them, you can then confirm the date they'd like it and the price, take a holding fee and make arrangements with them for moving in. Sometimes the first person to view a room will take it, but I'd say, on average, you need to conduct three viewings to secure a tenant.

What I would say is: trust your gut. If, while you're showing someone around, you feel unsure about them – for any reason, – then don't hesitate to put them off. The last thing you need is a troublesome tenant who either doesn't get on with the other house sharers or who stops paying rent, so don't feel bad about turning them down. Never accept a tenant you're not sure about, just because you want to fill the room – another tenant will come along soon enough.

## Part two: checking your tenant out and checking them in

### Referencing

The degree to which you reference your prospective tenant may be dictated by your mortgage lender, but may be entirely your decision.

If I was renting out a whole property on a single AST for at least six months, then I'd certainly carry out credit checks and take up references, but when someone's only renting a room in a house, it seems a bit of a waste of time. I take a month's deposit, ask them to complete a personal information form, and trust my instincts.

You can take a copy of their passport or driving license (but check how data protection regulations may affect you), and speak to their employer to confirm their status, but further referencing is simply not a good use of your time, and doesn't stop people disappearing without paying their rent. If you're in the HMO business, you have to accept that at some point you will be ripped off by a tenant, but it doesn't happen very often.

## Before check in

Once you've received the holding fee from your prospective tenant, you can start preparing the AST. Calculate the deposit still owed and the remaining rent for the current month and make sure that the tenant is clear on the amount they have to either bring with them in cash on the day they move in, or transfer in advance.

The two other things it's important to make clear in advance are:
1. individuals' belongings are not covered by your insurance, so the tenant must make their own arrangements if they want cover
2. the TV licence only covers the communal area, so if the tenant wants to have a TV in their room, they're responsible for arranging their own licence.

## Check in

If, for any reason, the tenant doesn't settle the full amount due, don't check them in, and tell them they'll have to rearrange for another day, once they do have all the money. As a general rule, when room renters fall behind with their payment, they rarely get back on track, so you absolutely don't want to start like that.

Assuming the money side is fine, go through the agreement, highlighting any particularly relevant conditions and restrictions, such as no smoking, notice periods and room access. Sign two copies of the agreement and have the tenant do the same. Confirm the monthly rent and give them a standing order form with your bank details on, for future payments. Always ask your tenants to pay by standing order – it's quick, easy, and it means there is a clear record on your bank statement. You can waste a lot of time trying to identify cash payments, sometimes not quite for the full amount, that appear in your bank without any reference.

Lastly, there's the inventory. Using an independent inventory clerk when it's only a room check in isn't really worth the cost, although you may want to use a clerk the first time so that you have a professional template. I now use an app on my tablet computer that allows me to take lots of photos and add written descriptions, then I email the whole document to the tenant.

Whatever you decide, you need to make sure you've detailed the condition of the ceiling, walls, floor/carpet, fixtures and fittings and all the contents. Any damage must be clearly specified, and I'd suggest you take a photograph of anything significant, so there's no argument at a later date. Also note on the inventory how many keys the tenant has been given and make sure you both sign the document. You must also give the tenant information on the scheme you're using to protect their deposit.

After you've checked them in and made sure they know where everything is and how white goods, etc. work, make sure you file all the paperwork, update your records and lodge their deposit funds with your chosen deposit protection scheme.

# Checklist

# Filling your rooms

Have you done all these things?

## Marketing

- ☐ Started as early as possible
- ☐ Listed rooms on spareroom.co.uk (and possibly also uk.easyroommate.com and gumtree.com)
- ☐ Identified other advertising outlets that work well locally
- ☐ Set up a system for tracking enquiries

## Checking in

- ☐ Taken holding fee
- ☐ Carried out referencing / identity checks
- ☐ Agreed move-in monies
- ☐ Gone through AST with tenant
- ☐ Taken an inventory
- ☐ Settled tenant in
- ☐ Filed paperwork

# PART THREE:
# MANAGING
# YOUR INVESTMENT

# Chapter 11

# Managing your HMO

Once your property is tenanted, it needs managing – and HMOs more than any other kind of buy to let – so the key to doing it successfully is organisation. As your business grows, you'll be able to bring on staff to deal with the day-to-day management, but chances are you'll be doing it yourself in the beginning.

## Your maintenance team

Having a good team of contractors is key to managing maintenance issues and making sure they don't escalate into major problems. When little things aren't fixed and tenants feel they're being ignored, it creates a lot of bad feeling, so you need to know your team will act quickly.

One of the most useful people to be able to call on is a really good handyman, who can take care of all sorts of jobs around the property, and also be the first port of call if there's a problem with the boiler or electrics, rather than you incurring a callout charge from your plumber or electrician. Tenants tend to be quick to complain without having a proper look at the problem, and it's often nowhere near as big an issue as they reported, or something they've inadvertently done, like turning off an electric oven at the mains socket.

Even if there is a serious problem and your plumber or electrician can't get to the property until the next day, sending your handyman round to give the tenants peace of mind that something's being done usually goes a long way towards keeping them happy.

And you can keep your team happy by paying them quickly. One of the biggest complaints you hear from self-employed contractors is about clients taking too long to settle invoices. If they know that you'll always pay when you say you will, and you don't mess them around, they'll be loyal to you. Thank them for jobs well done and make sure you remember them at Christmas time.

## Regular checks

There are a number of checks that have to be carried out at regular intervals, so you need to set up some kind of diary alert to make sure you don't miss them:

- **Routine inspections.** You'll be seeing some of the property on a reasonably regular basis, as you check tenants in and out and deal with any other issues, but you should make formal inspections of the whole property at least twice a year. You'll need to give the tenants at least 24 hours' written notice that you're going to be entering their rooms, and try to do it at a time when they're not there, so you're not disturbing them. Note anything that needs updating, repairing, replacing or replenishing, so you can schedule the work, e.g. repainting a hallway or buying some more plates. Write to the tenants to let them know your findings, tell them about any work that's going to be taking place, and remind them of their obligations if any clauses in the agreement appear to have been violated, e.g. smoking in the property.

- **Fire alarm testing.** You need to test your fire alarm system regularly, note down the date and results of the test and keep the record separately from the property.
- **Gas safety check.** This must be carried out annually by a Gas Safe registered engineer, and the new certificate displayed in the property.
- **PA Test.** All electrical portable appliances (kettle, fridge, TV, etc.) must be tested annually by a qualified engineer.

## Change-overs

You need to have a slick system in place for when one tenant moves out and another moves in, as it can sometimes happen on the same day. The outgoing tenant needs to be checked out against the move-in inventory, then the room needs to be cleaned and made ready for the incoming tenant, who must be checked in with a new AST and inventory. Again, it's down to systemisation, preparation and having a team you can rely on to get things done at the right time.

1. When notice is given, diarise move-out day
2. Confirm with tenant that viewings will be taking place and that they'll vacate the room by 12 noon on their last day
3. Check room to estimate any repairs/updating that will be needed
4. Confirm handyman (if necessary) for 12 noon on changeover day and cleaner for 2/3pm
5. Re-advertise the room
6. Confirm with new tenant that they can move in after 5pm
7. Prepare new AST and inventory
8. Take original inventory to morning checkout, go through it with tenant, agree any deductions from the deposit, take back keys and note a forwarding address
9. Handyman & cleaner prepare room
10. Check in new tenant with balance of move-in monies, AST, inventory and keys
11. Return deposit to former tenant and lodge deposit for new tenant

Obviously, if there are any serious repairs to be carried out, you might need to postpone the move in for a day, or agree with the new tenant what work will be carried out and when.

Even with the best preparation in the world, this won't always run like clockwork – some people are late, others are early – but I've never had any major issues. People are, for the most part, reasonable, and small delays can usually be smoothed over.

## Refreshing and updating the property

It's generally the case that when you put someone in a nice environment, they'll treat it nicely. Conversely, if you put a tenant into a shabby property that looks as though you don't really care about it – maybe because you're not the one who has to live in it – they're not going to bother looking after it either.

You'll pick up things that need doing when you carry out your quarterly or six-monthly property inspections, but ask your property manager, cleaner and handyman to let you know if they think something could do with refreshing or replacing while they're going about their business in the meantime. Sometimes paintwork needs a touch up, the bathroom could do with a new shower curtain or a carpet would benefit from some professional cleaning. If you can make on-going improvements before the tenants even notice or think about mentioning them, they'll really appreciate it and, as well as treating the property well, they'll be less likely to complain about little things.

It's not just décor – refresh your appliances as well. If you buy the more budget-range kettles, toasters and microwaves, they may not be as hard-wearing as more expensive models, but you can afford to throw them out and buy new ones every couple of years. Regardless of how much you've spent on a kitchen appliance and how hard-wearing it is, when six people are regularly using it, it suffers wear and tear and starts to look shabby.

And it's the same with larger items of furniture. Budget on the basis that you'll probably replace sofas and armchairs every five or six years because, while they might still be usable, they'll be looking tired. If you want to keep charging top-level rents as more recently refurbished properties (including some of your own!) come on to the lettings market, you have to keep your HMO looking smart.

## Handling tenant issues

Following on from what I said above, if you treat tenants with respect, they'll usually reciprocate. Of course, there will always be the occasional problem tenant, but there's a lot you can do to mitigate the chances of issues flaring up or non-payment of rent.

It really comes down to communication and ensuring the tenants feel they're being listened to – don't ever ignore a complaint. If it's a maintenance issue they're complaining about, then your contractors should be able to deal with that fairly quickly. If they can't, find out when they will be able to get to the property, and let the tenants know.

When a tenant is either consistently late paying their rent each month or has stopped paying altogether, it's important you don't let yourself get caught up in any sob-stories. This is business - you're not running a charity – and the tenant signed an agreement to the effect that they would pay their rent on time every month. Give them a few days to pay everything they owe, then issue them with a Section 8 Notice to Quit and start advertising their room. Nine times out of ten, this results in the tenant leaving without any further discussion (and also without paying the rent they owe – but their deposit should go some way to reimbursing you for the lost rent), but very occasionally they'll dig their heels in, seek advice from an organisation such as Shelter, and refuse to leave. In that case, you can try to reason with them and assure them that if they leave you won't pursue them for what they owe; if that doesn't work, you'll have to begin eviction proceedings.

I'd strongly advise you consider using the services of an eviction specialist (or solicitor), rather than trying to handle it yourself. There is a particular order to the paperwork and a specific way things need to be done, and if you get one of the elements wrong, the tenant could claim illegal eviction, and you could be forced to begin the process all over again. For the amount they cost, eviction specialists are worth every penny. I should stress, though, it's extremely rare for a tenant in an HMO to see this all the way through to court – they're far more likely to back down and leave when they realise you're serious about the eviction proceedings.

What's sometimes more difficult to deal with is a serious problem between two or more of the house sharers. One of the most common complaints you'll get is about noise – one tenant being inconsiderate and repeatedly shouting, crashing about or playing loud music very late at night, disturbing other tenants. If it's several against one, then you can go ahead and give the culprit a warning about breaking the terms of their agreement, but if it's just one person's word against another, you can't be biased.

Issues like that can self-regulate – i.e. the tenant tones down their behaviour or chooses to leave as they're not getting on with the rest of the house – or the problem may need to be escalated. Don't hesitate to call the police if you're at all concerned about things getting out of control, and make sure your tenants know they can do the same. That might sound extreme, but you're a professional landlord, not there to arbitrate in personal disputes or take on someone who's causing a disturbance and possibly breaking the law. Having the police deal with these issues will ensure you and your other tenants aren't endangering your own safety, and make it clear to everyone that such behaviour won't be tolerated.

# Checklist

# Property Management

Have you done all these things?

- ☐ Have a good team of reliable contractors who'll act quickly
- ☐ Set up system for tracking regular checks
- ☐ Systemised the changeover process
- ☐ Recorded age and condition of all furnishings and white goods and prepared to update/replace them every 5 years or so
- ☐ Set up issue log for tenant complaints

# Chapter 12

# Managing your business

An HMO generates a lot of paperwork and relies on constant figure tracking and analysis, so it's imperative you have a good administration system and a good administrator to manage it. If that's not your forte, then employ someone who *can* keep on top of everything for you.

## General administration

Filing paperwork correctly so it can be located when needed is something of a skill and if you don't do it every one or two days as your business grows, you can easily get in a mess (although some of this paperwork can be 'off-loaded' to a bookkeeper periodically). These are just some of the things you'll need to file:

- Purchase and mortgage documentation
- Refurbishment invoices and receipts
- Guarantees
- Utility bills
- Gas and electric certificates

- Tenant paperwork
- Rent receipts
- Bank statements
- Receipts for expenses
- On-going maintenance invoices

...and the list goes on.

Given that you're going to have an average of two tenants checking in and out of each room every year, you also need a good 'dead filing' system for archiving paperwork. As the number of properties you own grows, so does the paperwork, and you might quickly find that the area you originally designated as office space is a bit small! Landlords tend to start in a small box room, progress to converting the garage into an office, then realise they need other premises, particularly when they start taking on staff and needing more office equipment, such as better printers, a photocopier, shredder, etc.

## KPIs

I said in Chapter 2 that I focus on three main things - profit, ROI and yield - all of which I'm constantly trying to maximize. Having systemised the business and taken on capable staff to essentially run the day-to-day operation, I'm free to do what I'm best at: ensure my investments give the best possible return.

# Increasing profit

There are only two ways you can increase monthly profit: secure more rental income or/and reduce costs. Let's start with the slightly more straightforward one. You should have a complete breakdown of your costs on your main viability analysis spreadsheet, so it's simply a case of working through those and seeing if any reductions can be made, without asking anyone on your maintenance team to take a pay cut!

Your biggest monthly outgoing is always going to be your mortgage, but the costs of switching to a new product can be relatively large, so it's not something I do very often. I have a good relationship with my broker and am confident they're keeping an eye out for a deal worthwhile taking. What you need to focus on yourself are utility and telecom service providers and your insurance provider, and it really is worth getting new quotes every few months and regularly switching to get the best deals. A few pounds saved every month, across all the properties in your portfolio, can stack up to a significant amount every year.

Also keep an eye on your maintenance bills for repairing white goods, and make sure you don't end up spending more on fixing them than they're worth. Again, having a good supplier that you can trust to be honest with you about this is a big help. And don't be afraid to ask for discounts for buying multiple units. When suppliers know you're a landlord who's likely to be able to give them regular, on-going business, there are usually deals to be done with them.

When it comes to securing more rental income, there are three things I look at: increasing rents, increasing occupancy levels and renting things other than simply bedrooms:

1. **Increasing rents.** This isn't something you can – or should – do just because you think you can. While tenants will pay the best market rents for the best rooms, you need to make sure you don't price yourself out of the market. Keep an eye on what the competition is offering and charging because, while your refurbishment and furnishing might have made your property one of the best in the area when you started out, landlords are providing better and better quality accommodation as time goes on. At the same time, you must try to ensure you increase your rents at least in line with inflation, otherwise your profits are decreasing in real terms. It's a tricky line to walk, though, because you can only charge what people are willing to pay. My advice is to make sure you track the top, bottom and average rents in the area and be aware of inflation, so that you're always able to compare your returns accurately with both local averages and other investments.

2. **Increasing occupancy levels.** It's virtually impossible to consistently achieve 100% occupancy, but you should certainly be averaging at least 95%. As I've already said, voids will make a big impact on your profit, so you must do everything you can to avoid them. Retaining tenants is the cheapest and easiest solution, so make sure you fix

problems quickly, take care of the property, and have a good relationship with your tenants, so they don't have any reason to leave your property for someone else's. People always move on at some point, but try to keep each tenant for at least 6 months. When tenants do leave, try to have someone ready to move in right away, even if it means taking slightly less rent. That might be contradicting the last point (!), but you have to consider the implications of having an empty room for a week or two, 'losing' you rent, versus lowering the price by £5 or even £10 a week. It's almost always worth the slight reduction, not only in term of immediate rental income gained, but also because if you have rooms standing empty, existing tenants might start to feel there's something wrong with the property, and there's better to be had elsewhere.

3. **Renting out other things.** I know several landlords who make extra money from renting out garages and box rooms that are too small to use as bedrooms. That might be renting to current tenants or to other people - if something like a garage or storage unit is separate from the house. You can also generate additional income through having coin-operated washing machines and tumble dryers, although this has to be considered against the rent tenants are already paying for facilities. The point is, think laterally and make sure you're maximizing the potential of every square foot you've invested in.

## Return On Investment

Increased income and reducing costs, as outlined above, will result in a better ROI, but you should also periodically look at the amount of capital tied up in each property and assess whether it might be worth releasing some of it. Back in the early 2000s, when the market was hurtling up, it was often possible to remortgage and release all the capital you'd originally put in – and then some. With the market the way it is at the moment, you're not going to be able to do that, but you could still get some money out after a few years.

In order to work out whether that's a viable and good investment move, your analysis spreadsheet needs to be up to date and set up with the correct formulae so you can immediately see:

1. With the increased mortgage cost, am I still achieving the monthly cash flow I need?
2. Will I be able to invest the money released in such a way that it gives a better return?
3. What is the cost (fees and other charges) of facilitating the equity release?

This is where, again, you'll realise the benefit of having a financial advisor who is also a property investor, because they'll be able to quickly work the figures, understand exactly what it is you need to consider and give you informed, relevant advice. Your knee-jerk reaction might be to say that you don't want to increase your mortgage costs because you need the monthly cash flow for income, but what if you could make as much or even more overall from reinvesting some of the capital in another property or even a different investment vehicle?

Ultimately, if you can get to the point where you have none of your own money invested in a property that's still giving you some monthly income, while also appreciating in value, you'll be getting an infinite return on investment.

## Yield

Yield is the figure that allows you to see whether you're investing in the right kind of property – both in terms of type and location; gross yield is the rental income as a percentage of the property's value, and net yield is the profit as a percentage of value. I almost never look at other people's gross yield, because it doesn't take into account either how much money is invested or any costs, so is pretty meaningless when you're trying to compare two investments.

For example, because rental income is two to three times higher for HMOs than similar properties rented as single units, the gross yield is significantly higher. A detached house with four bedrooms and three reception rooms, worth £200,000 might rent to a family for £1,000 a month, giving a gross yield figure of 6%, while renting six individual bedrooms might achieve £2,400, giving a gross yield of 14.4%. But if the landlord of the single unit owns the property outright and therefore doesn't have monthly mortgage payments, while the landlord of the HMO is highly geared and has all the additional costs (utility bills, council tax, TV license, increased maintenance - handyman, cleaner, gardener - and more management costs), the net yields and monthly cash flow could be not that different. What will be very different is the ROI.

So I'd suggest you forget yield as a tool for comparing your properties' performances to other people's, unless you know that their investment model is the same as yours. What I use net yield for is comparing the properties in my portfolio with each other – that's where it becomes really useful, and it's something I'm constantly tracking. My costs don't tend to vary from one HMO of the same size to another, but the property values vary, as does the rental income. Looking at the net yield figures, I can see at a glance which properties in which areas were the better buys, from a cash flow perspective.

Of course, the caveat is that you have to take the yield figure in context with the capital growth figure. The yield figures might suggest you'd be better off selling a property and reinvesting the money into one that has a better income:value ratio, but if the reason for the lower yield figure is that the property has grown in value more than others in your portfolio, it's probably worth holding onto.

# Capital Growth

Whether a property grows in value or not is pretty much out of your hands. Yes, you can make sure you maintain it well, and could extend, convert or renovate to add value, but once your HMO is up and running, it's in the hands of the market. Nevertheless, you must keep track of what's happening to property values, to make sure that you not only know how much your own portfolio is worth, but also can see which of your properties are growing more quickly in value.

As I said in the section above, you can greatly increase your ROI by refinancing and pulling out some of your invested capital, so keep track of exactly how much equity you have in each property, assuming you'll always need to keep 25% in. Set up your spreadsheet so that you can easily see:

- purchase price
- invested capital
- current value
- total equity
- amount you could pull out (total equity, less 25% of current value)

If certain property types in certain areas have grown more in value over the last few years, look at the economic drivers, and what's likely to happen in the future, and that will help you see whether it's worth making further investment there.

Most of the professional landlords I know keep a balanced portfolio, with some properties which generate a high level of monthly income and others which aren't so good on cash flow, but are much better in terms of capital growth. And I'd suggest that tracking your KPIs, so you can make sure you consistently maximize your returns in a variety of ways, and spread the investment risk, is a very sensible investment strategy.

*One more little note...*

Of these four key metrics, the one you'll hear investors most often mention is yield. What I'm saying is that yield needs to be taken as just one part of an overall picture which includes profit, ROI and capital growth, and it will be more or less relevant to you, depending on your investment objectives. So if someone says they're getting a better yield than you, understand that the conversation is only just beginning!

# Checklist

## Managing your business

Have you done all these things?

- ☐ Set up a good general administration system
- ☐ Made sure your property analysis spreadsheets are up to date & you have diarised:
  - ○ cost reviews
  - ○ current property valuations
  - ○ rent reviews
- ☐ Understood your key KPIs:
  - ○ profit
  - ○ ROI
  - ○ yield
  - ○ capital growth
- ☐ Know what sources can quickly give you a snapshot of the current market
- ☐ Arranged with your financial advisers how often you will review your business

# PART FOUR:

# NEXT STEPS…

# Ready to apply what you've learned?

## Great! Here's even more from Nick Fox Property Mentoring

Thanks for taking the time to read this book - hopefully you've found it helpful and are inspired to put some or all of it into practice!

If you'd like to extend your knowledge, the next step is to check out our website, where you'll find lots of free information and details of our mentoring packages.

We offer a range of options to suit all needs, from short intensive taster sessions to more comprehensive packages that will give you a deeper understanding of property investment and the buy to let market, focusing on the rewards and implications of building an HMO portfolio:

- Half-day 'HMO Education and Tour'
- One-day 'Intensive HMO Property Mentoring Course'
- Two-day 'Intensive HMO Property Mentoring Course'
- 12 months' full access to and support from Nick Fox and his Power Team

Whichever package you choose, you can be assured that Nick's commitment to your personal property goals are absolute. Nick and his team get a real kick out of watching others grow their property portfolios by helping them implement the most successful methods that have been tried and tested over many years.

As skilled and experienced professionals, we present our mentoring sessions in such a way that they're easy to understand, while enabling highly effective learning. The acute insights and practical methodology on offer will help you to take your property business to the next level and secure financial independence for you and your loved ones.

Check out our website **nickfox.co.uk** or call us on **01908 930369** to find out more.

Find us on
FACEBOOK Nick Fox Mentor
TWITTER NickFoxPropertyMentoring
EMAIL hello@nickfox.co.uk
TEL 01908 930369

NICK FOX PROPERTY MENTORING
Suite 150, MK Business Centre, Foxhunter Drive,
Linford Wood, Milton Keynes  MK14 6BL

# Write a review and get free stuff!

If you've enjoyed what you've read, why not tell other people and bag yourself some free stuff in the process?

Simply write a review of this book – or any of the other books in the 'SUCCESS' series – and publicise it via:

- Amazon
- iTunes
- Facebook
- Twitter
- A blog

… or any other online or offline publication.

Then email an image or link to us at hello@nickfox.co.uk.

We'll thank you via Twitter and you'll get back some exclusive property investment tools or samples of our latest materials to help you stay focused and up to date in your investment journey.

Thanks in advance and we hope to hear from you soon!

# Some recommended reading

When I mentor clients, I give them a huge list of books I think they should read – some about property, some about the mindset you need to succeed in business and life – so here are the first five of those titles to get you started. You may have already read some of them…in which case, I'd suggest they may be worth a second look!:

Rich Dad, Poor Dad, by Robert T. Kiyosaki
Rich Dad's Cashflow Quadrant, by Robert T. Kiyosaki
The Millionaire Next Door, by Thomas J. Stanley
Wage Slave to Financial Freedom, by Neil Mansell
Think and Grow Rich: The Original Classic, by Napoleon Hill
Goals, by Brian Tracy
Goal Mapping, by Brian Mayne
The Dip, by Seth Godin

# Even more...

## ...from Nick Fox Property Mentoring.

Thank you for taking the time to read our book; we hope you've found it helpful. If you'd like to extend your knowledge, please check out our website, where you'll find a wealth of free information and details of our mentoring packages.

We offer a range of mentoring options to suit all needs, from short intensive taster sessions to more comprehensive packages that will give you a deeper understanding of property investment and the buy to let market, focusing on the rewards and implications of building an HMO portfolio.

## Various choices available include:

- Half-day 'HMO Education and Tour'
- One-day 'Intensive HMO Property Mentoring Course'
- Two-day 'Intensive HMO Property Mentoring Course'
- 12 months' full access to and support from Nick Fox and his Power Team

Whichever package you choose, you can be assured that Nick's commitment to your personal property goals are absolute. Nick and his team get a real kick out of watching others grow their property portfolios by helping them implement the most successful methods that have been tried and tested over many years.

As skilled and experienced professionals, we present our mentoring sessions in such a way that they are easy to understand, while enabling highly effective learning. The acute insights and practical methodology on offer will help you to take your property business to the next level and secure financial independence for you and your loved ones.

Check out our website **www.nickfox.co.uk** or call us on **01908 930369** to find out more.

# Read on...

Collect the set of books by Nick Fox to help you achieve financial freedom through property investment.

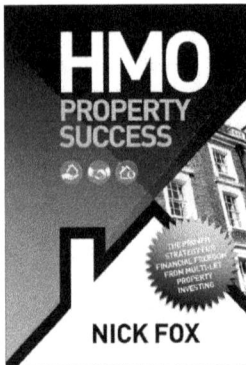

## HMO PROPERTY SUCCESS

Do you want a secure financial future that starts sooner, rather than later as you're approaching retirement? By investing in multi-let properties, you can double or even triple the level of rental income generated by single letting, and realise positive cash flow from the start. In this book, multiple business owner and investor, Nick Fox, clearly guides you through the steps to building an HMO portfolio that delivers both on-going income and a tangible pension or lifestyle pot.

ISBN: 978-0-9576516-0-9
RRP: £9.99

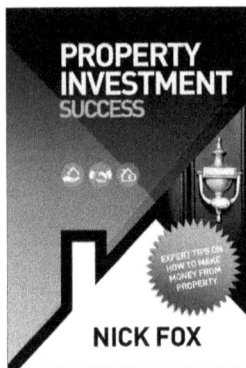

## PROPERTY INVESTMENT SUCCESS

How does your financial future look?
If you haven't reviewed your pension provision for a while or aren't completely happy with how your current investments are performing, you should take a closer look at property. In this book, Nick Fox discusses the pros and cons of traditional pensions and makes the case for property as a robust alternative investment vehicle.
He looks at how property can deliver different kinds of returns at different times and shows how you can build a tailored portfolio that perfectly satisfies your own future financial needs.

ISBN: 978-0-9576516-4-7
RRP: £9.99

**nickfox**
property mentoring

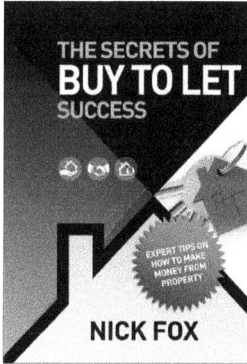

## THE SECRETS OF BUY TO LET SUCCESS

Are you looking for a sound investment that can give you both income and growth on your capital, but nervous about the future of the property market? This book will put your mind at rest. In The Secrets of Buy to Let Success, Nick Fox shares his knowledge and expertise about the market, guiding the reader step by step through the basics of building a solid and profitable property business - even through an economic crisis. If you're completely new to property investment, this book is a great place to start.

ISBN: 978-0-9927817-2-9
RRP: £9.99

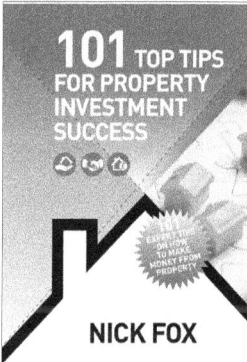

## 101 TOP TIPS FOR PROPERT INVESTMENT SUCCESS

Whether you're looking to focus purely on HMOs, build a varied portfolio of rental properties, or employ a number of different strategies to make money from property, '101 TOP TIPS' is full of useful information that will help keep you at the top of the property investment business.
Nick Fox has spent the past decade amassing a highly profitable buy to let portfolio and continues to invest in a variety of property projects and business ventures. His tailored mentoring programmes have helped many aspiring investors realise their own potential in the property field.

ISBN: 978-0-9935074-9-6 I RRP: £9.99

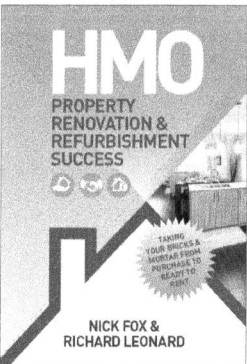

## PROPERTY RENNOVATION & REFURBISHMENT SUCCESS

Successful renovation and refurbishment relies on spending the right amount of money in the right way, so are you ready to hone your budgeting, planning and project-management skills? Alongside the deposit, this is where the biggest chunk of your investment funds will be spent. You need to analyse the figures, budget correctly, plan the work in detail and ensure it's carried out properly so that your buy to let performs as you need it to. Not sure how to do that? Then this is the book for you!

ISBN: 978-0-9927817-6-7
RRP: £11.99

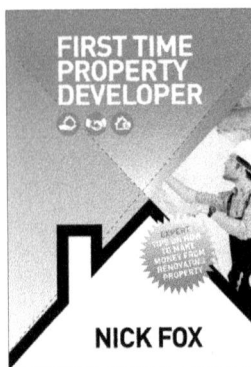

## FIRST TIME PROPERTY DEVELOPER

Interested in developing property for profit ? Don't know where to start? Let experienced property expert, Nick Fox, lead you through the process. Nick will show you how to find the property, add genuine value to it by developing and refurbishing and then explain how to sell on for profit or rent out for income.

ISBN: 978-0-9576516-4-7
RRP: £9.99

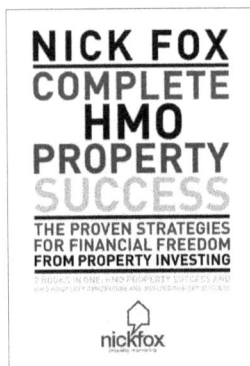

## COMPLETE HMO PROPERTY SUCCESS

This HMO 'superbook' is essential reading for anyone who's starting out in property investment and wants to generate income.

It begins by looking at investing in Houses in Multiple Occupation as a business and takes you through how to successfully source, refurbish, let out and manage a highly cash-positive portfolio.

The second part then focuses on the all-important renovation stage. It details how to budget, plan your works, manage your project and carry out the refurbishment in such a way that your HMO performs as you need it to and you get the returns you're looking for.

A prolific and highly successful investor, Nick's personal portfolio extends to more than 200 properties, both shared accommodation and single household lets – and he also has interests in several development projects around the UK.

ISBN: 978-0-9935074-0-3 | RRP: £19.99

Available now online at
www.amazon.co.uk & www.nickfox.co.uk
Books, iBook, Kindle & Audio

Find us on FACEBOOK Nick Fox Mentor TWITTER NickFoxPropertyMentoring
www.nickfox.co.uk EMAIL hello@nickfox.co.uk TEL 01908 930369
NICK FOX PROPERTY MENTORING
14 Wharfside Bletchley Milton Keynes MK2 2AZ

**nickfox**
property mentoring

# Testimonials

This is just some of the positive feedback I've received from happy mentoring clients over the past few years:

*"I met Nick a number of years ago and was immediately struck by his deep knowledge and experience in the field of property investing. No problem is ever too great a challenge for Nick - his creative entrepreneur spirit is a joy to behold. He is both dynamic and detailed, great fun to work with and quite truly inspirational. He is now my business partner and good friend."*
**Richard Leonard**

*"Nick and his team are the real deal. Their knowledge and help in moving my investment project forward has been invaluable. Without their expertise I would not have been able to reach my personal property goals or milestones."*
**Richard Felton, UK**

*"Great book, great guy and great results for me after I read 'HMO Property Success'. I've now replaced my job with passive income from HMO properties. Thanks, Nick!"*
**C.Clark, Bedford**

*"Nick has clearly got a huge amount of knowledge in his field, and having his support and experience has given me the increased confidence to make my first steps into investing."*
**Craig Smith, Edinburgh**

*"Nick is a very experienced property professional. His practical advice on setting goals, the pros and cons of this type of investment and how to minimise risks and properly manage a growing portfolio are essential in what can be a very complex investment. Nick's mentoring is not a get-rich-quick formula but a clear and concise way of demonstrating how a solid property investment strategy can be put into action. And the results are well worth it."*
**D.Wright, Aberdeen**

*"I have spent money in the past on various property courses, where you are taught in a group in a classroom, and those have not really helped me. This one-to-one mentoring with Nick was brilliant, as I was actually seeing his business and properties, meeting tenants, getting lots of advice and seeing what worked well and what didn't in a live situation. I have booked another two days with Nick in my home city next week, to look at various properties and hopefully start my journey as a full-time property investor, and I cannot wait! I highly recommend this type of mentoring!"*
**James Robinson, Hull**

*"Both Sarah and I cannot express how much help Nick has been to our property business over the last two years. His support and knowledge have been invaluable. We would thoroughly recommend his mentoring to any budding investor."*
**Stuart Lewis, Northampton**

*"Thank you so much for your patience, professionalism and general understanding during our three-day mentoring programme. The visit to see how your office and HMO business runs was incredible and so, so helpful. Without it we would have been at a complete loss. With your guidance and help we have now purchased our first HMO property and look forward to keeping in touch to show you our profitable progress!"*
**Rebecca Santay-Jones, Harrow**

*"I first met Nick in the autumn of 2012 when I was looking for someone to guide me through my first HMO purchase. Nick's mentoring was invaluable and gave me such a good grounding - not just in HMOs, but in how to run a successful property business - that I have been able to move forward with real confidence as my business has grown. Even now, if there is something I am uncertain of, or I just want to bounce an idea around, I'm very grateful to have Nick in my corner. He has such wide-ranging experience in the industry and I value his opinion greatly. The income my portfolio already provides gives me the option of going part-time in my day job and in the coming months, as I grow the business further, I fully intend to become a full-time*

*property investor and landlord."*
**Andy Potter, Fareham**

*"Today's experience has been brilliant – it really opened up my eyes up to the world of HMOs and made me see properties in a different light, in terms of understanding just how much potential each one has. Your experience has accelerated my learning and shown me how important it is to have the right mindset when getting into this area of property investing.*

*As a kinaesthetic learner, I really enjoyed the hands-on experience of going from property to property and getting a flavour of how you see and do things. Your openness and honesty is what I appreciated the most and has reaffirmed to me that I have made the right choice. Looking forward to getting that first property!"*
**Gabriel F, Enfield**

*"Nick has clearly got a huge amount of knowledge in his field, and having his support and experience has given me the increased confidence to make my first steps into investing."*
**Craig Smith, Edinburgh**